A BRITTLE GLORY
An Autobiography

I have seen the moment of my greatness flicker,
And I have seen the eternal Footman hold my coat, and
  snicker,

(*The Love Song of J. Alfred Prufrock*
by T. S. ELIOT)

A
BRITTLE GLORY

An Autobiography

PAUL WRIGHT

WEIDENFELD AND NICOLSON · LONDON

Published in Great Britain by
George Weidenfeld & Nicolson Limited
91 Clapham High Street
London SW4 7TA

ISBN 0 297 78971 6

Filmset by Deltatype, Ellesmere Port
Printed in Great Britain by
Butler & Tanner Ltd
Frome and London

Acknowledgements

The writing and publication of this book has been surrounded by kindness and the task of thanking those who have helped me is one of the most agreeable that I have to undertake.

Jacqueline Wheldon encouraged me to write the book in the first place and gave me much valuable advice on how to go about it. Her son Wynn's meticulous research put me right on many facts and figures. My friend and former colleague Nicholas Gordon-Lennox did his best to make palatable a critical attitude, to my mind verging on the pernickety, adopted by the Foreign and Commonwealth Office towards certain parts of the text submitted to them in accordance with the regulations.

I was lucky enough to secure the help of the distinguished literary agent George Greenfield who read the manuscript at an early stage and has since devoted many valuable hours to achieving its publication. His faith in the book has never faltered. My Editor, David Roberts, has patiently and skilfully tried to make sure that nothing I wrote would embarrass his company. Jeffrey Sterling has consistently kept my morale higher than it deserves to be.

My sister, Sylvia Yeatman, has given me useful help in jogging my memory about the past and brushing up my family history. My daughter, Faith, has been a constant and constructive critic, giving me the kind of advice, sensible and unsentimental, which only a fond daughter can give to a father.

Finally my wife, Babs, has had to live with me not only while the book was being written but through nearly all the years which it spans. The fact that she is still by my side is witness to her loving support, without which much of what these pages record would not have happened and the book itself could not have been written.

PREFACE

Contrary to popular belief, diplomats are human. Hands that grasp cocktail glasses, striped-trousered bottoms reposing on gilt chairs, eyebrows that lift in quizzical interrogation, tongues that effortlessly master a dozen dialects; all these, in so far as they are not creations of an obstinately romantic Press, are composed of all too solid flesh. However hard he tries, in the interests of his profession, to conceal his emotions, the diplomat loves, hates, fears and hopes much like other men. Indeed, he may be said to be rather more familiar with the seven deadly sins than the average man, although his knowledge of their corresponding virtues tends to become less precise with time. The myths that surround his life and work are a necessary burden to him, part of his public persona, recognised by his fellow professionals yet concealing from all but his closest companions the reality of his human fallibility.

Many books by, or about, diplomats tend to concentrate on this public persona; they tell of great issues cogently argued and brilliantly resolved; of revolutions promoted or foiled; they drop names like heavy, uncut jewels on a marble floor. Others are less ambitious, eschewing the great sweeps of History to concentrate on those private dramas which play so much greater a part in a diplomat's life than the world of protocol suspects. This latter is certainly the kind of book which I hope the persevering reader will discover – not so much a peek behind the scenes as a probe beneath the skin. Diplomacy is one of the most hierarchical of professions and its myths and mystique consequently intensify sharply towards the summit. So, of course, do the human problems concealed by the magisterial presence, the gold braid, sword and the cocked hat of an Ambassador Extraordinary and Plenipotentiary. But as he gazes into the mirror when trying on this finery for the first time, the diplomat, middle-aged, with his career trailing behind him like a ship's wake, cannot be blamed if he reviews the past and wonders at the long sequence of design and chance, work and play, planning and coincidence which has led to this often uncomfortable eminence.

Professions are usually believed to have an ideal background from which most of its members are assumed to have sprung. Some are more stereotyped than others, but none more so, I suspect, than the Diplomatic Service. In spite of the most vigorous efforts to democratise this once most aristocratic of services, usually by the intake of young men from the so-called red brick universities and from the less exalted social and economic strata, who, incidentally, almost invariably prove at least as clever and reliable as their bluer-blooded fellows, it remains a general assumption that British diplomats are born into a Trollopian world of respectably old families with affluent prospects in land or money or both; and with minds so honed by the classical education provided by Eton and Trinity as to be more than a match for the most devious of foreigners – even the French.

An investigation into the background of some of the most brilliant of my colleagues will prove how false this preconception is. In my own case, there were elements which made my early years startlingly abnormal for one destined to reach the upper ranks of so distinguished, demanding and seemingly exclusive a service. It was greatly to their credit that they took me in, lacking as I did most of the conventional cards of entry.

But before the reader judges for himself what kind of a risk they were taking, he must meet my family and try to tune in to those now increasingly faint signals coming from the vanished world of early twentieth century England.

CHAPTER ONE

Travellers to or from inner London, as they inch their way along the grotesquely misnamed Hammersmith flyover, will have noticed a tall, thin church, now standing like a Sarsen stone left by superstitious planners in the midst of a modern housing development. It is St Paul's Hammersmith; and if it survives the physical and perhaps spiritual shock of finding an early version of a motorway running past the vestry window, it may be remembered by those few who can conceivably have the slightest interest, as the church in which I was baptised.

It was an appropriate location; I was to be called Paul after my great-grandfather, a Suffolk parson with an Old Testament reputation feared but secretly enjoyed by his descendants; and the church was hard by my birthplace – a fourth floor flat in one of those mansion blocks, as they were called, no doubt in an effort to disguise their comparatively lowly status on the domestic housing ladder, with their uncarpeted flights of stone steps which lead up to mock-mahogany, brass-knockered doors.

The myth arose in my family that I was born in the middle of a Zeppelin raid – but I now discount this as being merely one of many legends invented, mostly by my father but with my mother's encouragement, to add colour to what might have otherwise seemed a drab, colourless existence. In any case, Zeppelin raids were not that frequent in May 1915. At times I have almost persuaded myself that I can remember later air-raids, being carried down wrapped in an eiderdown to the basement flat of some friendly neighbours, and the general air of excitement which war brings, even to the life of a three-year-old. But these are tales long told by parents, aunts and nannies, and not to be confused with historical truth. In them I was always the hero, being the only male (other than my father, who was, perhaps, a little too masculine for normal taste) in a feminine world, and accordingly was not only spoilt but cast in heroic or romantic roles for which I was obviously unsuited.

My father was, in my eyes at any rate, the dominant force in my early life. Typical of the mysterious, at times magical, aura with which he surrounded himself, he achieved this position while living apart from his family for a good proportion of the time. It was not that he and my mother were divorced, or even separated; such a situation would have been unthinkable, at any rate to my mother's strict middle-class unbringing; and it was only when I was myself grown up that I even suspected that their marriage was less than perfect. He lived during the week at Whites Club, of which he was the Secretary, in a bachelor flat which we were occasionally permitted to visit, creeping up the back stairs past the exciting smells and sounds which surrounded those who catered to the whims and fancies of the aristocratic life beyond the swinging green baize doors. His work was not exacting and left him time to indulge himself in the life of London's West End, which he loved as only a convert can love, and to supplement the token income with which the Club rewarded his services. However, he spent weekends and great occasions, such as Christmas and birthdays with us, arriving with armfuls of presents and good things to eat from Fortnum & Mason, dispensing a kind of exotic charm which, even at an early age, I recognised as originating in a very different world from that in which we lived.

I suspect that his eyes, like those of so many Scotsmen, had always been directed towards the great glitter of London. The third of seven sons, he was born in Inverary in 1867, where his father was a writer to the Signet and for some years Provost of the town.

His early intimacy with the Argyll family, achieved in the democratic Scottish way by neighbourly intercourse and shared basic education, together with the salt water of Loch Fyne, had suggested a wide world waiting beyond the Western Isles, and propelled him away from home at an early age, varying from thirteen to sixteen according to his mood. By the most devious routes which the merchant marine could devise, he landed up in South Africa where he became involved with Cecil Rhodes in circumstances, and in a capacity, about which he was careful never to be precise; and he had been forbidden to return to Africa – on pain of death, as he quaintly put it – after contracting Blackwater Fever as a young man.

Although a dominant feature of his personality was a deep mistrust of all foreigners and of 'abroad', I do not think he counted Africa as abroad, nor the numerous dialects which he was reputed to have spoken fluently as being foreign languages. Europe, on the other hand, aroused his deepest suspicions, and I have heard him, when challenged to give reasons for his dislike of some otherwise harmless Englishman, say, 'But have you ever heard him talk French? Talks like a Frenchman!' Conclusive evidence, in my father's view, of some fundamental weakness of character. In truth, his world was contained in a quadrilateral bounded by Piccadilly, Haymarket,

Pall Mall and St James's Street, and remained set in the period when this was at the centre of an Empire's capital. He made no concession to the rest of London – let alone to the countryside which he loathed, visiting it only on rare occasions when we were staying with my grandparents in Hampshire, and then dressed as if about to take one of his numerous lady friends to lunch at the Ritz.

My father's mind was like a computer, extremely efficient but totally uncreative. Moreover, having himself been a note-worthy athlete, a reserve cap for Scotland at rugby, an amateur boxing champion and, well over the age of sixty, (he was 48 when I was born,) playing an aggressive game of tennis at Roehampton Club wearing a cardigan and a grey trilby hat, he saw no reason why his son should not follow, and if possible excel, him in these pursuits. Our relationship suffered a series of crises as, one by one, he tried unsuccessfully to teach me to kick or strike various kinds of ball, to box, even to play golf at which, needless to say, he was better than average; and he would give up, discouraged, perplexed and finally furiously indignant, that fate should have landed him with so hamfisted an offspring. These extremes were somewhat moderated towards the end of his life when I had won a prize or two at school and given other demonstrations of comparative success in the academic world.

But all this was, of course, private to our relationship and my father would not have dreamed of betraying by so much as a glance his real feelings to any outsider. He had a profound sense of rectitude regarding loyalty to King, Country, Clan and Family, and somewhat rigid notions as to the way a gentleman behaved. His advice to me about life in general had always been enshrined in mysterious rules which he handed down with an air of finality similar to that which must have pervaded Mount Sinai. The concepts of negotiation or flexibility were foreign to his nature; if the rules did not fit the circumstances, it was the latter which must be altered, however gigantic an effort this might entail. But since loyalty was central to his code of behaviour, I could have counted, and indeed always did count absolutely, on his public support; and this was comforting to me because, however unhappy were our efforts at establishing a relationship of private and mutual respect, I loved him dearly, and had craved his approval even after I had grown to know that in certain respects I would never completely qualify.

How he met and married my mother was another, unexplained mystery. It was, according to legend, at a concert in Bury St Edmunds that he had first seen the slim, beautiful Miss Mercier, a gifted amateur musician, seated at the piano on the platform. He vowed, then and there, to make her his wife. What he was doing in Bury St Edmunds, let alone at a concert (he disliked music) remains obscure, like so much of my father's early life. But there he was. 'He swept me off my feet in the green room,' my mother used to tell me, thereby conjuring up in the literal mind of a small boy the picture of my father, his moustaches bristling with . . . what? . . . excitement, I suppose, like at a football match, giving my mother a kind of rugger tackle, both bathed in the sickly light reflected from the green walls of this mysterious room.

The Merciers were a Huguenot family. My grandfather, although perfectly normal by medical and psychiatric standards, was sufficiently eccentric for his family to believe that it would be unfair to saddle him with the burdens of everyday life. This view was dramatically strengthened when the family firm of stockbrokers, in which he was a partner, ran into severe financial difficulties. There is no evidence that he was directly or indirectly more responsible than the others; but his business habits and general attitude to life were not such as to create that degree of confidence necessary to exonerate him altogether. He was, accordingly, pensioned off by the firm at an early age and settled out of harm's way in a small house in Hampshire with no indoor sanitation and no electric light, but with a garden which his extraordinarily green fingers proceeded to beautify, and with a piano at which, usually wearing a hat, he happily extemporised often startlingly beautiful music. A further consequence of this supposed inability to cope with reality was a generally agreed family opinion that his two daughters, my mother and her younger sister Winifred, would be better brought up by their grandfather, the Reverend Paul Stedman, Rector of Thurston in Suffolk, whose huge family spanned an age bracket which could easily accommodate two more little girls – indeed, my mother's youngest aunt was hardly older than she was. These aunts – my great aunts – played an important role in my early years. Some spinsters, some widowed, they lived together for many years, rather like a small religious order, in a large house on the edge of Barnes Common. They spoiled me horribly, adding an extra, indulgent dimension to my already female-dominated world, and entering convincingly into my childish fantasies in which I was the perpetual hero. My grandmother shuttled uncomfortably between her daughters in Suffolk and her husband in Hampshire; later in life, she became a semi-permanent invalid, retaining until the end her beauty and the devotion of my grandfather.

Thus Margaret Ellen, my mother, and her sister grew up in the calm, civilised world of a late Victorian country rectory, the one destined for the tempestuous experience of marriage to my father, the other for a spinster life of great academic distinction and a permanent place in the history of English education, ending her career as Principal of Whitelands College.

4

Both possessed beauty and brains, my mother, however, having the lion's share of the former, no doubt to compensate for her younger sister's exceptional brilliance of mind. They were very close to each other, but my mother was always the more conventional, in spite of her later choice of so colourful a mate. It was through her eyes that I first saw life as the intensely hierarchical world which was her inheritance from her childhood – a cosy, ordered society in which everyone knew his place and appeared to be content with it – one respected but did not resent those above; one basked in the warm glow of compassion for those below. My mother used to classify our friends and neighbours by their position in what seemed to me, in my puzzled innocence, to be a huge tallboy. 'They're not quite out of our drawer, my dear,' she would say of some hapless family, although precisely how far up or down our own particular drawer was placed on this immense piece of social furniture was never clear to me. I do not think this stratification had any great effect on my mother, for she had close and devoted friends in all walks of life. She was what, in those days, people called jolly; although beneath the surface there was a current of melancholy, brought on no doubt by the strain of marriage with my father, and perhaps due to a wistful, gentle jealousy of her sister's seemingly so much more desirable career, which made her often pine for the security of the Suffolk rectory and the long-remembered, golden summers.

But to tell the truth, I saw little of my parents during those early years. Even my father's slender income was sufficient to allow us a cook or maid and a Nannie – indispensable keys to opening and occupying a drawer of the correct elevation. Thus, to a large extent I lived the nursery life so beloved by Victorian novelists, the remoteness of my parents being enhanced by their unnatural, but to me as yet unsuspected, separation. My father would occasionally appear, Zeus-like, in evening dress to say goodnight to me, his stiff shirt front crackling as he bent over my cot, smelling very nice and distinctly expensive. My mother was largely a tea-time phenomenon – except when we had a party and I was roused, cross but grateful, to listen to some singer perform ballads of appalling sentimentality while gazing soulfully at my mother who, coquettish but competent, accompanied him at the piano.

My real life, which was of course in those early days the secret inner life of the child, took place in the nursery. Its central figure was Nannie, who could have been said to dominate my physical and mental world, were not such an expression quite inappropriate for so gentle a person, in whose milky blue, myopic eyes glowed the unearthly light of a love purer than any which I have since experienced. Unfortunately, the pendulum of purity, in Nannie's case, had swung over and remained fixed at a point not far short of obsessive religious mania, the main effect of which was to compel her to steer her little charge ever nearer the Kingdom of Heaven. If I was good, she promised me, Jesus would appear to me. All my life I have feared the supernatural, and although then only five or six years old, I had no doubt of the need to take vigorous counter-measures in the face of this horrifying possibility. I began with some evasive action; for example, turning to the wall the picture of the Good Shepherd which hung over my bed, so that its Original would not be tempted by the unearthly light which shone from His Halo to materialise as soon as I had been tucked up for the night. This was clumsy, however, and somehow seemed too physical, since the effort required to reach it was often too much for tired little arms and legs; not to speak of the need to turn it back before morning – a precaution often forgotten and causing great histrionic displays of surprised innocence. No; a far safer, effective tactic was, I soon realised, simply not to be good. The one thing about Our Lord that had been made abundantly clear was that He knew a bad boy when He saw one, and would have nothing to do with him until he became good again. So I set about devising ways of being naughty enough, at least once a day, to ensure beyond all possible doubt that no Appearance would or could take place – but, of course, not sufficiently naughty to incur that human wrath in the shape of a disappointed Nannie, or worse, an enraged parent, which passeth all understanding. As can be imagined, the first experiments in so delicate a technique were not a great success and the grown-ups must have been baffled by this inexplicably sudden rash of naughtiness. But I soon learned the trick of this early example of the graduated response sufficiently well to banish the worst of the bedtime fears.

I am not sure how Nannie ever came into our family. From the start it must have been clear that a permanent state of open warfare was bound to exist between her and my father who, whenever asked to define his religious views, would describe himself, in his picturesque language, as a devoted and practising Atheist. It seems, nevertheless, that Nannie had the last word and became enshrined in family history as the only person to have succeeded in getting the upper hand of my father. In order to tease her and test her loyalty he used to affect horror at the sight of his only son – not without reason, for at an early age I was cross-eyed and bandy-legged – and he would call upon God to explain why he should have been afflicted with such an heir. At last Nannie's holy patience ran out, and during one of my father's tirades, fell to her knees in prayer beside my cot, or pram, or wherever my poor, misshapen little body was resting. My father stopped in mid-sentence, puzzled, like a bull whose charge has been deflected by something unfamiliar. 'Praying won't help the poor little blighter,' he said;

to which Nannie produced the doctrinally classic rebuke, 'I'm praying for you, Sir.'

When I first went to school, at the age of about six, Nannie left us to realise her long-cherished dream of joining the Church Army. We had postcards and letters from strange places until the war silenced all further communication. When my mother died in 1951, my sister and I tried in vain to trace her, but even the Church Army professed to have no knowledge of her whereabouts, or even if she was still alive. I had half expected a reply to our enquiries to arrive couched in suitably Old Testament terms, such as, 'Regret to inform you subject was taken up by fiery chariot on Feb. 24th last.' I feel sure that provision must have been made for Nannie and my father to continue their battles in that Hereafter which he so resolutely denied; they both enjoyed them so much that Paradise, for which both, I believe, qualified in their separate ways, would be less than Heavenly without them.

My sister, Sylvia, was the fourth member of this family quartet, but owing to the immense gap of eight years in our ages, she remained virtually an unseen presence during my babyhood, inhabiting an unimaginably sophisticated world in which books were read, games played with other children, even journeys made on trams and buses and, wonder of all, school was a normal daily occurrence. The principal emotion which at that time she aroused in me was resentment that her birthday occurred on Christmas Eve, thus effortlessly doubling the number of presents she received (and, incidentally, causing terrible confusion about Father Christmas) and, still worse, being placed firmly in the centre of the stage during this most family of festivals. We never quite managed to bridge this eight-year chasm, and throughout my youth and adolescence I could only admire from a distance her considerable musical and artistic talents, her glamorous friendships, her schoolgirl successes in the classroom and on the tennis court. Thus deprived of the companionship which a more compatible age would have naturally provided, I grew up with most of the disadvantages which the only child suffers, but few of the benefits. I dreamed my dreams and played my lonely games in this sheltered, feminine world until it was shattered by the impact of reality in the shape of school, at what seems to me now to have been an exceptionally early age. That the experience was not as traumatic as might have been expected was undoubtedly due to the Froebel Institute whither my now straightening legs carried me, at first reluctantly, and then with growing enthusiasm as I began to get the hang of community life. I was thrilled to discover that there were other children of my own age with whom I could play, and that some of them were girls; and once even, in a secluded corner of the playground on a hot afternoon, that girls were made differently. The staff invented marvellous games for us to play, which satisfied my passion for dressing up, my nascent desire for order and a proper hierarchy – a kind of medieval pageant in which everyone had his or her place and function under the benevolent tyranny of a purple-clad, crowned headmistress (every inch a King); and my somewhat hesitant sense of adventure – Red Indians, this time with a much-befeathered, wampum-bedecked head-mistress as Chief. I was picked for my first and only starring role during a long, permanently stage-struck life, in a play of ghastly archness called *Paddly Pools*; and I must have done quite well at my lessons for in due course I graduated to a prep school called Gladstones, and became the proud wearer of a green cap and blazer emblazoned with a scarlet Maltese cross. Here I discovered that the Froebel had protected me from the worst of the world; that learning was not the fun it had so deceptively seemed; that making friends inevitably meant making enemies as well; that there were two sides to every coin and you could never count on winning the toss. It was also here, however, that I began to learn those moral and social precepts which went to make up what was then called the Public School ethos; like many prep schools, Gladstones specialised in preparing boys for a particular public school, in this case Westminster, whither I was destined, subject to a long list of provisos concerning my own behaviour and academic performance, and the state of my father's income, all of which had to be at their most favourable for me to achieve the Valhalla awaiting me beyond the gates of Deans Yard.

By this time we had moved to a house in Chiswick, which was a little more spacious than the flat and had a garden in which my mother could recapture a little of her country childhood and my father demonstrate his contempt for nature unadorned by stone, brick or concrete. He was once charged with the responsibility of planting some bulbs; only when, late the following summer, a few lank green shoots struggled to the surface, did it become evident that, whether from ignorance or by design, he had planted them upside down. No-one who has lived in suburban London of the twenties and thirties can fail to marvel at the accuracy of Sir John Betjeman's evocation of the precisely structured, coniferous life that flourished there. The smell of damp privet on a summer's evening, of tarred fencing and autumn bonfires; the clatter of teacups beside tennis courts and the lazy applause from the pavilion as Pam's Old Malvernian brother hits another four – playing for Woking, imagine! All these were the background for those constant worries about what to wear and when, how to behave, the correct dress, the done and not-done thing that played so disproportionate a part in the middle-class life of that now vanished

England. When the strata are laid bare by the social archaeologists, evidence of the astonishing gulf between those times and the present day can be seen; such as the fact that it was not only possible to travel first class on the District Line, but that my parents were compelled to pay for me to do so on my daily journey to and from school so that I should not be tempted to disgrace the cap and blazer by contact with the lesser, third class breeds – a practice to be continued throughout my school life, for the Westminster daily uniform of top hat, stiff collar, tails and umbrella were thought to be equally out of place in a third class carriage. Even to this day, I have vague subliminal anxieties about being incorrectly or inappropriately dressed and feel uncomfortable in America where there are few rules or conventions about dress even on the most formal occasions. I still hesitate to penetrate into that uncharted, but nevertheless clearly definable area known to my father as the West End, unless I am wearing a dark suit; and it is not so many years since the hat was as essential a part of my wardrobe as the trousers.

My arrival at Westminster in the autumn of 1928 confirmed and strengthened these tendencies. I became part of that great industry for the production of administrators of an Empire on which the sun was already setting in a deceitful way, largely unnoticed by those who hoped to bask in its slanting rays. But there were other things about Westminster which served to keep fluid the young minds which, at other similar institutions, were still being stamped in the rigid mould first cast by Dr Arnold. Being in the centre of a great metropolis, a rich, exciting life beyond the still narrow school syllabus was available to us; music, the visual arts, the theatre, opera and ballet; and we were encouraged to explore these seductive sights and sounds by the many gifted men which the position and reputation of the school attracted as masters. Above all, it was the exceptionally active and diverse musical life within the school which watered the slender, delicate plant of my talent, such as it was, and made possible the strong, if rather erratic and still amateurish growth which flourishes today.

I was born musical, an inheritance from my mother, and this talent was discovered at an early age by the exceedingly unwise Christmas present of a drum, which gave the family almost unendurable provocation, except for my father, who although tone deaf and definitely anti-music, liked noise. However, I demonstrated a near-perfect sense of rhythm and began attempts to imitate my mother at the keyboard as soon as I could reach it. Accordingly, I was soon being given piano lessons. My teacher was a Miss Greaves. Even now I can conjure up the sense of her physical presence, warm and loving, although the only features that I can actually recall were her thick, pink lips and the long string of large amber beads which looked edible and made a clicking sound as she moved. She taught me marvellously well. At the age of eight I played one of the less difficult Hadyn Sonatas at a recital given by her pupils in a little hall in Notting Hill Gate. I was sick before the performance and again after it. I knew that I had not played well, and my failure sowed the seeds of a complete and, on the whole, justified lack of confidence in myself as a performer. Nevertheless, I persevered with my music, loving it and feeling that somehow it set me apart from other boys. At the age of thirteen I switched to the French horn, thus gaining invaluable orchestral experience and leaving the keyboard to find its own level in jazz, at which I later discovered that I was rather good, becoming much in demand at parties.

Thus, while still a schoolboy my basic musical education was as a promenader at the much-loved Queen's Hall, then more like a club than the nightly football match-like atmosphere which our descendants have created at the Albert Hall. I heard Chaliapin sing Boris Godunov and Rachmaninoff play his own works; I listened regularly to Malcolm Sargent's delightful analyses of Mozart's masterpieces at the Robert Mayer Saturday Children's concerts at the Central Hall, Westminster.

The French horn, however, turned out to be an instrument on which it is not advisable to perform a solo at the school concert. I was encouraged, against my better judgement, to undertake this act of foolhardy courage, which resulted in reducing the entire school audience to tears of helpless laughter as I burbled and hooted my way through a highly romantic piece by Max Reger, being not far short of tears myself by the time I came to a final, merciful cadence – a comic interlude unique, so I have been told, in the school's annals and only to be surpassed once when, a year later, a boy with the singularly appropriate name of Craze, attempted a serenade on the trombone. I was rewarded for my devotion to music by having permission, grudgingly but not infrequently given by my housemaster, a tone deaf puritan, to go up into the organ loft in the Abbey during our daily service and to watch Osborne Peasegood, the sub-organist and one of the great performers of all time, playing the service which included a voluntary, usually one of the great Bach Preludes and Fugues, with the effortless ease of a fine horseman riding a thoroughbred stallion. A moment which still sends a thrill racing to my fingertips occasionally came when, just before the last hymn, Ossie would turn nonchalantly to me and say, 'Want to drive?' (Like many organists, his real love was the internal combustion engine.) And he would slide along the bench to make room for a small bottom, legs that could hardly touch the pedals and were none too confident of using them, and arms which could barely reach an upper

10

manual of the beautiful monster on which I was permitted to encourage my school mates to stand up, stand up for Jesus.

I was still very uncertain of my place in the national chest of drawers, suffering agonies of embarrassment at both ends of my daily, first class journey on the District Line. Although my tails were rusty-looking and spotted, my collar inky, my top hat like the back of an angry cat, this sartorial splendour seemed terribly out of place as I dragged and scuffed my way through the acacia-lined avenues of Chiswick, dreading the onslaught of some predatory gang of local boys. On arrival at school, however, I was assailed by doubts as to whether my modest circumstances would be accepted by boys whose parents had motorcars and country houses, with pocket money to burn and the assurance which affluence brings. However, the life of the school was so active and diverse that there was not much time for brooding on these psychological dangers which, indeed, were only brought to the surface by a particular circumstance, such as the embarrassment of seeing my father turn up to watch a football match, exuberantly but grotesquely over-dressed in a top hat, or my being forced to ask a boy home in return for metropolitan or country hospitality much grander than I could offer.

Westminster was to open many gates for me, but none with more immediate and startling impact than that which led to the heart. Hitherto my emotions, like my behaviour, had conformed to the normal rages and frustrations which spring up in childhood like summer squalls and are as quickly forgotten. I had friends and playmates, of course, but their value to me lay in what they represented by way of toys and games, places to go and things to do, rather than in their personalities of which, together perhaps even with their sex, I was largely unconscious. But suddenly, at Westminster, I experienced love. It hit me a blow from which I staggered, completely uncomprehending, into a blissful, almost holy, world of total devotion to another human being, excluding all else save the desire to serve, worship and obey.

The object of this crushing burden was a boy three or four years older than I, endowed in my eyes and, since his achievements matched my vision, presumably those of the school, with all virtues, all talents, all beauty of spirit. He played soccer and cricket for the school; he was a senior monitor and clearly destined for academic laurels; he was very musical, could paint and it was claimed he had even kissed girls. I have only the haziest recollection of what he looked like. He treated my worship, which I was torn between disguising and confessing, with an amused tolerance extending so far as giving me help with my music lessons and asking me home for the weekend.

A great deal of over-heated nonsense has been written or imagined about homosexuality at English public schools. In my day it was far less regular or accepted a phenomenon than is popularly believed. In any case, as for most manifestations of the human social animal, it is unwise to generalise; these things occur in unpredictable cycles. While I was at Westminster, close and often sentimental friendships between older and younger boys were fashionable, but they rarely entailed any physical expression beyond arm linking or surreptitious hand-holding in the cloisters at evening; more often, perhaps, violent ragging which brought two sweating and perplexed bodies momentarily into close contact.

At that age, a very young fourteen, I suppose, I was totally innocent. My mother had turned aside from the appalling embarrassment of putting me wise to the complications of sex; my father believed in nature taking its course, egged on by a few sly digs in the ribs long after I had suffered the agonies of self-education. An attempt by an old friend of the family, one of my mother's many lugubrious admirers, to act *in loco parentis* in this delicate field had resulted in a description of the sexual act so disgusting and seemingly irrelevant that I had dismissed it as impossible the minute the door closed behind his red, coughing face. That was just before I went to Westminster; but at an earlier age I had undergone a horrendous experience which, technically I suppose, disqualified me as a virgin. My parents developed a friendship with a junior master at a prep school kept by my godparents; a bluff, jolly, uncle-like figure who, I am now convinced, must have been the original model for Evelyn Waugh's Captain Grimes. My unsuspecting mother welcomed the signs of growing friendship between this manly, cricketing fellow and her lonely little son.

But the first real shock of my life and, for all I know, of hers too, was awaiting us when, one night before dinner, he climbed the stairs to say goodnight to me. He sat on the edge of my bed and began making some remarks about my private parts which I thought were meant to be funny. However, he quickly followed them up my whisking down the bed clothes with a deft movement like that of a practised conjurer, undid my pyjama cord with an efficient tweak and proceeded to commit an act of gross indecency, as the Law would have put it. After a few seconds of outraged and unbelieving silence, I let out a piercing yell and burst into tears. My parents must have guessed the truth, or something like it, for I do not remember being questioned about or, indeed, ever discussing, the incident in later life. No doubt the jolly uncle, like his fictional counterpart, was asked to leave the school quietly to prevent a scandal, and was re-engaged by some other unsuspecting establishment where he continued his libidinous career.

With such a background, it was not surprising that I was something of a puritan and it was thus an appalling shock when, after some school play in which my hero and I had both acted, and flushed with the half-pint of beer allowed on such occasions to the senior boys, this God-like creature who occupied the centre of my small world attempted to give physical expression to our relationship. I was mortified, being convinced that it was somehow my fault that this terrible thing had happened. I wept for a moment in his arms, gasping out my shame and sorrow, and then fled, my pounding feet carrying me full tilt into adolescence. In fact, his timing could not have been worse for I had already become interested in girls and begun to perceive the advantages of heterosexual love. My prime incentive was, I believe, at that stage not so much the urge of adolescent sex, still very guilt-ridden, but rather the surprising fact that girls appeared to like me.

My last year at school was one of almost unrelieved happiness. I had given up the struggle to become a games player, although attaining the dizzy rank of reserve goalkeeper for the First XI. I had passed my exams with credit if not distinction and had found, in John Bowle, a master who provoked and satisfied an intellectual thirst, weaving before us a tapestry of history and contemporary literature illuminated by his own imaginative genius. I had come to some sort of terms with what had now become the girl problem, courting first the sultry, nubile daughter of a prominent QC, into whose bedroom I would creep in the small hours and watch over her, consumed with guilty but as yet chaste lust while she slept, or perhaps pretended to. Other, more mature friendships, or affairs as we liked to call them, followed, some of which survive those torrid early years and have become a precious part of the emotional furniture which I hope will last me the rest of my life.

I left school with no clear idea of what I could or should do next. Certainly, a university was out of the question; I was short of scholarship standard, and my father's income showed signs of an alarming decrease in real terms. This alone ruled out most, if not all, professions and inhibited the search for a well-placed job. Having cruised happily along the same middle-class tramlines followed by my contemporaries, I had suddenly become derailed and left disconsolately beside the tracks while they raced ahead to Oxford, Cambridge, Dartmouth or Sandhurst. Certainly, the thought that I might end up in the Diplomatic Service, had it occurred to me, would have seemed as remote a possibility as that of my sister marrying the Prince of Wales. Although, as a matter of fact, she did make a good and happy marriage before I left school. Her husband, Harry, was a brother of that Julian Yeatman who, even at the time of their wedding, was engaged with his friend Sellars in the production of their masterpiece *1066 And All*

That; and whose sister was married to Leon Goossens, the famous oboist, then and still one of my heroes, the finest instrumentalist of his day.

Early in my schooldays, and later in spite of the ludicrous disaster of the horn solo, I had cherished the dream of being a professional musician. But even if I, and others, had felt sufficient confidence in my talent to undertake what was, at best, a hazardous career, there was no money to sustain the several years of non-productive training which was an essential preliminary. Nevertheless, the musical life of London was a kind of Eldorado, glimpsed and occasionally touched during my schooldays. Once free and technically grown-up, I plunged into it with an abandon which concealed growing doubts about my future place in the Pantheon of English music. After I left school I kept in practice on the horn, playing in amateur orchestras and occasionally standing in as sixth or eighth horn in some professional orchestra – in those union-free days – which gave me a kick but very few ha'pence. On those occasions I would travel about trying to look, and behave, like the popular image of a professional brass player; I wore a green shirt and black slouch hat, carried my horn in a black velvet bag and drank, silent and morose, far too many pints of bitter than were good for either my playing or my health. In this way I rubbed shoulders with professional musicians, a shadowy figure to them no doubt, on the fringe of their busy lives, but with a little self-deception and plenty of nerve I was able to count myself one of them.

One of my first love affairs combined many of the sweets of life as I saw them in those distant days, although the episode was not without a touch of the bizarre. I fell heavily for a female tympanist, a relationship which drew forth many a knowing chortle from my more erudite friends who had done their Freudian homework. I was unabashed, for I lusted after her with my mind as well as my body, sitting at her feet (literally, of course) by the gas fire in her bed-sitting room while she talked of music and musicians, and stroking her ankle, the only part of her desirable body which I was allowed to touch – I did not count kissing, as I could never reach her lips before she had wriggled away in an embarrassment titivated, no doubt, by the fact that she was a year or two older than I. I helped her cart her unwieldy instruments all over London and at weekends we would set forth in her sporting two-seater for the Chilterns over which we would stride together, whistling musical quotations at each other, my heart thumping with desire and the hope that this time, somehow, it might be satisfied. But the most that I was permitted was an occasional glimpse of her knickers as she swung herself up and over a convenient (and, as I thought, lucky) branch of a beech tree. She was a regular tomboy and her attitude to the English countryside was typical of that romantic mysticism popular in the early

14

thirties. Still, she was gifted and helped form such musical thought and knowledge as I now possess. She founded and conducted a small, mixed voice choir in which I sang and which often performed new works by such then modern composers as Elizabeth Lutyens and Benjamin Britten.

It was in this way that I came to know Britten and thus to experience at first hand the rare, elusive quality of genius. I cannot remember the precise beginnings of our friendship, only its full maturity in which we spent a lot of time together walking, talking and making music. In those days, he lived in a small flat in the Cromwell Road and we would often go back there after some concert or party; I would hunch myself in one of the uncomfortable, rickety armchairs while he sat at an upright piano pouring out inspired improvisations on popular themes, musical jokes, pianistic pyrotechnics and, after a sudden hush that presaged a change of mood, some of the loveliest, most original sounds I had ever heard. It was impossible not to be aware of the extreme unusualness of his mind and the manner he translated his thoughts into music; there was a force about him which, I believed even then, could not fail to have a profound effect on our generation. With a lesser person I might have played the Salieri, asking sulkily why I could not have been equally gifted, or fortunate, or admired. But with Ben I was seldom tempted by envy, for I guessed that he had been chosen by the same mysterious hand that had touched the shoulder of Mozart, Beethoven and Schubert, and that I had not been so chosen but must always count myself lucky to have been warmed by those creative fires.

Paradoxically, it was my concern for his genius and future greatness which caused our only quarrel. Ben was a pacifist. When war in Europe was looming he decided to go to America. I am sure that he was not running away; it was rather that he felt that his work would benefit from the experience of life in the States. But he wanted nothing to do with a conflict which he regarded as irrelevant if not obscene. I respected his pacifism, although I did not share it. But I argued against his going, for I was convinced that our country was about to experience a profound crisis and believed that the work of someone destined to be perhaps the greatest composer of the century would suffer in some way if he were not here to share our national agony. Ben, of course, rejected all this at the time; and since I probably put my case badly, rejected me as well. We parted with a sadness soon to be anaesthetised, like all other emotions, by the yellow vapour of war as it crept relentlessly across Europe. After the war, when he had returned to the land where, as he recognised, his roots really lay, we saw each other briefly, but our relationship was never the same. We sent each other Christmas cards; I wrote to him from the Congo after first

15

hearing a recording of the War Requiem; he replied briefly but in terms which made me wonder whether something could not be salvaged. But we were too far apart, geographically as well as in our ways of life. After I retired, I planned to go to Aldeburgh to see him, and he would have welcomed me. But it was too late; he was ill and shortly to die. I think of him now with mixed feelings. I was probably wrong about his going to America and I was foolish not to have made a greater effort to remain close to him, above all to see him before he died. But I rejoice in the memory of a precious friendship, and of genius spread before me like a field of wild flowers, careless in its profusion, and infinite in its variety.

The glorious sense of freedom, as the beginning of a school term that I did not have to attend came round, was marred by my nagging doubts about the future and the clearly pressing need to find a job. At this point, not for the last time, the course of my life was given a nudge by that hidden force which, like a magnetic field, emanates from the old-boy network. An imaginative but eccentric business man, J. Spedan Lewis, had inherited a thriving retail business which he proceeded to turn into what we now know as the John Lewis Partnership. He had been educated at Westminster and was, in many ways, in advance of his time, believing that there was a place in industry and commerce for those who were still quite seriously called gentlemen by reason of their drawer of origin and educational background. Accordingly, the firm contained a number of these trainees who were destined for the upper management if they qualified satisfactorily in what was a vigorous apprenticeship. Somebody knew somebody who knew somebody; my old Westminster tie was carefully worn at an interview with a smiling, quick-eyed man, Michael Watkins, who turned out to have been a master at the school before he was spotted by Spedan and snatched to stardom. I was hired on the spot and told to report to the dress materials department the following Monday. My parents were relieved, although my father was, I think, disappointed that I was not embarking on a career more to his liking – such as that of golf professional or something in the catering business, where I could have been more useful; and I was thankful to have my mind made up for me. My heart was full of hope and my stomach of butterflies as I clocked in at nine o'clock and was told that my wages would be 15/6d a week. I was seventeen and a half, desperately shy and ambitious to succeed.

The Partnership had the outward trappings of democracy; an elected council, distributed profits, a fluid social life in which all partners, as the employees were called, mixed on an equal footing in various sports (at a subsidised country club in the Thames valley), theatrical and musical activities. But in reality it was a benevolent dictatorship presided over by an autocrat who permitted his policies to be debated and jokes about himself to be printed in the *Gazette*; but whose word, in fact, was law and final. My slightly bumptious personality and musical talent (I began composing lyrics and music for the annual satirical review), together with the pink and black Westminster tie, soon attracted his attention, and I became a kind of Court Jester, not necessarily destined for high office but assured of a place in the sun and secure from arbitrary dismissal. Spedan was kind and imaginative, and his little court circle enjoyed trips to Glyndebourne, and winter sports in Switzerland, all at his (or the firm's) expense. But he exacted a full return for our wages, the meagreness of which was not successfully concealed by the trappings of enlightenment. We worked from nine to six on weekdays and from nine to one on Saturdays; often longer, without any overtime. But we did not complain; on the whole it was a relatively trouble-free life. I left my parents' roof (by now a flat in Chelsea) and found a series of bedsitters, gradually improving in furnishing, service and location as my weekly wages crept up the scale until, suddenly, I was being paid monthly, an advance in status equivalent, in those days, to direct promotion from lance corporal to field officer.

Meanwhile, my friends were enjoying the secluded pleasures of Oxford or Cambridge. I would visit them at weekends, dipping into the university life in a tantalisingly unsatisfactory way. But I was not jealous of them, for I believed myself to be much more sophisticated, to have a superior knowledge of the real world, and hence to be several laps ahead in a race which we had started together. I did not then suspect the disadvantages which I would later suffer from having missed the intellectual bonanza they were enjoying. I was content with my world, in which I had already become a personality in my own right, and my lack of a degree did not seem to present a barrier to promotion, given patience and a determination not to roam beyond the permitted boundaries of behaviour. I inched my way up the ladder – serving behind the counter, running the lifts, working in the store-rooms and packing bays; as an assistant to first one buyer, then another; and a short, extraordinary period as private secretary to the Marquis of Carisbrooke, who had been engaged by Spedan for a function about which neither he nor I was clear. This, my first experience of royalty, gave me a ring-side seat, so to speak, at the Abdication in 1936, since the Marquis was gloriously indiscreet and regaled me with tales of the goings-on at Fort Belvedere and other royal residences which I found deliciously implausible until history revealed most of them to have been largely accurate; and rubbing his small, exquisitely-shaped hands with glee when it was at last clear that a new, and for him especially, more favourable reign was about to begin. As well as Marquises, my life contained the classic contrast of shop girls – for I found the pretty girls behind the counter irresistible, with their pert little figures and broad Cockney humour. However, as social students of that period will know, they were almost universally prim when it came to anything approaching a crunch, and I was seldom permitted more than a surreptitious pat on a neat behind, or a sticky kiss on firmly closed lips at the end of a rehearsal for some Partnership show.

As if to complete this Jekyll and Hyde existence, I had also got myself onto a number of Lists. At this period, the social life of upper class London was each year crowned by a wreath of debutantes and studded with dances and other entertainments at which the daughters of the aristocracy and the upper classes, sanctified by presentation at Court and protected in their certified virginity by elderly females, either related or of impeccable reliability, would be placed in the marriage market to capitalise on such looks, personality, talent and wealth as they might genuinely possess or be made to appear to own. Naturally, this activity required a number of young men not only as eligible suitors, but as the counters with which to play the game. I became one of the counters whose names made up the Lists so carefully kept and continuously vetted by anxious mothers. On several nights a week during the Season, I would fight my way home from Oxford Street, change into white tie and tails – the self-same suit which had graced the school concert platform for the hilarious horn solo –and report for duty at some Belgravia dinner party. I often hardly knew the girl I was supposed to escort (let alone my hostess), and was not above abandoning her, once safely landed at the dance, for some closer, more attractive partner. In the early hours of those soft summer mornings, I would deposit my girl of the evening dutifully at her front door, perhaps with a snatched, lipstick-smeared goodnight kiss, and often having had to borrow the taxi fare; then, with my top hat Bertie Wooster-like on the back of my head, I would saunter across the dawn-dewed park to my bedsitter, feeling, as my father would have said, a helluva-lad, to snatch a couple of hours' sleep before clocking-in at nine o'clock as a drapery salesman, while my friends of the previous night slept it off before resuming the round of pleasure. I kept as quiet as possible about my real life, knowing that it would take too much explaining to bridge the apparent gap and would undermine that mothers' confidence which was an indispensable passport to this glamorous world. I had a reputation for being 'SIT' (Safe In Taxis), which meant not only that I could be relied upon to respect the precious daughter's virginity between dinner and dance, but that I was considered socially acceptable and generally List-worthy. I was occasionally confronted with an awkward moment when my hostess of the night before caught my eye across the counter in John Lewis or Peter Jones when purchasing satin for a petticoat or gingham for new nursery curtains; I did not always succeed in convincing her that I, too, was a customer. But no serious harm was done, and I gradually found that those girls and their parents whom I cared about understood my situation, took my job seriously and even hinted at a sense of admiration on which I was, of course, quick to capitalise. 'How amusing,' they would say, 'to work in a shop – and such useful experience.' I was not above conveying the impression that I had consciously chosen this eccentric, and otherwise unacceptable, way of life.

CHAPTER TWO

Most of my generation must admit that the central decades of their lives might have been very different had it not been for the outbreak of World War II. Certainly in the mid-thirties there seemed no reason why the pattern of my life should alter. Apart from some echoes of my adolescent dreams of fame – that very special kind of versatile success of which Noel Coward was the unique, brilliant and much imitated example – I was content with my lot. The higher rungs of the John Lewis Partnership ladder were becoming dimly visible as I gazed up; I could afford the modest pleasures of those unsophisticated days; and I had no desire for marriage, which would, in any case, have been beyond my economic reach, although it was a game of pretence which I played with one or two girls to give depth to an otherwise rather shallow emotional life. But those of us who by this time had discovered, however tentatively, what certain parts of our bodies were really designed for, lived in constant anxiety about the risk of pregnancy – that unspeakable disgrace which carried disaster for all concerned, living or as yet unborn. Days, sometimes weeks, were passed in agonized suspense, even some rudimentary planning against 'the worst' happening, until the blessed relief came, the telephone call, the quick note slipped under the door – 'It's all right, it's happened' – and the sun came out again to ornament the gay silks, the long flashing legs and shiny shoes which had played such a part in the original temptation.

The coming of the war slowed down this glittering express train. The brakes were suddenly applied with that ominous sound which meant an amber light had been passed and trouble lay ahead; soon the train would shudder to a halt and lie, panting and perplexed in the open countryside, waiting for some quite unprecedented happening. I was not, in those days, a very political animal and it was well into 1938 before I realised things were happening which might affect me and my life. I decided to join the Territorial Army with the mixed, muddled motives which characterised that confused period. I supposed naively that the more soldiers we had, the more chance of preventing war; but if there was going to be one, I wanted to be in on the ground floor. I walked down Davies Street one day with a friend and enlisted in the Queen Victoria's Rifles, a territorial unit of the 60th Rifles (the KRRC) which was about to form a second battalion. From my public school accent it was assumed that I shared the previous experience of school OTC with the other young gentlemen then enlisting; but this was not so, for the Corps was not compulsory at Westminster, and even as a small boy I was able to imagine better ways of spending my time than wearing, once a week, the scratchy and conspicuous khaki uniform with its fiendishly difficult puttees and studded boots which rang ominously on the ancient, peaceful gravestones of the Abbey floor.

This lack of experience meant some pretty fast footwork if I was to keep up with the military Joneses; but since the British Army, when confronted with a new situation, tends to go back to the beginning, I was able to pick up the rudiments of rifle drill and weapon training as we went along, and in due course was promoted Sergeant in the newly-formed battalion. I developed a quite uncharacteristic rash of patriotism and began talking about the Hun, the Colours, the Regiment (God Bless It), and generally using language more appropriate, as history now knows, to the war that had already been fought and won. I omitted to tell Spedan about my new, part-time military career. He was furious that I had not consulted him and threatened that, if war should break out and I went for a soldier (as people still said), I should never darken his door again. I responded as I imagined Kitchener or the King would have expected, by saying that if he thought I was going to spend the war buying mirrors and gimp (my job at that time) for probably non-existent customers, he had better think again. We parted on this discordant note; I never saw him again.

By the summer of 1939 our battalion was thought to be sufficiently well formed to spend a fortnight in camp. That August was cold and wet; Munich had been proved the false dawn that so many had proclaimed; we were ploughing into the night at an alarming but irreversible velocity. The betting in the sergeants' mess was that the outbreak of war would catch us still in camp, that we would never revert to civilian life until victory, which most people thought would take about six months, restored us as heroes to a world made even safer for democracy. Rumour was our daily and nightly diet. All German tanks were rubber fakes – a chap had skidded into one while on holiday in Austria; the Fleet was mobilised and steaming to China; London would be wiped out by aerial bombardment five minutes after the declaration of war; the King and Queen were preparing to go to Canada; the Maginot Line was invincible; the Maginot Line was indefensible; Hitler had been seen on the Siegfried Line – and so on *ad infinitum*.

We were not far out in our timing. I was on my way back from an extra week's holiday after camp had broken up when my mother read over the telephone a telegram ordering me to report forthwith to our regimental HQ, now set up in a large house in Grosvenor Square, from which the tenants had already fled. It was mid August, and we had been embodied – a biblical sounding term to describe the mobilizing of the Territorial Army. We were issued with our pitifully inadequate weapons, ammunition and transport. The crescendo of rumours reached a *fortissimo* climax a few days later as we climbed into civilian trucks, which smelt of fish and garbage, and drove off through cheering crowds to an unknown destination, varying in rumour between Flanders trenches and the South Pacific.

I had managed to telephone my mother to say goodbye, and felt quite a hero as we drove through the streets of South London. I would have preferred to have been marching, with a flower in my cap and a girl on my arm, singing a patriotic song, but in war, as I was discovering, you can't have everything. My heroic mood was abruptly deflated when we stopped somewhere in Battersea. I ran up to the front of the column to find out how long a wait we would have, and was told that we had arrived. My platoon's destination was the railway bridge which carried over the river the only direct link between the north and south systems. It was to be our task to guard this vital artery against enemy attack, although our potential assailant was never precisely identified. I was able to get through to my mother late that night. She shrieked with dismay, having no doubt steeled herself against a separation of months if not years. 'Where are you, darling, for God's sake?' she gasped. 'Battersea,' I said, 'but you mustn't tell anyone.' I heard the receiver fall from her hand and feared that she had fainted with shock. But she soon revived enough to say, 'Well, at least I'll be able to do your washing.' There did not seem to be much more to say, and since I was, in any case, short of change I said goodbye, probably rather too abruptly, and rang off.

We were there, billeted in houses round about, when war was declared on September 3rd. Immediately after Chamberlain's tired, sad voice had died away, the sirens went, in justification, it seemed, of those who had prophesied an aerial armageddon. I was in command but had no idea what to do; our battalion was spread out all over south London performing similar duties; there was no officer within miles; and I had no orders on the procedure in an air raid. Vague memories of the importance of civilian morale flashed through my mind. I ordered the platoon to fall in and marched them off, with instructions to sing cheerful, military songs. We had no sooner bawled out the opening bars of Tipperary when the All Clear sounded the biggest anticlimax of my life. We spent several weeks on the bridge, watching the troop trains roll southwards and gradually accustoming ourselves to a strange, wartime world that, nevertheless, seemed in some odd way familiar. When war actually came it was no surprise to me; I realised that I had known, subconsciously, for a long time that it was inevitable. In my childhood I had been fascinated by the World War I which I had seen through the romantic haze of stories in boy's papers, old bound copies of the *Illustrated London News* and my own reconstruction of the trenches in endless war games which I and my friends played, turning Barnes Common into a plausible-enough replica of the Somme, and pressing the odd Aunt or two into service as enemy forces. The British Army's modernisation was, in 1939, only skin deep – below the surface it was still the Army that had defended Mons, survived the unimaginable slaughter of the Marne, the Aisne and the Somme, and come singing home with poppies in their caps, to stand silent but proud in front of the Cenotaph while a single bugle called a note of sad greeting across the graves of those who had fallen for King and Country. Of new techniques and weapons we were unaware and the growing stalemate on the European mainland left us confused and impatient.

We were moved to the Docks where we spent an icy Christmas, still on guard against the unseen enemy, my only risk being a near escape from skidding into the river while delivering the rum ration on Christmas Eve. Early 1940 found us in billets in north London with more rumours of moves abroad. By this time I was under pressure to exchange my sergeant's stripes for an officer's pips – a move I was reluctant to make since I enjoyed the comradeship of the Sergeants' Mess, and the firm but friendly relationship with the riflemen, but had not formed any great opinion of the officer class as represented in our battalion. However, I could not hold out indefinitely and so at the beginning of May I found myself at an OCTU in Colchester. Within a week the Germans were sweeping through France, proving as much to their own astonishment as to ours that modern warfare had successfully arrived.

For the rest of that summer we awaited what seemed a certain invasion by the victorious Germany Army, the unbroken succession of glorious days and clear, starlit nights reminding us of the puny plight and massive failures of mankind. All day we followed our training course. At night, formed into *ad hoc* sections, we stood-to on the East Anglian beaches, armed with 1914-type rifles and six rounds each of ammunition, waiting for the Panzer Divisions to come storming out of the sea. We christened ourselves the Clacton Expeditionary Force, and doubted if we could win the race against time and get our commissions before the Germans came.

My friend Stephen Watts, destined, like me, for a black-buttoned commission, was in a section actually stationed on Clacton Pier itself. His orders were that when the enemy was sighted, whether by air or sea, he was to run to the landward end of the Pier where there was a public telephone, place two pennies (provided by the Quartermaster from public funds) in the slot and, when connected, inform the Adjutant that the invasion had begun. These ludicrous precautions may have been the cause of his making a remark, now famous, which nearly cost him his commission. During an inspection by an under-employed General, he was asked the kind of question which readily springs to the unfertile military mind: 'And what are you doing here, my good man?' The General nodded, beaming in anticipation of an equally military reply. He got a political one instead. 'Sir,' said Stephen, stiffening to attention, 'I am making a land fit for Pierrots to dwell in.'

In spite of many alarms, and an even more fantastic crop of rumours – charred bodies washed up on the Channel coast, parachuting nuns, spies who altered the hands of the church clock to help the Heinkels navigate, the slightly laughable, but nevertheless seemingly omniscient Lord Haw Haw – the Germans did not invade. I gained my commission and reported for duty to the regimental training battalion in Wiltshire. There I stayed.

Regimental life retained a number of peace-time features. We changed for dinner, ate from tables festooned with the regimental silver, and played snooker or billiard fives afterwards. We trained innumerable intakes of recruits and despatched them in due course to our battalions elsewhere in the UK or overseas. We helped the local Home Guard, feeling very professional; we spent occasional Saturday evenings in Swindon or Marlborough, and even more infrequent weekends in London, the mecca for all leave. Otherwise, lost in the beautiful English countryside like a permanent all-male houseparty, the war largely passed us by. It was a situation of which part of me was ashamed, for I recognised in myself a distinct unwillingness to thrust myself forward as a volunteer for active duty. But I seemed to have the knack of putting across the simple lessons then required by basic training, and I felt that I was doing my duty, if not a very glamorous or courageous one. I certainly did nothing to try to alter the course of fate, and remained ready to accept whatever its wheel might turn up.

During 1941 and early 1942 I developed a further, much more powerful reason for hoping that I would be left, unnoticed in my tiny corner of war-time England. I had fallen in love and was, as they say, courting. This delicate operation, made infinitely more difficult by the unnatural strains and separations of war-time life, was nevertheless successfully completed.

I proposed to Babs in the garden of the King's Arms Hotel in Marlborough, Wiltshire; wearing the crash helmet in which I had arrived but had omitted to take off. The reader will be able to judge what prophetically appropriate headgear this turned out to be. We were married on May 23rd, 1942, in Saint Faith's Chapel, Westminster Abbey.

Babs (or Beatrice to give her formal, seldom-used name), an only child, was born in New Haven for reasons which I could never quite fathom since the family house had been, and continued to be, on Beacon Street in the proper part of Boston. Her parents were Bostonian New Englanders, both of whose families could trace their origins far back to faded parish records and crumbling gravestones in the villages of East Anglia. Her mother was a strong personality, Victorian in outlook and puritan in manner; I sometimes wondered how Babs had ever managed to get herself born, let alone conceived. But this unworldliness was tempered by a delicious sense of humour and an uncanny instinct about human nature, both of which qualities her daughter has inherited to the full. My mother-in-law faced with great courage the appalling handicap of severe deafness and was a charming and intelligent companion to whom I was deeply attached. I never knew Babs' father, since he had died when she was fourteen. He was, by all accounts, an accomplished musician and gifted linguist. His career in international banking took him to Russia, China and Japan in which countries Babs spent her formative years, moving from Vladivostok to Tokyo to Peking as the demands of her father's work dictated, and picking up the languages with a child's lack of effort as well as acquiring fluent, idiomatic French, the only language in which she could receive any education. This multi-lingual childhood spent in an international community gave her an understanding of, and respect for, foreign customs, cultures and people far removed from the insular and bigoted outlook all too frequently a hallmark of Anglo-Saxon attitudes of the period and which was, of course, of infinite benefit to both of us in our future career. Although she did not retain any of her languages, except French, in any fluency, she can reproduce to this day certain limited phrases in rapid and faultless accents – scaring and confusing Soviet diplomats, for example, by beginning a conversation in what seems to them to be impeccably idiomatic Russian and then refusing to continue; or enchanting the children by singing lullabies to them in Japanese.

Babs is of medium height, auburn-haired, possessed of tireless energy and a determination not to be defeated by the trials and tribulations of this earthly life. Being, in addition, immensely capable, the more impossible the task the more she feels challenged to overcome any and all obstacles, often with the help of willing but bemused friends, relations or even total strangers wise enough to recognise that they are in the presence of a considerable natural force. Through it all she communicates an irresistible zest for life and a deep concern that others should share in her pleasures and triumphs. She is quickly moved to compassion for the deprived and handicapped and to outrage at injustice and cruelty. In the face of any such situation, her first instinct is the need for action – a quality which she inherits from her mother, whose immediate reaction on seeing the leaning tower of Pisa for the first time, late in her life, was to consider ways in which it could be straightened, and to wonder why no-one had apparently attempted to do so during the six centuries of its existence.

Babs' family moved back to the USA when she was fourteen, thus permitting her to complete her education in her native America (and American) and to round it off by a year at Oxford, where she combined studying English Literature under Neville Coghill with meeting her future (first) husband; and so fulfilling, I suspect, her mother's dream, to whom all things and persons English were lit by that rosy romantic glow which has done so much to diffuse the light of truth as it struggles to cross the Atlantic.

She duly married and in 1935 her husband, John Rathbone, was elected National Conservative member of Parliament for Bodmin, the youngest successful candidate at that election. Her presence at his side in the constituency was so effective that when he was killed in 1940 – one of the early casualties of Bomber Command – she was asked by all Parties to take his place, and was returned without opposition. She thus became the second American-born woman in history to be a Member of Parliament (Lady Astor was the first). I had known the whole family since before the war. When we married I inherited two beloved step-children, then sheltering from the Blitz with Babs' American family in the USA. The arrival of our own daughter, Faith, in 1943 set up a further record, since she became the first child ever to be born to a sitting Member of Parliament – a formulation to which, although constitutionally correct, Babs has always objected owing to its gynaecological implications. This remarkable family story has recently been carried on by the entry of my step-son, Tim Rathbone, into Parliament in 1974 as Member for Lewes; which made him only the second Member in history both of whose parents had been Members of the House of Commons. In spite of this highly Anglicised pattern of life – she had forfeited her American citizenship by taking the oath of allegiance required of all MPs – Babs has always maintained a fierce, although not uncritical, loyalty to America. Her reception by her first English family could hardly be described as enthusiastic; her mother-in-law habitually introduced her as 'my little American daughter-in-law with the incredibly small feet', an accurate description, admittedly, of one of Babs' most endearing physical attributes, but hardly an encouragement to strange relations to take her to their bosoms. She says that it was often several months before uncles, aunts or cousins actually looked her in the face, so hypnotised were they by the size of her shoes.

Female Members of Parliament were then rare enough, and not usually thought of as being marriageable. When I formed up to my Commanding Officer to seek permission to marry (still required by junior officers) and told him to whom, adding that as she was a MP there might (horror of horrors) even be a little publicity, he showed signs of acute distress, bending at the knees, pulling his moustache and staring silently out of the window. At last, with a kind of spluttering cough, he brought himself to say, with many courtly apologies, what was on his mind. 'Isn't she – er – ah – a little – um – well – shall we say – old for you, my dear boy?' He was crimson with embarrassment, as well he might be since, probably due to my own lack of precision, he believed my intended bride to be Miss Eleanor Rathbone, (an Aunt of John's) at that time an elderly, spinster lady MP devoted single-mindedly to the great social causes for which her life is rightly honoured and remembered.

Faith was born on 24 April 1943 in an upstairs bedroom in a house in Bridlington, whither the battalion had been moved with that appallingly inept timing so typical of war-time. We wanted to be together for the birth, and this seemed the only way. Within a fortnight, Babs was back in the House, and I was biting my nails, now thoroughly bored and longing to get away, anywhere, from a routine out of which I had wrung every possible variation, and whose remoteness from the real war was causing me increasing concern. The old-boy network once again came to my rescue. By dint of a few telephone calls from a CO now anxious to be rid of me, and a quiet glass of sherry at the Cavalry Club, I found myself at last posted away to a mysterious unit called 21 Army Group, said to be housed in St Paul's School, Hammersmith. When, ten days later, I reported to Humphrey Prideaux, my host who had so discreetly vetted me, he smiled shyly, saying, 'You might as well know what we are up to here,' and showed a map of the north-west coast of France, with beaches marked in code names. We were planning Overlord, and I had become a member of Montgomery's staff. Within days I knew most details about the invasion plans (except the actual date) and became immersed in the highly complex task of planning the orderly embarkation, landing and deployment of hundreds of thousands of men and their equipment on a hostile shore. We worked very hard, straining for a deadline we all could guess but never discussed. I was able to spend the few free hours I had at home with Babs in her little house in Dean's Yard, Westminster; but the burden of the terrible secrets I carried was so heavy that I scarcely dared share her bed lest I were to talk in my sleep. Humphrey was a kind but precise master, the finest staff officer I was ever to know; it was a happy, fulfilled time, stretching my capabilities to the utmost and teaching me things which, in my intellectual snobbishness, I had thought the army incapable of imparting.

This halcyon spell was broken when Humphrey was replaced by an officer less sympathetic in every way. On his first morning he gathered our little section together and, glaring at us with a disconcertingly unco-ordinated pair of eyes – you never knew which was looking at you – he growled, 'From now on, there are only two rules in this section – first, always get it in writing; second, never put it in writing. Got it? Right then.' Fortunately, our pre-invasion work was largely done, and one morning we woke up to the news that D-Day had arrived. We moved to Wentworth. I made a brief return trip over the Channel by air. Finally we boarded a large troop carrier and slipped out of Portsmouth to land, on a cold June dawn, at the now miraculously assembled and fully operational Mulberry Harbour.

So much has been written about the Normandy campaign, the dramatic fighting through France and Belgium to the Rhine, and of the subsequent campaigns until VE Day, that it would be superfluous for a junior staff officer who, on the whole, saw shots fired by accident rather than in anger, to add his reminiscences. My job was unspectacular but essential and exhausting: to help organise the supply lines for the ammunition, food, petrol and everything else which the army needed for its operations. We moved up not far behind the forward divisions. In Amiens, we had to dislodge by force the inmates of a brothel who believed that the arrival of the Allies would mean a slump in trade. I landed at Brussels airport while the retreating Germans were still fighting in the nearby fields, and took part in that great surge of relief which carried young and old alike out onto the streets and into the arms of complete strangers. My last winter was spent in Brussels, with a growing certainty of victory that not even the frightening seven days' wonder of the German Ardennes offensive could seriously undermine.

I remained incredibly healthy throughout the campaign, but succumbed to the political virus which, as final victory came in sight, seized the armed forces with the fever of an impending General Election, a form of national sport which some of them could hardly remember. On a brief leave, I had got myself adopted as a candidate for the Liberal party in Bethnal Green, next door to Sir Percy Harris, also a Liberal and a veteran Parliamentarian.

Babs, by this time, had decided not to contest her seat at the forthcoming election. This was a brave decision made in the interests of her family, for she loved political life and had been a successful and popular MP. What was more difficult for her to swallow was my adoption of a party against which she had fought long and hard by her husband's side in Cornwall.

But the mood in the armed forces was overwhelmingly for change. As things turned out, that mood found its expression in a massive vote for the Labour Party: but for those who, like myself, mistrusted both the major parties, the Liberals seemed to represent the kind of England for which we imagined we had been fighting. The party fielded over five hundred candidates and, in the uncertain silence which followed the cease-fire in Europe, was felt to stand a good chance of at least holding the balance in the new Parliament. I flew home the day after the Germans surrendered. Babs met me at Croydon airport with pretty well the last of her monthly petrol ration. As we drove into London, my reserves finally cracked: I laid my head on her shoulder and wept; tears of relief that it was all over; tears for all my vanished friends and for an old world never to be recaptured; tears of joy to be with Babs again, unthreatened by another separation; tears of plain fatigue now, for the first time, a permitted indulgence.

After VE Day, I got down to the task of canvassing my constituency in preparation for the election. The East Enders were wonderful people. All through the war they had shrugged their shoulders, sucked their teeth and got on with the job, undaunted by the appalling Blitz. I campaigned as a returning soldier who would look after the boys coming home, find them jobs and houses, and generally usher in a new society which would be fair to all. The slogan devised by my local Chairman (a road sweeper) and my Treasurer (a prosperous fish monger) seemed right: 'Good enough for Monty, Good enough for us' was shouted from the hoardings, beneath the picture of a puzzled young officer trying to look wise. I was politically naive and my agent, a shrewd, realistic professional, kept me as far away from the platform as he dared, sending me knocking on endless doors while Babs, with extraordinary loyalty considering her own political past, ran the office, dished out election literature and generally made things work with her wealth of experience and tireless energy.

I greatly enjoyed getting to know these gallant people for whom a Brave New World seemed to have been brought no nearer by victory. Indeed, peace seemed to have knocked them temporarily off balance. One old lady, in a very poor, badly bombed street, wearing a man's cap fastened by a large pearl pin through her abundant dyed hair, summoned me indoors and offered me what she called 'a cup o' tea and a nice piece of seedy cake'. After I had made my customary little speech, she gave me a shrewd friendly glance. 'You look like a nice young man,' she said, brushing cake crumbs off her bosom. 'I advise you to bugger orf from 'ere: we've always been Labour in this 'ouse and so we're voting for old Churchill.' The great man did, in fact, pay the East End a visit shortly before polling day. Enormous crowds cheered him wildly and then went into the polling stations to administer one of the most humiliating defeats in British electoral history.

In our local poll, I came a respectable second to Labour, the Conservative losing his deposit. Looking back I cannot tell how I came to deserve this act of mercy by a Providence which had clearly not equipped me for a political career. I should have been miserable as an MP, and my years in Whitehall were to do nothing to increase my respect for politicians as a breed, however much I was to love and admire individual specimens.

In accordance with a gentleman's agreement almost unthinkable today, but then taken for granted, I returned to the Army although technically and legally free, to serve out my time until my due date for demobilisation came along. I spent the last months of 1945 in the War Office in a part of the Joint Chiefs of Staff Organisation. In January 1946 I was a civilian once more, with a small gratuity, a free suit of clothes plus tie and raincoat, a wife and child (together with my two step-children who had returned to England earlier in the year, before D-Day, much to the fury of their American relations); and no prospect of a job. Spedan, in spite of his threat, had said he would take me back at my pre-war salary, an offer which I hope I managed to decline without revealing how derisory I considered it. I dabbled in Liberal politics, helping the party lick its post-election wounds by serving on a Committee which was to make recommendations for the future. Our report was entitled 'Coats Off for the Future and Hats Off to the Past', but once discussion of its proposals began in the Party Committees and Council, it seemed to me that a juxtaposition of hat and coat would have been more appropriate. The Committee's Chairman was Noel Newsome, himself a failed Liberal candidate and famous as a war-time broadcaster. He was offered the post of Director of Recruitment in the Ministry of Fuel and Power, and asked me to join his staff. I thus became a temporary Civil Servant and began to learn how to thread my way through the Whitehall maze, how to say yes when I meant no, and maybe when I meant neither. Our team included Robin Gordon-Walker, the brilliant younger brother of the future Foreign Secretary, who was to die tragically young, within two years; and an old Westminster friend of mine, Jack Triggs, who performed the near-incredible feat of being the brother-in-law of Joe Davis, world snooker champion, and son-in-law of Sir George Rendel, at that time British Ambassador in Brussels.

Increase in coal production, and hence of the workforce in the mines, was a high priority of the government. Noel had the ear of Manny Shinwell, the first post-war Minister of Fuel and Power, and of his junior ministers who included Hugh Gaitskell. When the formal nationalisation of the mining industry took place on January 1st 1947, the entire Cabinet assembled in Shinwell's office to toast the great occasion. It was my only glimpse of Ernie Bevin at close quarters, a man whose massive presence imposed itself on any gathering, and who had the grace and manners which come naturally to very great men.

As soon as the National Coal Board was formed, our team moved over to Hobart House and became the Directorate of Public Relations. My short, but intensive training in Liberal policies had convinced me of the validity of arguments in favour of selective nationalisation, particularly of the coal mining industry, and I felt lucky to be able to witness the first major experiment of its kind from so advantageous a viewpoint. It was deeply disillusioning. The new management differed from the coal owners only, it seemed to me, in their remoteness from the pithead amid the vast bureaucracy which rapidly developed. The Trade Union leaders viewed the Board with even greater suspicion than their past opponents, the owners, and from the beginning exhibited that deep, rigidly conservative outlook which was then, and remains, the British Trade Unions' unhappy contribution to industrial relations. Of the golden millennium, when there would be no more 'we' and 'them' but only 'us' there was no sign, as the two sides glared at each other across the sea of paper which littered the committee room tables. Central to all this was the miner himself. Like the vast majority of the nation, I had taken the production of coal for granted, assuming that its arrival in my fireplace, the light and power which it generated and the trains which it moved, were part of the natural order of things, and of no direct concern to me provided I was maintained in a relatively even temperature, and with adequate mobility; the disruptions to these attributes of civilization were temporary inconveniences which victory would cancel overnight. But that did not happen. Shortages became, if anything, worse after VE Day, and by the exceptionally severe winter of 1946/7 the nation was gripped by a major fuel crisis.

Our primary task remained recruitment, and I felt unable to make a sincere and worthwhile contribution without knowing much more about the miners' work and life. Accordingly, I visited coal fields in the Midlands, in Wales, in Kent, wherever I found that I was not unwelcome; I spent hours at the coal face, sometimes in old fashioned pits with narrow, back-breaking seams, or in those with broader, easier seams where the introduction of mechanisation had begun. I shared the pit-head baths, where these existed, with the miners and visited their homes. I was staggered by their skill and the danger of their work, by the nobility of their underground comradeship, the fortitude of their women; indeed, by all aspects of a job which few would undertake voluntarily unless, like so many in that aristocrat of heavy industries, they had been born to it. I was so absorbed in this work that Faith became convinced that I was actually a miner and registered bitter disappointment when I failed to appear off the commuter train at the end of the day with a grimy face and wearing a hard hat with a lamp on it.

We tried to build a place in the nation's heart for these gallant men; to portray them as a fourth service whose duties were as arduous, and whose existence as essential as the Royal Navy, the Army or Royal Air Force. We applied all the known techniques to bring this home to the public: an exhibition in Hyde Park with simulated pit-cage and coal-face, mass colliery brass bands conducted by Sir Adrian Boult, posters, articles, broadcasts, and public meetings. Recruitment improved, output figures crept up. But there was a hollow ring in it all, when the miner got his pay packet or his wife waited anxiously for news at the pithead.

No doubt our ideas were idealistic and took scant account of the industrial and commercial realities which the Board had to face. But whatever the reasons they could not, or would not, implement a policy which recognised our central theme. Our relations with the Board became strained, and our little team began to break up. First I resigned, mainly because I was dissatisfied and disillusioned with the Board's policy, but also because their idea of my future prospects did not coincide with my own. Robin had died, a tragic loss; Noel resigned a few months later. I had few regrets. In spite of my, by now, near-romantic attachment to the miners' cause, I felt that somehow I had not found my proper niche. So once again, the future yawned at me, empty of purpose, lacking that beckoning finger which is often more of a comfort than a challenge.

In spite of my unsettled career, we had managed to create some stability in our family life. We had bought a house in the West Sussex Downs. It was in a stretch of country with which I had fallen hopelessly in love when, as a small boy staying with a school friend, I had roamed the chalk hills, learning their ancient tracks by heart and, as a special treat, helping to excavate the site of a neolithic camp. The great beech trees along the embankment of the old Roman Stane Street as it crosses the hills on its course towards Chichester became my friends. I knew even then that one day I must live there, and fate was kind in making it possible so soon. The elder children were at school and Faith, even then acutely conscious of being much the younger, was straining at the leash to join them. Babs beautified our house with her genius for colour and style; we had a tiny flat in London where we could retreat into a grown-up world when the school holidays were over. It was all perfect, but extremely precarious without a settled job and income.

Napoleon used to ask one question only about officers proposed for promotion – 'Is he lucky?' On this basis, I would have qualified for high rank in the Grande Armée, by dint of often finding myself in the right place at the right time. The present stage was no exception. There lived in the next village to ours a man to whom I owe a debt which I never could have fully repaid, even if he had not died tragically in 1968. I had known Gerald Barry a little during the war, when he was editor of *The News Chronicle*, and he had taken quite a shine to Babs as a young and pretty MP whose views he respected. Few men in any age are gifted with vision larger than themselves and their times; and fewer still are given the chance of making their dreams come true. Gerald's dream was simple, but enormous: 1951 would see the centenary of the Great Exhibition of 1851, a watershed from which have continued to run streams of inspiration in the creative life of the country. Let us, he proclaimed, celebrate the occasion not only as our final emergence from the dark tunnel of war, but as a springboard for the nation's young creative talent which had for so long been denied an outlet. Let there be a Festival of Britain in 1951. He published several articles on this theme and talked endlessly to his friends, his arms waving expansively, his blue eyes alight with enthusiasm and his infectious laugh ringing out, unable to resist a precisely-placed quotation or a joke at his own expense. He made us see what England could do and be, given the chance, the knocking off of war-time shackles, the bold leap forward into a new age, trusting, as always, to the genius of youth. Largely due to Herbert Morrison, the Labour Government took up his challenge, greatly to their credit, in the spring of 1948 and agreed to finance a Festival of Britain in 1951, and appointed Gerald, who had already resigned from *The News Chronicle* earlier in the year, as its Director-General. I had listened to him pounding out his ideas as we tramped over the downs we both loved so much, and had become one of his most enthusiastic supporters. Knowing that I was at a loose end, he had suggested that I should join the team he was in the process of forming. Although in theory independent, the Festival administration was under government control, since considerable sums of public money were involved, and even at this early, enthusiastic stage, things moved slowly. We were due to visit Babs' family in America and consequently I had to leave England with my future unresolved, but inhibited from taking any more positive steps by my intense hope that a job with Gerald would materialise. It was a lovely summer evening on Long

Island when his cable arrived. 'Believe it or not, appointment as Festival DPR (Director of Public Relations) agreed. Begin September.' I have no record of my reply, but I can remember the welling heart from which it sprang, and the joy with which I tried to explain to Babs' sympathetic but baffled relatives what kind of a hand Fate had at last dealt me.

The history of the Festival of Britain has been adequately recorded elsewhere. What struck me most, when I visited the exhibition put on by the Victoria and Albert Museum in 1976 to mark its twenty-fifth anniversary, was how young we all were. I was standing behind two people who were looking at a photo-montage and discussing the personalities it depicted with the utmost frankness. 'Look at him,' one of them said, 'he looks a mere child.' I moved closer and found myself staring at my own photograph. It was a young man's show and, although modesty prevents me from saying that Gerald was a good picker, the Festival provided just that springboard from which, as he hoped, so many leapt into subsequent fame and distinction. Of the many friends which I gained at Savoy Court, our dingy offices just off the Strand, and have kept throughout my life, the memories which I share with two are as fresh today as they were when we all danced away the last night of the Festival in October 1951 under the Dome of Discovery with Gracie Fields wowing an audience of hundreds of thousands.

Hugh Casson, who was Director of Architecture, brought his original mind to bear on pretty well all visual aspects of the Festival, and particularly on the South Bank. Exhibitions, he used to say, are the nurseries in which tomorrow's architects cut their teeth – that is why they are regarded with suspicion by the Arts Establishment of succeeding generations. 'Don't forget what Nannie used to say,' he would declaim from any handy platform. 'Come, come, Master Hugh, we're not going to make an exhibition of ourself, are we?' He translated Gerald's inspiration into the fantastic shapes and colours that began to spring up on the South Bank, marshalling a flock of talented young architects who could hardly believe that what they saw emerging on their own drawing boards would actually be built.

The other Huw (Wheldon) represented the Arts Council. It was through his ebullient energy that the resources in music, theatre and the visual arts were gathered together and spread across the country in a series of regional Festivals. He pinched and pulled to make the money go round and took Gerald on a series of pep-talking tours to galvanise the local authorities. I often went with them and remember Huw briefing Gerald before a session with some city's fathers which promised to be awkward because they had been left out, or perhaps because they did not want to be included. 'Money for old rope, DG,' he would say cheerfully. 'You can't go wrong.' And between them they seldom did. They made a fine pair, tossing jokes between them like cricket balls and acting as lightning conductors for each other's ideas. It was, I think, at this time that Huw's great skills as a creative administrator and communicator were practised and perfected; they remained at full stretch, to our great benefit, until he died, shortly before this book went to press, leaving an aching void in the hearts of his family and friends.

Our feet were kept on the ground by Bernard Sendall, a young civil servant with a remarkable career already behind him, having been a Private Secretary to Winston Churchill and Brendan Bracken during the war. Our funds were controlled and accounted for by George Campbell, a shrewd but kindly Treasury official who seemed to delight in finding ways round his own regulations. Our friend at Court and in Cabinet was Herbert Morrison, Lord President of the Council, who took responsibility for the whole concept, defended it in Parliament, fought for its money and, more important, for the creative freedom essential if it were to become a living thing. The man who worked the ropes, so to speak, of this Deus ex Machina, was Max Nicholson, the bridge between us and the rest of Whitehall. King George VI took a close interest in all phases of the preparations. He visited our offices on more than one occasion and, with the Queen, toured the South Bank site during its construction.

But the ringmaster of this circus, if such a term can be applied to so remarkable a galaxy of talent, was Gerald himself. He hurled himself full tilt at obstacles which then melted away in his path; he did not recognise the words 'No' or 'I can't'. He was a perfectionist who would not rest, or let others do so, until the smallest details were exactly right. We spent weekends in Sussex planning, philosophising, arguing, until the outlines of the great canvas were clear and agreed. By an effort which was as physical as it was mental, he carried us along on the surging whitecaps of his own driving imagination. When the King came in State to St Paul's on May 3rd and opened the Festival with a speech from the Cathedral steps, Gerald, more than any of those who stood among the glittering throng, could say (and perhaps very quietly to himself *did* say), 'I did this: these are the opening bars of my Jupiter Symphony.'

These years passed for me like a brightly coloured whirlwind. The Festival totally absorbed all my energies for seven days of each week. Even my holidays were combined with its affairs, for my job was to publicise it on a worldwide scale to help redress the image of a sad, grey, rationed England inimicable to the tourists, who were beginning to infest the world as never before, like a rash of self-propelled, pre-packaged cameras. My budget was pitifully low, even by the less ambitious demands of the 1950s when television advertising had not put forth its Midas touch. Moreover, exchange control was rigidly restrictive; I had only a total of 100,000 US dollars for a complete campaign in the USA and Canada. Believing that the big bang was best for our purpose, I decided to invest almost the entire amount in a one-shot, four-page, full-colour advertisement in *Life Magazine* – the first time anyone had spent that kind of money on a single advertisement. I did the deal with C.D. Jackson, then Publisher of *Life* and married, by chance, to a family connection of Babs'. He had been over to London to see the preparations and had caught some of our enthusiasm. 'The only risk to this show,' he said, as we tramped across the vast building site which was slowly turning into fairyland, 'is that you and Gerald are going to blow your tops before it opens.' David Ogilvy, then at the start of his spectacular advertising career and anxious, I think, for the Festival account which he imagined to be much bigger than it was, wagged his finger at me and said that I was making a great mistake in taking such a huge risk. I think this was one of the very rare occasions on which he was wrong. The advertisement duly appeared, a startling, bright, intriguing affair which the entire readership of *Life*, estimated then at about twenty-five million, could not possibly miss. It also attracted attention as a novelty in its own right and C.D. Jackson at the eleventh hour, threw in the International Edition for the very little extra cash that I had over. Nobody can persuade me that this was not more effective than dribbling away our precious dollars in little packets in the newspapers or on the radio. In any case, the Americans came in significantly larger numbers than had been estimated.

I do not think that any serious assessment of the Festival's long term effect on what is so glibly called the British way of life has ever been undertaken. This is certainly not the place to attempt one. It is now clear that it was not the dawn of that Brave New World fit for all those (including Pierrots) who cherished the past values and future promise of Western civilisation. But I believe that without it our post-war lethargy would have lasted even longer, our science and technology would have developed more slowly, and that creative flowering of youth in the late 1950s and early 1960s would have been less exciting. At any rate, the end of the Festival found our ideals more or less intact.

Throughout the Festival and its preparations, I had seen a good deal of Herbert Morrison, and had become fond of this irrepressible cockney with his deep love for and understanding of London and the Londoner, his courage, and his total dedication to the principles of democratic Socialism (although he would have rejected that expression as denoting something

alien to British politics). But I could not have been considered in any way
an intimate of his, and I was therefore astonished to hear him speculating
out loud one day, as he gave me a lift after some Festival function early in
1951, as to whether he should accept the Foreign Secretaryship in
succession to Ernie Bevin, whose health was clearly failing fast. 'They'll
offer it to me, you know,' he muttered gloomily, 'and I suppose I'll 'ave to
take it for the sake of the Party.' He looked out of the window and shook his
head. 'But it's not right for me, is it?' I was paralysed with embarrassment,
not being in the habit of receiving such private confidences from Cabinet
Ministers, and thus not knowing whether his question was rhetorical or
required an answer. He saved me by telling the driver to pull up, and said,
'I'll 'ave to drop you 'ere, young lad. Good luck and – er – no gossip, eh?'
Hopping smartly out of the car, 'Thanks so much for the lift, Lord
President,' I said, 'and good luck to you too.'

Morrison's instinct was right. Before the Festival ended, he became one
of the least effective Foreign Secretaries of this century, a tragic waste of
those great talents which had enriched the post-war domestic scene. The
little twist of fate, however, was not without its advantage for me.
Although no longer constitutionally responsible, Herbert continued to
regard the Festival as his child and came to help us celebrate its final
moments on the South Bank. At one point he put his arm through mine
and said 'You boys 'ave done a good job. What are you thinking of next for
yourself?' 'I haven't had time to make any plans,' I said, and added, not
quite on the spur of the moment because Babs and I had talked vaguely
about the future once or twice, but more or less as an afterthought, 'I'd
rather like a job abroad, if there's one going; in America, for instance.' He
grunted and looked at me for a moment. 'Well, you'd better come round to
the office and 'ave a cup o' tea when all this is over.' A decisive moment in
my life had arrived – we were all singing *Auld Lang Syne* with Gracie
Fields, and I was feeling no pain. As soon as I could disentangle myself
from the immediate aftermath of the Festival, I telephoned the Foreign
Office and asked to speak to the Private Secretary, having little idea of what
an immensely grand person I was approaching. He sounded very dubious
on the telephone. 'Who did you say you were?' he asked, 'and exactly when
did the Secretary of State issue this – er – invitation?' I filled in the
background. 'If you will leave your number, someone will ring you back,'
said the voice from Olympus. I waited a week and then received a call from
a warmer-sounding young man giving me an appointment a few days
ahead. I was shown in by a not-noticeably less distant Private Secretary, to
find Morrison looking small and somehow lonely at his desk under the
portrait of George III in the great ornate room overlooking the Park. 'Well,

young man,' he said, evidently not prepared to waste time on polite conversation, 'I don't think we've got a job for you; but you'd better see our man 'Ooper, who'll fix you up if there's anything going. I've arranged it – they'll tell you outside,' he added, waving his hand towards the door. I was about to stutter my thanks and withdraw when someone came in with a tea tray. 'Oh well,' said the Foreign Secretary in a resigned sort of way, 'you'd better 'ave a cup – 'elp yerself. 'ow's Gerald?'

The tea warmed up the atmosphere, which I think was chilled only by Morrison's embarrassment at not being able to be more helpful. We chatted for a few minutes about old Festival times. I left him with the usual volleys of 'good luck' and was told, outside, that I should see Mr Hooper, (now Sir Robin Hooper), the Head of the Personnel Department, the following day. I did not know Robin, although he was later to become a good friend and colleague. But we had a curious link, unsuspected at that time. During the war he had been a Lysander pilot, flying Agents clandestinely in and out of occupied France. These daring operations had been masterminded by a neighbour of ours and controlled from his house in our village. Robin was awarded the DSO for this highly dangerous and gallant task, although it was years before I could penetrate his modesty sufficiently to get him to talk about it. He received me with great courtesy but made it clear that there was no chance of an appointment, of however temporary a nature, in the Foreign Service. 'If anything, we're cutting down at the moment,' he said sadly. 'But leave us your address and telephone number and if by any remote chance something does come up, we'll get in touch with you.' The classic situation of the unsuccessful audition – don't call us, we'll call you.

I was not a bit surprised, never having rated my chances very highly. I retired to the country where the accumulated strains of the Festival caught up with me. When you take your foot off the accelerator, the engine begins to cough if the mixture has been too rich. I went to bed with a high temperature, my defences overwhelmed by a particularly persistent virus. At what, in a more serious illness, would have been called the crisis, I was made to stagger to the phone by an urgent call from the Foreign Office. It was Robin Hooper. Was I still interested in a job in New York? I tried to control the grave disturbance this caused to my nervous system and to make my reply sound as normal and qualified as possible. Well, could I get up to London tomorrow? Oh, so sorry – well, early next week? I said I would do my best. After the initial stratospheric heights to which this news propelled my temperature, I recovered sufficiently to travel up to London in time for my appointment.

The job on offer was that of Press Officer to the UK delegation to the

United Nations, under Gladwyn Jebb (now Lord Gladwyn) of whom, I must confess, I had never heard. First I saw Ridsdale, the head of the News Department and Chief Foreign Office Spokesman. Rids (it was months before I discovered his Christian names) was a Foreign Office legend, having been the mouthpiece of successive Secretaries of State and hiding a very shrewd and experienced mind behind a delightfully off-hand manner. We talked as if after a good dinner, and I was surprised to find that he knew a good deal more about me than I did about him. After a bit, he said, 'Well, I think you'll do, if it's all right with Gladwyn. You'd better see him now, if he's free.' I was considerably impressed by this casual use of first names. Gladwyn was indeed free, sitting in a small office at an empty desk and apparently with time on his hands. I immediately noticed his socks, which were of maroon silk and disappeared up his long, elegant legs into a pair of well-cut trousers. I thought they were frightfully smart. I was also almost hypnotised by the way he rolled his eyes up into the dome of his forehead so that only the whites showed, giving an alarming impression of Buddha-like wisdom tinged with Christian resignation. He was charming, almost apologising for the unimportance of the job compared to what I had been doing for the Festival. He ended by saying, 'Well, I think you'll do, if it's all right by Rids.' 'But I've already seen Mr Ridsdale,' I said, envisaging a long period of shuffling between the two offices. 'Well, I should see him again and tell him what I say; see you in Paris,' said Gladwyn, rolling his eyes up as if to signify that his hour of meditation had arrived. This was the first occasion that Paris had been mentioned; it transpired that the UN General Assembly was, for the first and, as it turned out, last time being held away from New York and that the delegation (now to include the Wrights) would return to New York in February after it was over. A week tramping the tessellated corridors of the Foreign Office was sufficient to legitimise my status as an unestablished (temporary) First Secretary.

Although Whitehall was still groggy from the after-effects of the Burgess and Maclean defections, I cannot remember any noticeable concentration on assessing my rating as a security risk. I was, of course, asked for references, and assume that some kind of positive vetting procedure was completed. Nor was there time for any political preparation. By early November I was in Paris, giving daily briefings on British Foreign policy to the world's diplomatic correspondents gathered there for this unique, but not very exciting General Assembly. It was a case not only of diving in at the deep end, but doing so from the top diving board. I was secretly terrified, dreading the day on which I should find my own words in banner headlines heralding a complete but unauthorised change in HMG's policy. It never happened, of course, and perhaps the first lesson I learned was that it is the horse's mouth which counts and only rarely is the spokesman confused with the horse.

But to be a spokesman was glamorous enough, as was the sudden plunge into high politics, diplomatic society and a Paris for once attempting to disprove her reputation for xenophobia towards all but high-paying tourists – a task in which she did not entirely succeed. True, I was not a natural inhabitant of these shining worlds, and had the familiar sensation of being an outsider, an amateur, a spectator even, of a society inhabited by gilded professionals entirely at ease. But I learned fast; how to respond to the delicate nuances of rank and national status; how to juggle people (for we had to do our share of entertaining) so that all could give of their best and most useful, and none feel offended or unwanted.

The international world of those days (1951-52) was much smaller than now. There were less than 50 members of the United Nations, an almost cosy club in which everyone knew everyone. It was a world in which the wind of change was a hardly-discernible breeze on the cheeks of the old guard who were unwittingly presiding over the dissolution of the Imperial order. Our own Diplomatic Service was small, intimate, efficient and wise; it had the confidence and sureness of touch of the aristocrat to whom service is a natural way of life. It was also smug, relying on its upper-class traditions to protect it against the unthinkable pollution of alien, not to say Communist, penetration, and slow to recognise the first mutterings of the whirlwind which the policies and attitudes of the then non-communist world would reap.

I did not learn all this, of course, during six weeks in Paris, punctuated by a Christmas break, the New Year's Honours List in which I was awarded an OBE for my work with the Festival – ('Don't worry', said one of my new FO colleagues, 'people never remember what you got it for.') – and the death of King George VI which I recall chiefly by my hectic scramble to find a black tie to wear in the Security Council, which was meeting that afternoon; and the rapid drafting of an appropriate speech for Gladwyn which, in the end, he sensibly ignored and instead spoke movingly off the cuff.

In late February we crossed the Atlantic, the *Queen Mary* like some floating international symposium, and settled in New York, renting a spacious apartment in the since-famous Dakota building, then eccentric rather than fashionable. I became absorbed in my life and work, and soon felt as if I had been a diplomat all my life. This rapid transition was greatly eased by the kind and generous way in which I was accepted by my colleagues in the Delegation irrespective of my irregular and unorthodox background. But I was still vulnerable being, as a temporary, subject to dismissal at three months' notice. Indeed, this threat materialised late in 1952 in the form of a letter from Robin Hooper to Gladwyn saying that I must be sacked; a casualty, it seems, of that self-same economy wave which had initially impeded my appointment. Gladwyn reacted with the most flattering vigour, bombarding the unfortunate Hooper with daily letters extolling my virtues, calculating the waste to public funds of so short an overseas posting, and generally making such a fuss that I was reprieved. It was, no doubt, a case of peace at any price, a policy usually adopted internally when dealing with determined patricians at the summit of their careers.

This generous championship must have kindled Gladwyn's interest in my future, for it was at his insistence that, in the summer of 1953, I went in for the open competition for late entry in the Foreign Service, conducted each year by the Civil Service Commission, who awarded two or three places at the First Secretary level out of an entry which, in my year, was said to be in the region of 400 candidates. I had arranged to go through the selection process during my home leave. It consisted of one interview with the Selection Board, followed, if shortlisted, by a second and final one. I was bracing myself for the first interview when something blew up in New York and I was told to cut my leave short and get back as quickly as possible. In order to facilitate this, the Commission, somewhat to my surprise, agreed to combine my two interviews in one.

The dominant factor of that year's competition was, as I recall, the presence of large numbers of applicants from the former Sudan Political Service. Heavy competition, I was warned; implying that novices like me, *sans* degree, *sans* languages, *sans* experience, *sans* practically everything, did not stand much of a chance. I agreed with these estimates and so was not particularly apprehensive, despite a thumping heart, sweating palms and dry mouth, when I sat down to face a formidable horseshoe of grave, sober-suited men, presided over by Sir Paul Sinker, who immediately welcomed me by saying that I ought to know that the competition was very difficult this year – er – Sudan Political Service, you know, and all that. So what, I thought, and proceeded to treat the whole affair as if going in for the village cricket side, sixth wicket down in a friendly match on a fine Sunday. My innings reached its peak when Sir Paul, in a devious ruse, pretended to have been very much against the Festival of Britain and taunted me with having wasted my time on so frivolous and unproductive an enterprise. Indignant rather than alarmed, I laid about these googly deliveries, dredging up old arguments in favour of the Festival and carting Sinker's bowling over the pavilion rails. I thoroughly enjoyed myself but doubted whether I had done my candidacy much, if any, good. I told Babs afterwards that I thought I had no chance of getting in, and as we re-crossed the Atlantic, we began to think of plans for the future when my temporary assignment should come to an end.

There followed silence of a profundity only to be experienced when Whitehall faces action. Then, sometime late in November, there arrived a brown manila envelope of the kind used by the Civil Service to impart bad news; moreover, it was understamped, even for the sea mail which had caused its long delay, so that Babs had to find some odd change before the postman would relinquish it. On being opened, it was found to contain a circular letter beginning 'Dear Sir or Madam', which informed those whom it may have concerned (clearly not expected to be many by the signatory, whose illegible scrawl revealed neither sex, creed nor race) that the successful candidates in the recent competition for establishment in HM Foreign Service were: and then three names typed in, of which mine was the last. I was in.

Later in the day on which this news arrived, I went in to Gladwyn's office to tell him. After all, I owed a great deal to his support and I wanted to make sure he heard the result from me and not someone else. 'Oh really, how extraordinary,' he said, rolling up his eyes, when I diffidently informed him that I had made it; then, realising perhaps that this reaction, although honest, was inadequate, he added, smiling broadly, 'Well done – well done indeed.' It was as auspicious and happy an entry into the Service as I could have wished.

CHAPTER THREE

Becoming an established member of the Service had no effect on our everyday life visible to the naked eye. Just as my Confirmation had proved something of a let-down, – no shaft of light had struck me as I knelt in Westminster Abbey at the feet of the Bishop of Wakefield, no celestial voice had singled me out for a special welcome to the Church – so there were no immediate changes or benefits to show for my new, more secure status. My work continued in exactly the same way; my colleagues, having from the beginning treated me as one of the family, saw no reason to modify their affectionate tolerance of my unusual background; the outside world was unaware that anything had changed, and would have been baffled by attempts to explain my new circumstances or how they had arisen. Babs veered wildly between satisfaction at the prospect of a career which her mother had brought her up to admire and which would take her on many an exotic journey, and anxiety about its effects on the upbringing of the children.

But the capacious arms of the Service were slowly preparing to embrace their newest child and draw him into the Whitehall nursery. It was probably due to Gladwyn's insistence that I was left another year in New York, having built up such a case for my indispensability he could hardly acquiesce in my immediate withdrawal; and perhaps the rudimentary economic sense of getting value for having shipped me, my family and my effects across the Atlantic had also dawned on the FO. But as soon as he was nominated to Paris, my days in New York were numbered and I survived long enough only to help ease in his successor, Sir Pierson Dixon, a gentle, gifted man with whom I would have liked to serve much longer, and whose tragically premature death seemed to leave a scar on his whole generation. So back to London we went, in the spring of 1954, Babs to settle us into our Sussex life once more, and I to the Foreign Office where, as a very low form of diplomatic life but no longer representing an endangered species, I had the distinction of taking over a desk in the junior (or Third, as it was traditionally called) room of the Central Department from Michael Palliser. With the deceptive ease and shrewd kindliness which characterised his brilliant career, he initiated me into the ways and traditions of an institution in whose corridors the ghosts of Lord Curzon and Ernest Bevin still pursued their not dissimilar goals, and the descendants of their servants behaved with the same spacious, mannered ease as if unaware of the speed at which the real world outside had changed. Our Department dealt with the affairs of Germany, the West still partitioned into Zones of Occupation and anxiously awaiting a Sovereignty which would, in fact, underline its division from the drab servitude of the East and foreshadow the Berlin Wall.

I quickly learned many lessons. How to handle papers and submit them to my superiors in such a way as to render the process of decision-making as painless as possible; and often, how to increase the chances of getting what one believed to be the right decision. This included such simple but essential skills as pinning papers together so that the points of the pins should not be exposed and wound the practised thumb of an Under Secretary, thus causing a bellow of pain and, perhaps, a momentary failure of judgement. How never to call anyone 'Sir', but somehow to contrive that the Christian name, even if it were Sydney or Albert should sound respectful. I was amazed at the deceptive air of informality which pervaded the ornate rooms of the senior officials; for the Foreign Office, being in those days small and intimate, was extremely efficient. During a crisis it purred like a Rolls Royce and answers could be extracted from it in the time which most other Departments took to formulate the questions. It enjoyed a superiority complex which rubbed off even on those few who, like me, had not been born to superiority. There was also a certain disdain for the expert, the atmosphere being more that of the university faculty than of the boardroom. But all this concealed a highly professional Service with a hard cutting edge and a ruthless insistence on decisive thought and action when British interests, or those of her allies, were threatened.

Familiarity breeds affection rather than contempt in me; I like routine. So I soon became happy in the Central Department (now renamed Western in the teeth of traditionalist opposition), filling my niche with the self-importance of the junior official, trying to solve the dream-puzzles about the future of Germany and Europe, growing daily more confident as my minutes and drafts were treated seriously as well as courteously by my superiors. My idea of the perfect Foreign Office official was fortunately embodied by my first Head of Department, Pat Hancock, (later Sir Patrick Hancock) a squash-playing, salmon-fishing old Wykehamist of startling eccentricity, with a mind like a scalpel and a dazzling turn of speed when the crunch came. He treated foreigners with a mixture of respect and amused tolerance which I thought exactly right and never allowed the political and economic problems with which we grappled to obscure his kindness and profound concern for truth and honour. He was very good to me, an ugly duckling thrust into his small but classy nest of cygnets. I learned a great deal from him. When he died recently his obituary in *The Times* described him as '*Una persona per ben*'; and someone said, 'He died like a gentleman.' It was well said, for that was how he lived.

Luckily I had not expected this halcyon period to last, so I was not surprised at the beginning of 1956 to find myself in the Embassy at the Hague as First Secretary and Head of Chancery. This was a real Embassy, and my first experience of diplomatic life at its most starchy. I paid formal calls, wearing a morning coat; attended white-tie dinners at which the *placement* was at least as interesting as the food. My Ambassador, a kindly martinet, instructed me in rituals which, even then, reminded one more of the Congress of Vienna than the Treaty of Rome. Babs was expected to wear hat and gloves as she called on diplomatic wives and Dutch ladies, learning when and how to leave cards and which corner to turn up. We had appalling problems finding somewhere to live, and spent eight weeks in one room in the Hotel des Indes, depressed by the gloomy winter and the low-lying, flat grey landscape.

But we were lucky that Dorothy Keast was able to come with us to this, our first real Embassy. Her presence helped to make life easier and more civilized as indeed it has done for the last fifty years. Dot (as she is always known) has come with us to every post except Cairo and the Congo and mastered their languages sufficiently to be able, for example, to tick off the milkman in sharp, idiomatic Dutch. She is a godmother to one grand-daughter and our first great-grand-daughter is named after her. In the Hague this small, indomitable figure seemed to turn her hand to anything needed and she has been doing so ever since.

Spring at last arrived with its incomparable Dutch flowering, and half a pretty eighteenth century house on a canal in which we could at last settle. The children came and went from their various occupations in England. We made many Dutch friends and explored the country-side by land and water. By the middle of 1957 we were sufficiently dug-in and content to make me suspect that a move might be in the offing. It came quite quickly. John Henniker-Major, the Head of Personnel Department, had backed my entry into the Service and kept a watchful eye on his protégé in whom he appeared to have some confidence. I still think of him as the best Head of Personnel the Service is likely to know. With that invisible but indispensable element of chance hovering over me, I ran into him one day when I was briefly in London. It was precisely the moment at which he was looking for someone to fill a particularly tricky job. 'You'll do,' he said, guessing rightly that the Hague had little more to offer, and we were back in London in time for Babs' birthday on June 17th.

I spent the next six months as FO Liaison Officer with the BBC External Services, a job intended to quell the storm which raged between Bush House and Whitehall in the aftermath of Suez, and which had been exacerbated by my predecessor who had occupied most of his time in complaining about the modest size of the office allocated to him by the BBC and, above all, its lack of the carpet to which, by Civil Service regulations, he considered himself entitled. These months spent shuttling up and down the Strand on the precarious bridge I was trying to build, left me with an affection and respect for the External Services which I was never to lose, in spite of the incidental problems which their wholly justified insistence on telling the truth caused for HM Representatives abroad; and which, indeed, had been the cause of my present task. Then I was promoted with flattering abruptness, given charge of the Information Policy Department, and replaced at Bush House by a member of my own new staff. The Heads of Department in the Foreign Office make up the gear box, so to speak, of the whole machine. During the next three years I was very much at the centre of affairs – if not actually making policy, at least responsible for explaining and justifying it on a world-wide basis. The hours were long and the strain considerable, but I was nevertheless genuinely surprised when Derek Hoyer Millar then Permanent Under Secretary (now Lord Inchyra) telephoned me a day or two before the Birthday Honours in 1960 and congratulated me on a CMG which would appear against my name.

Meanwhile, we had been posted to Cairo. The Suez affair had taken place while we were peacefully browsing in the Hague; but it had deeply shocked and upset me – I can remember bursting into tears at seven o'clock in the morning when I heard on the BBC that we had cast a veto in the Security Council. It had seemed to me to be all wrong, the wrong war in the wrong place at the wrong time against the wrong enemy – the last petulant fling of an Imperialism which my generation hoped we were out-growing. Its shock waves had already catapulted me to London, promotion and a gong; now they were to fling us outward again to Cairo, the epicentre of that futile storm. Colin Crowe had been sent to Egypt about eighteen months earlier to begin the difficult and delicate task of restoring our relations and rescuing what was possible of British interests from the wreckage. His time there had been a classic example of patient diplomacy, carried out under very difficult physical conditions – the Embassy and its effects were still in the care of the Swiss and he had to work at first from an hotel room, and in the face of Egyptian suspicion and hostility. I was appointed his number two, to reach Cairo in time for him to take a well-earned holiday. His efforts had so far succeeded that our initial presence – a British Interests Section – had been transformed into a Diplomatic Mission with Colin recognised as Chargé d'Affaires.

August is not the ideal time to arrive in Cairo. The temperature hovered around a stifling 100 degrees Fahrenheit. Our senses were assaulted by unfamiliar noises, smells and tastes, and by the beauty of the great river which flowed beneath the window of our room in the new Shepheard's Hotel, splendid but insanitary. Here we spent our first few days before moving into the Residence where we camped in one room, not wishing to give the impression that we were anticipating the last step in the slow dance with our hosts – that of the restoration of full Embassies with real Ambassadors at their head. Colin duly went on leave; we found a flat to live in and were joined by Faith, now a beguiling seventeen and destined to cause havoc amongst the most susceptible of our colleagues, not to speak of the Egyptians, who regarded her as fair game. She played a masterly hand and emerged unscathed but greatly experienced, with fluent French and kitchen Arabic.

I felt something of an impostor in charge of a post which included Geoffrey Arthur and Tony Parsons, both brilliant Arabists with far more experience of the Middle East than I. They were tolerant and friendly and we managed to keep things on an even keel until Colin returned. I was relieved to hand over to him, the pleasure of my first command having been somewhat reduced by the constant fear of making some false move which would undo all his patient and painful work. Indeed, in spite of the flag flying on the bonnet of my car, a barely perceptible modulation in attitudes, an extra duty allowance and a good deal of worry, I had little sensation of being in charge of a Mission, still less of what it must be like to be that be-plumed, be-medalled figure, the object of all ambition – a genuine, vintage, Château-bottled Ambassador.

On Colin's return the pace quickened. We found the Egyptians, who had for some time been anxious to restore relations provided the political price was right, now increasingly ready to settle the issues which any agreement would have to cover. But so complete had been the rupture that these were many and complex; the de-sequestration of British assets and compensation for their owners; the number and siting of Consulates; the resumption of trade and of air services; the timing of the arrival of Ambassadors in London and Cairo. The solutions to these now flowed steadily forward, due not only to the emergence of the necessary political will, but also in large measure to Mohammed Heikal, then editor of the newspaper *Al Ahram*, and a close confidant of President Nasser, through whose subtle mind, and in whose modest little office, nearly all discords were eventually resolved. At the last minute, when documents were in print and Colin was on the point of departure, he received a message from Heikal late one night, asking him for an urgent meeting. This sounded as if it might be the last minute hitch we had all feared. Colin subsequently told us what took place.

On his way to Heikal's office, he reviewed the remaining possible areas of misunderstanding. Among them was the continued detention in an Egyptian prison of a British subject named Mr Zarb, a political casualty of the disastrous adventure. It was a tricky business. The Egyptians were touchy about it and there could have been a minor storm in the UK if things had gone wrong. Rather than make his release a condition of the entire agreement, it had therefore been decided not to press the point in the hope that feelings of humanity would prevail and that before, or at the moment of, the new Ambassador's arrival, his freedom would be granted; if not, we would be on much stronger ground to press for it when we were once again at peace with one another. So he had dismissed this as a complicating factor and had arrived *chez* Heikal baffled and apprehensive. The great man was affability itself; sorry to drag Colin out so late at night, urgent message from the President himself, must be dealt with at once, and so on.

'Not at all,' Colin said, sitting back and waiting for the blow to fall.

'Well,' Mohammed continued, 'the President and I have been thinking that we ought to give you a present in recognition of all you have done for our future relations.' Colin heard distant alarm bells going off at that stage, remembering regulations about the giving and receiving of presents by Civil Servants, rules which many foreigners regard as incomprehensibly restrictive to fruitful intercourse, as it is understood in their own moral climates.

'But when it came to deciding what to give you, we were stumped. So we thought that the best thing would be to give you a cheque to buy something for yourself. Here it is, with our best thanks and good wishes!' And with a grin, handed Colin a plain white envelope. Colin was transfixed by the implications of this exceedingly awkward development. Knowing that he could not refuse such a gift out of hand, his one desire was to get away as quickly as possible and think out how to cope with it. So with as much grace as he could muster, he thanked Mohammed, thrusting the envelope into his pocket, and made a move to leave. He was not to be let off so lightly.

'Aren't you going to open it?' Mohammed asked. Feeling, and probably looking, guilty, Colin retrieved the now crumpled envelope from his pocket, tore it open, and pulled out a sheet of paper on which was written the single word 'Zarb'.

This humanely humorous gesture was not, of course, without strings. We had to guarantee that Zarb would leave Egypt within twenty-four hours of his release and that there would be no publicity. This was accomplished and the episode crowned Colin's remarkable achievement. He left the country amid applause, and sensibly never returned for a curtain call. I again remained in charge to await the arrival of Sir Harold Beeley, who had meanwhile been nominated as our new Ambassador.

During this waiting period, I started to smoke again having given it up, with enormous effort, several years before in London. When subsequently asked why, I was able to say with well-rehearsed casualness that it was Nasser's fault. He sent for me very late one evening, as was the Egyptian habit. I had guessed what the trouble was – a particularly snarky broadcast by the BBC Arabic service which had received a lot of unflattering comment in the Egyptian press. I was eventually shown into his office about midnight.

There was nothing half-hearted or hesitant about Nasser. Whatever role he chose to assume – he was a born actor – he played to perfection. This evening, for some reason, it was, or began by being, the quiet-spoken statesman with the charm and manners of a Harley Street specialist, and a voice reflecting sorrow rather than anger. He much regretted having to call me out so late, how good of me to come, how difficult life was for us statesmen, please sit down, would I have some coffee (of course) and then – the fateful question – would I like a cigarette? Pulling out a crumpled packet of Parliaments from his pocket, he leant across the table with his most ingratiating smile. Well, I thought to myself, suppressing my mild surprise that he smoked at all (I had never seen him do so in public), this is going to be a difficult half hour; I am over this grubby little habit now, a grown up, self-reliant adult whose nicotine slavery has long since passed. Why not? So I took a cigarette and allowed him to light it as my already trembling hand held it to my lips, Whereupon, Nasser switched off the charm abruptly and proceeded to give me a bad time about the BBC, HM Government, and all things and persons British, while I wheezed and coughed and spluttered my way through the classic defence of the BBC's independence and integrity. We parted amicably, Nasser recommending that I see a doctor for my cough; I reported the whole episode to London in a very low key and, such is my strength of character, was smoking twenty cigarettes a day within a week.

Harold Beeley arrived on schedule, an event rightly regarded by the Egyptians as historic. They laid on an elaborate ceremonial for his presentation of credentials, driving us through streets packed with rent-a-crowd spectators and lined with troops, in a convoy of ancient Rolls Royces whose grey plush interiors smelt strongly of a byegone, horse-driven age. A Guard of Honour was mounted in the Palace courtyard and an Egyptian Marine band played the jolly, imperial tunes learned in more spacious times – Tipperary, Hearts of Oak, and Hooray Hooray Hooray Hooray For the British Grenadiers. They played them very well. Harold and Nasser talked privately for nearly an hour, and afterwards we were presented formally to the President, who enquired kindly after my bronchial condition. Thus, Egypt and Great Britain were together again, bickering like old friends rather than eyeing each other with silent, surprised hostility as new, unfamiliar and reluctant enemies.

Once Harold was installed, it was clear that, as an Embassy, we were over-staffed. I was the obvious candidate for redundancy and so was offered, and accepted, a posting to Paris – not to the Embassy, but to the UK Delegation to NATO. Personnel Department believed they were handing me a plum as compensation for my early removal from Cairo, but it turned out to be, in many ways, the most difficult of my posts; relentlessly long hours, masses of paper-work, a large delegation to administer (I was Head of Chancery again); besides which, a good deal of Parisian glitter gets rubbed off if you have to live there as a not-very-highly-paid foreigner. There were rewards; the civilised delights of a great city and easy access to the rest of France; some new and lasting friendships; and valuable experience in my career. Moreover, it was here that Faith met her first husband Julian, the son of my Ambassador, Evelyn Shuckburgh. It was a case of 'his daughter married the boss's son', and caused some interest and amusement in Foreign Office circles. My old friend and former boss, Sammy Hood, looked at me thoughtfully and said, 'I hear that you have contracted a dynastic marriage'. It was, alas, a marriage not destined to last, although it produced two much loved grand-children, Matilda and Benjamin, before, to the great regret of many, the parents went their separate ways, without bitterness and remaining good friends.

But by the summer of 1964, with three years of hard slog at NATO and one grand-daughter to my credit, it was time to move on. The post of Director-General of the British Information Services in New York was vacant, and for once there seemed general agreement that I was as well qualified to fill it as anyone in the Service, requiring, as it did, a certain expertise in the information field, together with knowledge and experience of the USA.

I plodded round Whitehall on a series of visits designed not so much to brief me on aspects of British foreign policy as to improve my name-dropping capacity when I got to New York. It is useful when trying to convince someone of the authenticity of a background briefing to be able to refer, casually, to the last time you were with the Prime Minister. These calls culminated in a delightful quarter of an hour with Rab Butler, then Foreign Secretary, who lived up to his reputation for indiscretion by staring gloomily across the park and making no secret of his conviction that the Tories would lose the election which was certainly coming. As I left, he said, a little wistfully I thought, 'Keep in touch, dear boy, keep in touch.' How I wish I had.

We slipped away from London without any fuss and found ourselves sailing into New York harbour on a golden autumn morning. The mysterious Ferris wheel of our career had come full circle and brought us to a point, familiar yet challenging, from which it was at last possible to discern a glint of gold braid on the far horizon and to catch the sound of trumpets practising for a fanfare which might, after all, ring out one day for Their Excellencies.

CHAPTER FOUR

The concentration of diplomats in Manhattan is dense. In addition to the large secretariat of the United Nations and the national delegations, which have increased as independence has spread across the world like the blushes of a bride, most countries maintain Consulates and some, like Britain, commercial or trade-relations offices as well. The Head of the UK Delegation to the UN is the most senior diplomat, but the Consul-General is the Queen's representative. I was third in the hierarchy, but also held a rank in the Embassy at Washington, since my responsibilities were national rather than confined to New York. All of us were career diplomats save Hugh Foot (Lord Caradon) Head of the UN Delegation, who was a political appointee. Our relationship with him was odd, to say the least, for it was his father, the distinguished Liberal statesman Isaac Foot whom Babs' first husband John had defeated in Bodmin in the 1935 election. Moreover Hugh himself had become one of Babs' constituents when she took over the seat. Nevertheless he brushed aside this complicated political past in his generous way and, with his wife Sylvia, gave us friendship and support which we have valued ever since.

British Information Services (BIS) itself is a descendant of the wartime organisation which employed such legendary figures as Bill Ormerod. People tend to associate 'Information' with Intelligence, but BIS is not concerned with anything more sinister than presenting the facts about Britain in as favourable a light as possible, and trying to correct the distortions which prejudice, genuine but over-enthusiastic concern, or plain ignorance produce.

In the relief of finding a square peg to fill an essential or important square hole, the feelings of the peg are often overlooked. But in my case, since the hole was New York, I felt very comfortable. I love America and Babs was born there. To live in New York and to be a part of its brilliant, multinational culture, its mixture of cynicism, sentiment and faith, its dazzling speed and brutal realism, its extremes of heat and cold, its contrasts of beauty and squalor; to walk down Park Avenue early on a

spring or autumn morning and feel your spiritual and physical batteries
being recharged; all this I had been lucky enough to experience already.
My love affair with this remarkable city became so compelling that when,
in 1965, I took on extra duties in the Embassy in Washington, I managed to
persuade all concerned that New York was the right place from which to do
both jobs.

But my infatuation, like most love affairs, had its disadvantages. I
usually had to spend one day a week in Washington, usually accomplished
by means of the Shuttle, a superbly American institution which worked
like clockwork when not interfered with by God (the weather) or man
(strikes). I would leave our apartment in mid-Manhattan at half past seven,
walk on to the first available plane (no tickets, no booking) at La Guardia
and could normally rely on being in the Embassy in Washington not much
after half past nine – sometimes, with the wind behind me, so to speak,
even sooner. Coming back it was the same. I could go to an early cocktail
party with a correspondent in Washington at five o'clock and be in
Manhattan for a late dinner at the Waldorf Astoria at nine o'clock.

Life in America is open, relaxed and uncluttered by artificial barriers of
class and status, although wealth supplies a powerful substitute for these
leavening qualities. It is true that the American male, with his drive to
succeed and doubts about his own virility, can sometimes be a bore; and
some American females tend to be predatory, especially about British
diplomats. But these are essentially minority traits and are offset by many
qualities which we, in the old world, have lost in the welter of wars and in
the social and industrial jungles which we have created for ourselves.
Americans believe passionately in the future and can thus afford to be
enthusiastic about the present. Indeed, the average American's passion for
quite ordinary things ('for the discovery of the Alphabet', as Dame Freya
Stark once said) is something by which only the most hardened cynic can
fail to be touched, or even to admire perhaps a shade wistfully. This
eagerness is particularly addressed to the acquisition of knowledge of all
kinds and there is a reverence for professionalism in all walks of American
life at which only the grossly complacent should scoff. They have come to
terms with the twentieth century and recognise that, however much to be
regretted, the amateur is fighting a losing battle against the pressure of the
technocratic society.

A powerful ingredient in the American character, certainly that which
makes an immediate and lasting impact, is a warm generosity of spirit
which displays real concern for a neighbour or traveller to a degree not
known in Europe since the Middle Ages. At first it is hard to believe in the
sincerity of those instantaneous invitations from complete strangers to

lunch, dinner, breakfast – use the pool, the car, stay the night, be my guest. But it is for real, as they say, something which in the vast majority of cases is done for the purest of motives and not to impress or to keep up with anyone. I used to puzzle a great deal about this great rush of friendship before which I have seen my more reticent British friends quail in bewildered resentment of the intimacies implied. It is partly a manifestation of the fact that Americans really believe in democracy and want to make it work. Indeed, the word 'undemocratic', often used so loosely as to be applied to such things as not cleaning your teeth after every meal, is one of the worst things that can be said about anyone or anything, because it is taken to mean 'un-American'. The British, while in favour of democracy in theory, dislike it in practice. They spend time and money circumventing the will of the majority by perfecting the art of getting things past any elected body, from Cabinet to Parish Council, in the interests of what they call practical realities. Americans, of course, also try to do this and sometimes spend even more time (and money) on it than we do, but over there it goes against the grain; democracy is a reality and they are readier than we are to accept its results.

Another, and perhaps more pervasive characteristic is that however civilised and sophisticated American society may appear to be, the frontier is still not far distant; there is a feeling that the Indians have not long been driven westward. Nobody who has travelled the four-lane highway between Boston and New York, and has seen on the outskirts of a more-than-usually built-up area a sign reading 'Caution, Thickly Settled' can believe otherwise. This folk sense of the frontier and its demands still permeates the American subconscious. In huge under-developed countries you need your neighbour and making sure of his friendship is part of your survival kit. That vestigial emotion is in turn why Americans are so often confused and unhappy when they come to Europe, and especially to Britain, and fail to find that same spirit in our small, overcrowded island with its houses and gardens separated by hedges and walls and fences. They do not realise – why should they? – that *our* neighbours are all too often a nuisance, too close for comfort and unhealthily interested in our private affairs.

BIS NY was virtually an independent command. Part of its success lay in the fact that, although a government agency, it was not obviously a part of the local resident British bureaucracy and could often pose, with honesty and success, as the journalists' friend and champion in his perpetual battle against the Establishment. With this went a certain professionalism in the media world rather greater than that usually found at embassies in other countries. A Labour Government was in power virtually throughout my posting. At the time of my appointment in 1964 a general election was clearly not far off. I was hurriedly despatched to demonstrate to sceptical Americans, by arriving before voting took place, that I was not a political animal and the creature neither of Mr Harold Wilson nor of Sir Alec Douglas-Home, whichever should win. This probably worked, and certainly gave me greater flexibility in defending a British Labour Government's policies against the inevitable American mistrust. By the mid-1960s most Americans had, I think, learned to distinguish socialism from communism, and indeed had become less paranoiac about the latter. However, they still intensely disliked the idea of socialism, tending to believe that it must, in time, lead to the greater evil and blaming all Britain's economic ills, of which the 1960s had a generous share, on the political colour of the Labour government. Thus my principal function during this period was to persuade informed American opinion, and through it as great a slice of the public as possible, that Mr Wilson and his colleagues were not possessed of horns, tails and cloven hooves, that Labour policies made economic sense, should be given a chance to work and were not in any case dictated solely by the demands of doctrinaire socialism; that the British workman was not as idle or bloody-minded as the Press of both countries portrayed him; and that, in general, the clichés about silver linings, lights at the end of the tunnels, bottoming out, British resilience, and so on, deserved to be taken seriously.

All this called for considerable mental agility, for many of us were by no means convinced of the total validity of all the arguments we were compelled to use. But the government of the day is the best government we have, and civil servants, especially those abroad, must either support its policies in public and try to make them work, or get out of the way. This is called loyalty, a somewhat old-fashioned term. It may also be called courage, for it can involve staying in the kitchen however hot it becomes. The national mood of those days was neatly summed up by Lord Harlech, who was Ambassador when I arrived, although to be replaced after what was, for me, a regrettably short time; 'We British are a strange people,' he said, in the course of a speech. 'We never see the writing on the wall until we have our backs to it.'

New York was inevitably the principal battlefield in this struggle for it contained two major elements in American public life who needed convincing if confidence in Britain was to be maintained – firstly, the financial establishment of banks and the stock market; and secondly the media. Thus to New York came all the senior government ministers, to see and be seen, to speak and listen – in short, to be exposed, as was the ambiguous expression. It was mainly I who had to arrange the exposure.

Their visits punctuated my life and largely determined our tactics (strategy, alas, was made in Whitehall and Westminster) giving me a unique opportunity to observe their public and private performance. On the whole, Labour politicians were, I believe, better at dealing with the Americans than their Conservative opposite numbers. The Labour Party of those days took America very seriously and since Churchill's and Eden's retirement from politics, outbid the Tories in enthusiasm for the Atlantic Alliance. Labour foreign policy was rightly seen by Washington as being essentially conservative; the ghost of Ernie Bevin still stalked those corridors which ran parallel in the Foreign Office and in the State Department. Moreover, that attitude of slightly patronising *bonhomie*, unhappily characteristic of so many British visitors was, I thought, rather less evident among our Labour clients than their Tory counterparts.

It was not surprising, therefore, that despite reservations about our domestic and economic policies, Labour ministers were well received and listened to with attention and respect. In addition to the media there are in America a bewildering number of Societies, Councils for Foreign Relations, for Economics, for Public Affairs. They give you a good meal in pleasant surroundings, and provide platforms for experts, or well-known public figures, thus furnishing the opportunity for the discussion, seminar, colloquy or workshop so beloved by all Americans. The lecture circuit is big business and the grading of platforms and speakers a complicated but exact science. New York was no exception to any other city in this respect; indeed, many of its organisations, such as the Economic Club and the Council on Foreign Relations, have national importance and command a wide and influential audience. It was part of my job to arrange for our ministers to address these bodies as well as to meet American bankers, editors, columnists and other leading figures (opinion-moulders was the correct jargon) for more private, off-the-record talks.

Of course, I was not always successful; competition from other nationalities and other problem areas was fierce. It was sometimes difficult to explain to British politicians why their words and deeds were not automatically front-page news, and why prime-time TV could not always be persuaded to devote entire programmes to a favourable account of the British economy. Even in the 1960s American interest in British affairs could be greatly overestimated.

Since many of my visitors are still active in politics, I shall not risk the attempt to draw up a full league table for effectiveness of impact. Variations in circumstances and other criteria would, in any case, make the task almost impossible. I suppose Harold Wilson, as Prime Minister, was the best value. (I speak, of course, strictly from the export point of view.) Americans respect the horse's mouth and as horses go, he was a good one – urbane, unflappable, authoritative, never at a loss for an answer, and with the right mixture of dignified informality which Americans hope for but do not always get in British public figures. His visits let me in on some unusual experiences. Being part of the team in Washington as well as in New York, I was swept into the White House with the rest of the entourage when Wilson first arrived, and witnessed him and President Johnson mauling each other in front of the TV cameras like a couple of playful, gallery-conscious bears. I was also present when George Brown telephoned from London at what must have been two o'clock in the morning for him. Wilson listened impassively and at one point, putting his hand over the mouthpiece, turned to Burke Trend (who, with the Private Secretary, was the only other person in the room) and said, 'He's resigning again.'

Sir Burke Trend was, at that time, Secretary of the Cabinet, and probably the most influential Civil Servant in the land. Certainly, Harold Wilson took few steps without him by his side. I forget how he responded, probably with a silent nod of the head which said, in effect, 'Don't worry, I've got that under control' – no understatement, for in those days it seemed that Trend was the still centre of the turning world of British Government; he was always informed, never in a hurry, calm, wise, practical and courteous.

I also caught my first close-up view of Mrs Marcia Williams (later Lady Falkender) in action. She was part of the Prime Minister's party; and while most of the Embassy staff, being civil servants, were too junior for her to notice, there was hardly anyone who failed to notice her. The Embassy administration made the fatal error of taking the word 'Secretary' in her title literally, with the result that she found herself listed, billeted and transported with the other visiting short-hand typists. Needless to say, she had this put right in a flash and assumed what she regarded as her proper place in the entourage for the rest of the visit.

It was later during that same visit that the high spot of my relationship with Mr Wilson was to be reached. He was due to make a major speech to the Economic Club of New York at a dinner at the Waldorf Astoria. It was an important forum, but an organisation whose conservatism and sense of occasion was such that they would not allow TV cameras into the Ball Room during the dinner. I did not altogether blame them, but since on this occasion Wilson had something important to say, and we needed all the coverage we could get, I had to think of some way to circumvent this little hazard. Wilson was invariably co-operative about such things, and after I had fought, and won, a battle with the networks who disliked compromises, he agreed to get dressed an hour earlier and pre-record parts of his speech under an embargo. My problem was then to reach him in order to decide which parts of the speech would have the best impact. This last conference took place in his bedroom while he was changing into a dinner jacket, with me perched on the bed, choking back my disappointment that a Prime Minister's underclothing should be so unglamorous. We rushed down to the Waldorf where a mock rostrum had been set up on a dummy stretch of top table. The PM delivered, cold, some stirring passages about British Economic Recovery to an appreciative audience of cameramen. He did it very well and, indeed, performed admirably later that evening on the real occasion. All this did not result, however, in more than about sixty seconds of network time. Wilson did not complain; but I had to justify the exercise to his disappointed and less realistic staff by pointing out how much it would have cost to buy even that short time commercially.

Most of the Cabinet visited us at least once, each with his idiosyncrasies and special needs. Mr Callaghan came several times, first as Chancellor of the Exchequer, later as Home Secretary. Always ready to take advice, he patiently trundled about the East Coast and sometimes further afield, speaking at lunches, dinners, symposia, on TV shows and even early morning radio chat programmes. Nothing was too much trouble. His bluff, cheerful manner did a good deal to restore and maintain confidence, and his message did not seem to vary whichever office he happened to be holding at the time: 'Don't worry, Britain will be all right.'

Curiously enough, the Americans *did* worry. However Anglophobic many might be in theory, they disliked in practice the idea of a Britain so weak that they would be left alone to cope with the Germans and French in an alliance of which they were still so reluctantly the leaders. They were scared of socialism, believing it to be both infectious and contagious. The reassuring role which people like Jim Callaghan played in those years cannot be overestimated. Indeed, he even reassured us, the officials, as he sailed serenely through session after session of loaded, anxious, frequently hostile questions.

Roy Jenkins was also a confidence builder, though in a different way and to a different audience. Whereas Callaghan's appeal was based largely on his reputation, cunningly contrived I dare say, for honest pragmatism rather than academic brilliance, Roy's visits were a continuous display of intellectual pyrotechnics. He was a superb performer on TV and his exaggerated drawl and endearing inability to pronounce the letter R greatly pleased the Americans and fortified their belief that all British spoke, or ought to speak, like that. Much of his time was spent at universities or with quiet groups of the intellectual establishment; and at weekends he sought out and was welcomed by the more internationally-minded hostesses of the eastern seaboard. These visits were not without their fall-out of artistic temperament. I remember being called up very late one night by his Private Secretary, who passed on a complaint by the Chancellor about having been let down over an appearance on some TV show. 'Is he angry?' I asked.

'Well,' I was told, 'he's not exactly swinging from the rafters yet, but steam is beginning to come out of his ears.' But such storms did not last long and he was a loyal friend to those civil servants whom he liked and in whom he had confidence.

George Brown was the fourth of this quartet of Cabinet visitors – the double bass, one might say. His earlier visits were remarkable chiefly for the rumours of his probable behaviour which preceded him. In the event, it was almost always more effective and less outrageous than expected, but even his persuasive and courageous tongue, together with the much smoother and more precise tones of Sir Eric Roll, were unable to convince the Americans that the National Plan – (remember the National Plan?) – was the solution to all our problems. This particular visit, and a call paid on him subsequently in London, were my first experiences of this most complex of political personalities. During his later visits as Foreign Secretary, I was much closer to him and, like all of us involved in his official life, suffered many anxious moments. I gave a lunch for him to meet the leading publishers, editors and columnists in New York at which, after a good deal of clowning with me playing the self-appointed fall guy, he gave an extempore review of past and present British foreign policy of a brilliance matched only, in my experience, by Anthony Eden at his best. Since this day had been preceded by a night of carousing with some nameless, perhaps faceless, old friends to the alarm of his Private Secretary and his detective, to whom George was by now a past master at giving the slip, his performance was all the more impressive.

Nothing about George Brown in those high, heydays was half-hearted or indecisive. He was either on the crest of a wave or in the eye of a storm. He embraced a cause with zest and courage, but discarded it without sentiment when proved wrong. He began by displaying, to an extreme degree, the traditional Labour Party dislike and distrust of the Diplomatic Service, to whose morale he did considerable harm in the early stages. But I suspect that he ended with an equally exaggerated respect, and perhaps even affection for it. Certainly, he was always one to stand up for us in Cabinet. That, at any rate, was the note which he sounded in a touching little speech of thanks which he made to us all at Hugh Caradon's apartment after dinner and before catching the night plane to London at the end of a particularly difficult session at the UN. I drove out to Kennedy Airport with him afterwards and we had a bet about the outcome of the forthcoming Republican Convention. By the time I had to pay up (he won of course – he was usually right about such things) he had at last succeeded in resigning, and was on his way to the House of Lords and a comfortable niche in the hall of legends from which he will no doubt continue to baffle political historians.

Apart from senior politicians and businessmen, one other main category of visitor, members of the Royal Family, must be mentioned. There are few spectacles more amusing than the sight of American men and women – to whom Republicanism is a religion, July 4th 1776 its consummation, the Declaration of Independence its Holy Writ and King George III the embodiment of evil vanquished – struggling with each other for a sight of, let alone a chance to meet, one of his descendants. Small wonder that we are sometimes accused of exploiting our Royal family; and since, as a family, they possess a kind of collective sense of duty which allows them willingly to be exploited, small wonder that the whole exercise is unfailingly successful! A Royal visit requires an enormous amount of meticulous preparation, and usually a good deal of juggling with protocol, since few nations share our obsession with punctuality and ceremonial. The results are invariably worth it. I have seen tycoons of Wall Street and the Press heel over like schooners in a hurricane before that mysterious charm, so uncontrived but so deeply professional, which a Royal occasion dispenses.

Such powerful concentration of interest, however, has its disadvantages. Any institution outwardly so perfect, it is argued, must have hidden flaws and thus it is only human to try to detect and expose them. In this respect, the American Press was more than human and gleefully spent large sums chasing crowned and coronetted hares. The result was usually a rumour about the private life of a member of the Royal Family, the more improbable the faster spreading. As a diplomat and civil servant, this sort of thing always fussed me; such matters were not strictly my concern, but they were, or became, public affairs about which I, being the recognised official spokesman, could hardly remain silent. No-one likes his nation's dirty linen washed in public, especially if the linen is, in fact, spotless.

Late one spring afternoon in 1967 I was having a meeting in my office before rushing home to give a drink to the resident British Press Corps to meet Jennie Lee, who was over to sing the praises of the Open University. All that day a most tiresome rumour had been running to the effect that Lord Snowdon's marriage to Princess Margaret was breaking up; that he had left London precipitately without saying where he was going; and that he was at this moment in New York, incognito and in hiding. I had been strenuously denying this all day, saying in effect, 'Nonsense – impossible. No question of Lord Snowdon being here. Yes, you may quote me.' As far as I knew, this was the truth. I was not a little discomforted, therefore, when my secretary broke into the tail-end of my meeting to say that someone claiming to be Lord Snowdon was on the phone. Suspecting that my leg was being pulled, I was just about to pick up the phone and indulge in some reflections on my caller's ancestry when one of those little gremlins whose sole function is to stop diplomats making fools of themselves gave my sixth sense a tweak. 'Yes?' I said rather tentatively.

'This is Tony Snowdon,' said a cheerful, and unmistakeably authentic voice. 'I'm in a bit of a jam and Pat Dean says you're the only person who can help me.'

Flattered by this otherwise unhelpful attitude on the part of my Ambassador, Sir Patrick Dean, I probed the Snowdon position sufficiently to confirm that he was, indeed, in New York. On arrival that morning he had made a beeline for the offices of *Vogue* (for whom he was working at the time), but had been spotted by some alert reporter, since when *Vogue* had been besieged. He was aware of the growing rumpus: what could or should he do? I said that unless the story was substantially true, I strongly advised him to make some kind of statement since silence on his part would be taken as confirmation. After some hesitation, he agreed. There was to be no press conference. I would, I said, arrange on the old-boy-net for the Reuter's correspondent and also a reporter from the American APN to get themselves into the *Vogue* offices unobserved. We wrote, and later gave them, a strongly worded statement which had been cleared with Princess Margaret by telephone. I was struck then, as so often during the week that followed, by Snowdon's good sense and deep concern for the image of the Royal Family.

So far so good, but meanwhile I had to face the British Press, already gathering at my apartment, who would not be exactly thrilled with me when they found out what I had done. I arrived home to find them waiting and suspicious. Naturally, a good deal of my time was spent with newspaper correspondents, American and British. I believed that my main responsibility was to the former; the latter did not always agree. I liked them all personally, but many were trouble-seekers, their editors and proprietors in Fleet Street being convinced that only bad news sells newspapers. This made for a delicate relationship; I was not particularly concerned with what the British public was told about America as such; but I was constantly anxious to ensure that the criticism of the Embassy and its Service, and of the performance of British VIP visitors, especially

61

members of the Royal Family, should be as fair and informed as possible.

Jennie Lee was in her room when I got home, and I slipped in to warn her what was afoot. A good deal of HM Government's business abroad goes on, one way and another, in bedrooms. Of course, she played up magnificently and the one correspondent who *did* ask her about the Snowdons' marriage got exceedingly short shrift. For once the timing was in my favour. Before the party broke up I got confirmation that Snowdon had done his stuff, so I was able, innocently, to tack on a short announcement at the end of the proceedings without revealing that he had already made a statement. The Head of Reuter's Bureau never let me down, and the Press departed, leaving me for once smelling reasonably rose-like. By then, our Royal had gone into deep cover. Next day, the popular Press, deprived of a juicy scandal, decided to turn on the other circulation-boosting tap – romance. It had long been the Snowdons' plan to meet in New York at the end of that week and to go on together for a holiday in the Caribbean. The Press refused to accept that these arrangements had not been extemporised in the light of public speculation, and began to talk about the 'great reconciliation' which would take place at Kennedy airport, implying a sudden dash by a love-sick Princess to the side of her contrite husband.

This rubbish made it clear that we would be in for quite a production when HRH did eventually arrive at Kennedy in a few days' time. We worked out a scenario, which Snowdon insisted on clearing at each stage with Kensington Palace. We went into great detail – should he go on to the plane first? Should HRH say anything? Where could they spend the time between flights privately? And so on. On the great day, I smuggled Tony (as he had now become to me), disguised by a pair of glasses and a hat out to Kennedy in my own car and into the VIP lounge by a series of back doors. I had been accused by some of exaggerated fears but I was vindicated when Princess Margaret duly arrived to be greeted by a greater number of reporters, photographers, and TV cameras than at any other occasion in the history of the airport. Our little playlet proceeded according to script, and after about an hour the Royal pair departed for the Caribbean, leaving behind a smug Press determined to be dewy-eyed and a number of sticky articles which might have come straight from the pages of a child's fairy story. Before they left, Princess Margaret saw me alone with Tony and thanked me with warmth and, as Sam Goldwyn used to say, charmth. It is sad that what was, so far as I and the world knew in 1967, no more than a malicious twinkle in the eye of the Press should turn out to have been prophetic: and that these two people, so gifted in their different ways, should have had to separate. It would be a mean-spirited person who did not wish them both well.

The middle sixties saw the peak of the Permissive Society, and foremost among the waves of new habits, fetishes and behavioural extravagances was, of course, the whole drug-taking scene (it is even now difficult not to employ the jargon which formed an important part of this new culture). Babs and I had become very interested in the arguments that raged round the pros and cons regarding the legalisation of marijuana. We talked far into the night about these things, feeling once again like undergraduates, deeply involved in controversies which, for us at any rate, were purely theoretical and had better remain so. This is, incidentally, one of the many delights of social life in the USA; a passion, almost adolescent in its intensity, for abstract discussions.

However we were both painfully aware that in this particular case our confidently expressed views were, in reality, based on nothing more than hearsay since neither of us had knowingly come within a mile of a joint (a word we tossed about with an assurance as if bred from years of pot-smoking), and it seemed unlikely that we should do so in the future. But from an unquestioning belief that any kind of drug-related activity was totally excluded on grounds of professional probity, I began to drift into an attitude which admitted the possibility that perhaps I owed a wider duty to humanity to try out this experience so as to be the better informed when discussing it. It was not that I felt in any way attracted to the act of drug taking as such, or that I had any doubts about my ability to resist their addictive effect. But at that time I was impressed by the arguments in favour of the legalisation of marijuana although not, of course, of other harder drugs, and began to see no reason why I should not discreetly experiment. I talked the whole question over with Babs who, I found, thought much as I did and was all in favour of a little deviation from our excessively correct public and private life.

I accordingly consulted a great friend, a musician, who lived in Greenwich Village and who preferred smoking pot to getting sloshed on alcohol or ruining his lungs with nicotine, although I must say that his attitude to these latter activities could hardly be described as austere. He was immensely tickled by the idea of introducing two such characters to the vices of Lower Manhattan, and offered to take us to a party the following Saturday night where, he said, the joints would be going round like hot-dogs on Memorial Day. 'Right,' we said, 'we'll be there.' Wondering a little what we had let ourselves in for, we settled down to wait for the weekend. But we were to be baulked of this relatively innocent debauch, for two days later a scandal broke in the American Press involving a member of the Royal Family who had narrowly missed a police raid in connection with drugs at a party on the West Coast. My heart quailed, and my imagination supplied headlines ready-made – 'British Aide in Drug Scandal', 'Pot Rap for Limey Diplomat', and so forth. No, I thought, this is a silly risk, and forthwith I called our friend to cry off.

'Not to worry,' he said cheerfully, 'I'll just give you a couple of joints and you and Babs can try them one evening at home.' I felt that I could not refuse so generous an offer, and so he presented himself at the office the following afternoon and handed me over two rather seedy-looking objects wrapped in a piece of Kleenex with no more fuss than if they had been a couple of refills for a Parker pen. I went home with them burning a hole in my briefcase as if they were already alight.

When Saturday night arrived, Babs and I had a quiet dinner together, with nothing to drink so as not to spoil the effect of the pot. Then we settled down on either side of the fireplace in the study. I produced the joints. We looked at each other and burst out laughing. The idea of these two middle-aged persons by themselves, solemnly sitting and looking at each other while they puffed away at a couple of joints seemed suddenly unbearably grotesque. I threw the two cigarettes into the fire and mixed us a couple of drinks. Thus ended our only approach to one sub-culture of our times. The incident, when I confessed it subsequently to Faith, was always laughingly referred to as the 'Parents' Non-Trip'.

Such had been my life and work during my time in America. After four years, however, I had to face the fact that I was what was usually termed 'vulnerable', that is likely to be posted to a new job. I had reached the stage in my career when the next move would be crucial, setting the pattern for the rest of my service; and although I had no wish to leave the USA, where I was happy and fulfilled, I knew that it was time to move on.

Our summer holiday in 1968 had been spent, as in past years, on Martha's Vineyard, the enchanted island off the coast of Massachusetts which had not, at that time, been visited by the tarnished fame of the Chappaquiddick affair, nor the hoards of tourists that came to gape at the fatal bridge and to carve little souvenirs from its wood. Our time had been overshadowed by the thought, unspoken with our host and hostess but eloquent between us, that it would probably be the last of its kind; although we felt certain of being able to return to the USA whenever we could in the future, we both knew that it would never be quite the same after we had ceased to live and work there.

The American summer is one of the best things about life in America. Far more than just one of four seasons, it is the quintessential setting for the American Dream – where all young men are accomplished all-round athletes, sensational dancers, more than ready to meet the demands of twilight romance on the warm fragrant beaches, and are handsome in that extra-masculine way that advertises jeans and pipe tobacco. When the girl next door suddenly turns out to have all those qualities which autumn and winter somehow failed to reveal; a perfect figure, a soft, cool voice and the kindly wisdom of the ages. How they love their country, these Americans, and the fruits of its abundance which ripen from May to September – food and drink in unimaginable variety from the local store or packaged in the supermarket; sunlight and great distances; healthy bodies and clean, simple minds; freedom! Millions are air-borne at weekends, pouring out of New York, Chicago, Cincinnati, a hundred crowded cities, seeking relief from the great tall buildings which give off the stored-up summer heat like radiators. They are making for beaches, islands, country clubs and the grandparents' frame farmhouse, where wives and lovers are waiting with soothing words and Martinis, and children are impatient to be taught to swim, sail, play tennis and golf and to ride a horse. It is a time of shorts and sneakers, of lobster rolls and hot-dogs eaten casually on the move, of transistors in the firelight and the first damp fumbles of adolescent love. But all too soon it is Labour Day, the first Monday in September, which is the official end of Summer. The boats are beached, the rackets and clubs put away, and bronzed young men and women stand holding hands as the ferryboats leave for the last trip to the mainland. They smile at each other and wave at friends on the shore. 'Summer's over,' they say, mournfully but secure in the knowledge that it will come again next year. And so it is, and so it will.

Returning from the summer holiday always produces in me a feeling of unreality. My formal clothes, with their unaccustomed restraints, seem to belong to someone else; the familiar surroundings have a dream-like quality and I find it hard to accept that the daily, well-worn patterns of activity have actually been going on unchanged in my absence. New York in August is a bit unreal in any case. People stare at each other in frank amazement at finding another known face in the brooding, steamy concrete jungle; there are guilty, over-the-shoulder-looking explanations of why it is necessary. 'Uh, as a matter of fact to, er, well, sacrifice a day or two by the sea', to be present personally at the conclusion of some important deal.

Although I had left Babs for a few more days by the sea, summer was not over for me as I sat sweating on the way into town, wondering what the post, or rather the bag, would bring forth. In spite of much constructive and even joyous correspondence throughout my life, I have had my share of postal disappointments. Hoped-for, expected letters to which I have considered myself entitled by right fail to arrive; the wrong letters from the wrong people arrive punctually when least wanted; letters where the bad news is so deeply buried in the penultimate paragraph that two or three readings are necessary to confirm the subliminal feeling of disaster which they convey; letters badly or obscurely written, or lacking that longed-for warmth or future promise; bills, of course; and perhaps worst of all, letters which remorselessly call to mind duties unfulfilled and the thoughtless, indifferent cruelties of daily life. All these have been a feature of my post since adolescence and the substitution of a twice-weekly diplomatic bag for the village postman had done nothing to banish the jitters to which I am still a prey shortly before the expected arrival of mail from any source.

I left my car and padded across the hot pavement to the air-conditioned hall, into the elevator, and finally reached my office and the comforting, just intimate enough smile with which my secretary greeted me. Ann Stewart had been my PA for four years and had executed that most delicate of roles with grace and skill. The relationship of secretary to boss is a uniquely twentieth-century feature of human society. In no other age or civilisation has the male been able to enjoy so intimate, regular and, in the vast majority of cases, innocent a relationship with a female other than his lawful spouse with such lack of social or sexual friction. In the Diplomatic Service this is particularly so since an officer's PA is, in a sense, part of his household as well as of the office staff and should, if she is up to her job, have a good deal to do with his social life, itself an important part of his task. She is often the recipient of secrets and confidences which, for security reasons, many officers find themselves unable to share with their wives, although I was never inhibited in this respect and told Babs everything. Men who see the same woman daily, perhaps for more hours in the aggregate than they spend with their wives, cannot fail to develop a relationship in which the subtlety of the unspoken word can have full rein and unless the lady happens to be physically repulsive or mentally retarded – qualities which, needless to say, are never to be found in Foreign Office ladies – the situation provides many of the advantages and few of the drawbacks of a love affair.

Ann was no exception to this general rule. Good-looking, intelligent, yet not so efficient as to insulate me completely against the real world, she had those qualities essential for any successful PA. The important one was that she was almost able to persuade me that I was the wittiest, most attractive, super-intelligent man she had ever met and that she could not understand why I was not already Permanent Under Secretary. Well, flattery is harmless provided you don't inhale, as the late Adlai Stevenson once said. On the other hand, she was not slow to point out my errors of judgement and to save me from myself on more than one occasion. It goes without saying that she could spell; but for me this was an added bonus. There are certain words which create a sense of panic when they have to be spelt in the absence of Ann or a dictionary. Normally, I would dictate, thus avoiding the problem. Or I would scribble out drafts in my own hand, secure in the knowledge that Ann would silently and discreetly correct the spelling in the course of typing it out.

Given this relationship, it was, of course, impossible for Ann, when she greeted me in her outer office, to conceal that something was up. A suppressed excitement in her voice, a refusal to look me straight in the face, the palpable untruth of her 'Haven't had time to look' reply when I asked whether there was anything in the bag, told me plainly that an important letter of some kind had arrived. Sure enough, there it was, nestling innocently in my in-tray, but carefully placed on top of a pile of other letters and papers – an epistolary time-bomb.

There was no need for me to indulge in guessing games about my correspondent. Every letter in the bag has to be franked with the initial of the sender. In this case, both they and the type of envelope indicated that it was from my old friend Colin Crowe, now the chief Administration Officer of the Diplomatic Service and as such possessed of the pleasantly archaic, but nevertheless still accurate title of Chief Clerk. It was he who, among many other unenviable tasks, presided over the destinies of all, but particularly the senior, members of the Service. His letter looked somehow too official to be a mere postal pleasantry or delayed Christmas card. I opened it and scanned the contents in one continuous movement. Yes, this was it. A posting. Two words leapt at me from the page in that first reading: Ambassador and Kinshasa. My immediate satisfaction, not to say relief, at knowing that at last I had been given my own post was faintly overshadowed by a creeping uncertainty as to where exactly Kinshasa was, and of what country the capital. Place names in Africa tend to change with bewildering rapidity and lack of logic, and I had to consult an atlas before being quite sure of my future. I tried hard not to let Ann see exactly what I was doing, or why. Once having confirmed that Kinshasa (formerly Leopoldville) was the capital of the Democratic Republic of the Congo (now Zaire), I began to assess the pros and cons of this next and, for me, momentous move.

It was, of course, a major breakthrough to be able to put the magic letters H.E. in front of my name. To have one's own post is what all members of the Service aim for. I was fifty-three and could count on at least one other post after this one. So far so good, but I had some immediate reservations to offset this initial euphoria. A quick way of judging the importance of a post, and the scope and scale of its activities, was to look up the list of staff in the directory. In this case it was clear that, as Grade 3 posts went, it was of medium size and importance. It had its own Defence Attaché and a Counsellor as number two. There was one Consulate-General, at Lumumbashi (formerly Elizabethville). I was also to be accredited, non-resident, to Burundi, a small country lying to the east which would, I imagined, entail long journeys across the continent; and to Congo Brazzaville with which we had no relations at the time and which, although just across the river and visible from my house, I was never to visit.

In spite of all this rather promising information I found myself feeling vaguely disappointed – quite unjustifiably, since I had no valid reasons to have expected a larger post, let alone the promotion which that would imply, having held my present rank for only three years. But somehow I had subconsciously hoped that my move, when it came, would be rather more prestigious.

As it turned out, and as I saw later, I was wrong. It was just right for me at that stage; being an Ambassador proved far more difficult than I expected and I was glad in the end that I had cut my teeth in a post which was less demanding politically than it might have been. Indeed, I ended up by feeling what I should have felt in the first place, that I was lucky to get an Ambassadorship at all with the Service tending to contract. But on that hot August morning I confess to spending a little time coping with these gnawing little pangs of regret. They were quickly replaced, however, by more serious and respectable concerns. Kinshasa was a long way from anywhere; I had no idea what I would find in the way of living conditions, but suspected that they would be rugged. The climate was clearly difficult and there might be health problems. I wondered how Babs would take to it all. It would be asking a good deal of her and she would not, in any case, relish leaving New York, the home of most of her American family and where her elder daughter was also now living, married to the Italian Consul-General. Diplomatic wives have a more active and prominent contribution to make to their husbands' profession than is to be found in most walks of life. The anxious enquiry, 'What's *she* like?' is not frequently to be heard in, say, dentistry, the law or the arts. A diplomat's wife is a key part, and a working part at that, of his life and can affect her husband's career favourably or adversely.

I was greatly cheered and excited by the thought of Africa itself and by the prospect of living and working with Africans. I believed, rightly as it turned out, that Babs would be so too. I had liked those Africans whom I had met in other posts and I had visions of Wright, the trusted friend and counsellor of President and peasant alike, walking and talking at ease under the great African sky and reconciling Black with White, old with new, rich with poor, Left with Right. The prospect was cheering –

inspiring even – and I believed that it was a challenge that we both could meet.

By this time I had read Colin's letter several times, and had noted that he had not used that time-honoured word 'challenge' beloved by Chief Clerks and Personnel Officers to describe posts of an unusual unpleasantness. So I made a mental note to use it back to him in my reply; a good word, in fact, without which life would be much duller.

When news of this kind arrives a first, often desperate, urge is to talk to someone. Needless to say, this was not easy. A posting, in the early stages, especially an Ambassadorship, is a highly confidential affair and I could not run round to all my friends asking them what they thought. Nor could I reach Babs until the evening. However, there was, as always, Ann. I walked into her office and said with an assumed nonchalance that totally failed to convince her: 'Well, we're off, I'm afraid. I've just had a letter from Colin Crowe.'

'Oh yes,' she said, as if she didn't know. 'Where to?'

'Kinshasa,' I said, watching her closely and hoping to see a look of bewilderment come over her face. No such luck; of course she knew exactly where it was.

'Oh good,' she said briskly. 'My friend, Joyce, was there until last year and says it's much quieter now.' She paused, looking slightly embarrassed. 'You're going as . . .?'

'Ambassador,' I said firmly. Her relief was almost audible. She would have taken it somehow as a reflection on herself if I had not got a respectable job. I put the letter into my pocket (strictly against the security regulations) and mooned about the office for the rest of the day, making work for myself and trying to act as if nothing had happened.

When I got home that evening I called Babs. Having been brought up in the period when the telephone was an expensive and unreliable hobby, I have never got over a sense of awe at the marvellous efficiency of the American telephone system. Even the dialling tone gives one confidence. Operators appear positively to enjoy tracking down people called Cohen or Taylor (no initials) at an uncertain address in Chicago. I was speaking to Babs nearly five hundred miles away almost before I had finished dialling. I gave her quickly, clinically almost, the gist of our news. There was a short pause at the other end, a hint of an intake of breath.

'I think that's marvellous,' she said. 'I've always wanted to go to Africa – and you're going to be an Ambassador; that's very nice too.' I stopped her in full flood at this point, warning that it was still all very confidential and please not to chatter to anyone, especially to me over the telephone. I need not have worried; she was, after all, a professional like me.

'Quite,' she said. 'See you Wednesday night,' and hung up.

I sat back and marvelled at my luck, not for the first time. Such a wife was an asset of literally priceless worth, a gift beyond that of tongues, of riches, of the right connections, all of them desirable assets in themselves but as nothing compared with a mate who will accept cheerfully the prospect of three years in Central Africa over the long distance telephone. I knew only too well the sharp decline into which many of my colleagues' wives were liable to be plunged at the mere mention of any post other than Paris, Rome or Washington; Africa would have produced the vapours. But here she was, all set to go. She must have faced the major disadvantages in that first imperceptible pause and, true to form, decided that they could and should be outweighed by the prospect of our own post. So, as usual, she wasted no time in giving that first burst of confident support that I now knew I had been needing all along.

When life in New York got going again after Labour Day, we entered a limbo-like existence. We were allowed to say that we were leaving – and by then I had even managed to fix the date – but we were not allowed to say *where* we were going. Secrecy, or at the least discretion, is one of the main tools and principal drawbacks of a diplomat's life. It is not so much that careless talk costs lives, although this can, in extreme cases, be true; but it can cost reputations and careers. A diplomat must have in his armoury a reputation for discretion, since to be trusted is one of his most important qualifications. Nevertheless, I think that there is often an excess of secrecy about the work of the Diplomatic Service. Some diplomats tend to play their cards so close to their chests that they have difficulty in recognising the strength or weakness of their own hand, let alone revealing it to an opponent. But while the arguments of principle against excessive secrecy are strong, those in favour of discretion in particular cases are often stronger, and by their nature cannot be rehearsed in public. So the diplomat gets the worst of both worlds, often being forced to adopt a pose of mystery without explaining why.

My own circumstances well illustrated these difficulties. The process of nominating one of Her Majesty's Ambassadors is cumbersome rather than stately. A vacancy occurs, often as part of a general shuffle sparked off by unforeseen illness or retirement. The senior officials of the Foreign Office, sitting as a body known as the Promotions Board, then consider all the possible candidates, choosing one name (or possibly two) for submission to the Foreign Secretary and Prime Minister. With their blessing, the name is then submitted to the Queen for her approval 'in principle'. This useful phrase, when employed in Whitehall context, can be made to mean virtually anything; but in this case it really means 'providing the receiving government agrees', thereby indicating the next step, which is to seek such *Agrément*. (The French language is still used to describe these international minuets.) This manoeuvre is carried out by the embassy concerned, often by the outgoing Ambassador himself, whose loyalty and discretion are sometimes sorely tried when he contemplates (not perhaps without a trace of hope) what a mess his successor is bound to make of things. In due course – due being a pretty flexible word – the *Agrément* is given by the relevant government, who say that they will accept Mr So-and-so as HM Ambassador. For an *Agrément* to be refused is extremely rare and causes a fine old rumpus in Whitehall. The whole process starts again and this time the Queen is asked for her formal approval which, being the subject of Ministerial advice, is invariably given.

It is only at this stage that the prospective Ambassador's destination can be revealed and an impatient, not to say anxious, public informed that 'HM The Queen has approved the Appointment of Mr . . . as Ambassador Extraordinary and Plenipotentiary at . . . to succeed Sir . . .' Most appointments are not sufficiently important or interesting to make these restrictions any more than a bore to the individual concerned. Those really interested can always indulge in a little detective work, for life has to go on and preparations must be made, however surreptitiously. 'I hear that Ursula is buying cotton knickers – they must be going to Delhi to replace the Smiths.'

I had selected October 30th as our departure date from New York, which would give us just over three months for leave, and for preparatory briefing in London before we were due in Kinshasa at the end of January. This set a comfortable pace; it was a longer break than we had ever had before, and represented perhaps one of the first outward and visible signs of my new, as yet inward, status. The two months before we left the USA were, however, quite another matter. Although I intended to try to prevent the news of our departure getting out, I could not keep the lid on indefinitely. At the same time, I had been warned by the Foreign Office that the *Agrément* was unlikely to come through before our final departure, which would leave us, as so often, the monkeys in the puzzle.

The news actually began to leak at the end of September, which at least made it possible for us to get on with plans for leaving without any subterfuge. Moreover, our friends in New York, a society always on the look-out for fresh diversions, were presented with a new and apparently for them amusing parlour game entitled 'Guess Where the Wrights Are Going'. As time went on, I became less busy in the office and outside. There is no duck so dead as a departing diplomat. But by contrast our social life became increasingly hectic as those most generous of people,

New Yorkers, vied with each other in giving farewell parties for us. I had also to attend a number of more formal functions given, rather to my surprise, by such prestigious bodies as the Council for Foreign Relations, the Pilgrims, and the Editorial Board of *The New York Times* in my honour. At all these affairs, public and private, a lot of heavy jokes were made about the mystery of our future. It worried me a good deal that some of this speculation was flattering in the extreme, depicting for us a future far more glamorous and high-powered than I knew the reality to be. I felt something of a fraud and began to hope that the *Agrément* would, in fact, be delayed so that I should not have to face the disillusionment of our friends when they learnt the truth. However, there was no mistaking the warmth of feeling for us both. It dawned on me that we might actually be missed by quite a lot of people and, if friendship was a measure of success in diplomacy, as it often is, we could ease our withdrawal pains with the knowledge that we had not done too badly.

The process of clearing up and saying goodbye left little time for speculating about the future. We managed a couple of weekends in the country to see once again the breathtakingly spectacular New England autumn – the Fall, they call it, as if the season had something to do with the Garden of Eden, which was surely less colourful than Vermont in October. We settled the future of our devoted and beloved Chinese couple, Li Wong and Su Ying Tsao, who had achieved their long-cherished ambition of US citizenship, leaving them comfortably installed in an apartment which, although a long way up-town, had a view of New York like the title shots of a TV programme. The farewell parties became more frequent; I performed on a radio chat show to which I doubt whether many listened since it was at half-past six in the morning. The staff of BIS gave me a handsome electric clock. We tried, with little success, to reduce the enormous accumulation of things – books, records, clothes, stationery, objects of art and utility – which seemed to have multiplied of their own accord during our time in New York and without each one of which, on careful examination, life would clearly be impossible. The packers arrived and we had the familiar, insoluble problem of what to keep out with us for the last few days, the journey home, and in London until the main load (which would be shipped direct) joined us in Africa.

All this time I had also been in contact with London, planning my pre-African programme and briefing. I began to be conscious for the first time of a subtle change of mood, a hesitant note of polite formality which was creeping into the correspondence. 'Would you care to . . .?' 'You may wish to . . .' 'Would it be convenient if . . .?' 'It would be most helpful if you could spare the time . . .' This matched a new kind of attitude detectable among my friends and staff in New York, a certain respect, generous or grudging according to taste, which I could only put down to the fact, now dawning on me, that there was something odd about the label Ambassador. Even though it could not yet properly be used in my case, and was unsupported by any known destination, it seemed to carry of itself a mystical charge to which people automatically responded with a kind of reflex, invisible bow. It astonished and alarmed me, the more so since many of our friends appeared determined to make the most of what they obviously considered to be reflected glory. And since they still did not know where we were going, some were no doubt reinsuring against a future in which they saw themselves as guests in a handsome, impeccably-run embassy in a glamorous capital. But I had no time to do more than add these unfamiliar sensations to the growing list of things to think about on the voyage home.

As our departure came to be anticipated in terms of days rather than weeks, the signs of this new attitude multiplied. The Manager of Cunard gave us a special lounge on the *Queen Elizabeth* for a farewell party to which came not only our staff and personal friends, but the Consul-General and many of his foreign colleagues, a representative of the Mayor of New York, many friends from the American and British Press, now no longer chasing a story, past battles forgotten, but merely wishing us well for the future; and finally, of course, the Tsaos, wailing as if at the funeral of a Chinese grandfather.

The aeroplane has robbed human parting of much of its drama. The squalid muddle of an airport and the abrupt, clinical take-off by a sealed metal tube filled with sweet-chewing humanity cannot compare with the grandeur of that slowly widening gap of water, at first hardly perceptible but in time to become an ocean, as a great ship begins to throb with life and one by one the threads which bind her to the shore strain and snap. We stood on deck and watched the famous skyline grow remote and misty, blurred by the October evening and perhaps by tears that we had not dared to shed earlier. The past can be awe-inspiring when you see it forming before your eyes. In the ship's barely perceptible wake as we sailed slowly down the Hudson River were four years of intense living – work and play, love and friendship, opportunities taken and missed – a continent of memories stretching back, in Babs' case to childhood. It was one of those definitive moments in our lives which we had known would come. We could not fail to recognise it when it did.

Ahead lay a new life. 'Here comes His Excellency,' I thought to myself. 'I wonder what he will make of the job.' Afraid even to attempt to answer this question, we stumbled down to our cabin and found it so over-flowing with flowers and luggage that we could only go in one at a time until this clutter of past and present had been sorted out. By the time we had finished, New York had vanished over the horizon and we were ploughing into the future at a steady twenty-six knots as the evening darkened into night.

CHAPTER FIVE

Atlantic crossings by ocean liner are fast becoming the substance of boring tales which, to our grandchildren, are or I suppose soon will be a history lesson. What comfort; what luxury! For five or six days stewards and stewardesses were at hand to serve sumptuous and indigestible meals, tuck legs on deck chairs into very smart blue and red rugs, bring bouillon at eleven o'clock, organise deck games by day and Bingo (which somehow acquires a respectability undreamt of on land) by night. There was dancing, flirtation, pursuit and conquest; gambling and private meditation; and endless blessed time to do nothing for hours on end. We had been allotted a first class cabin in which the space not taken up by two huge beds, of that depressingly sexless kind that only the British can contrive, was occupied by our luggage.

So well treated were we that I began to have my suspicions. Sure enough, it had got about – how I am not sure, perhaps by an excessively eager clerk who had made our bookings – that I was no ordinary mortal but an Ambassador, albeit one as yet without an embassy. Those tell-tale signs were there: a table booked in the Veranda Grill for 'Ambassador and Mrs Wright', and a slight inclination from the hips by the head waiter. I am not, I hope, prig enough to pretend that I was not enjoying all this, and Babs was not above using the magic title on carefully selected occasions inspired, she assured me, by pride but also I suspect by a shrewd knowledge of human nature. Nevertheless, it seemed awfully premature; my appointment had not yet been announced, and I pictured a frowning Queen saying to her Private Secretary, 'Isn't he rather taking Us for granted?' I was also anxious about what my compatriots on board would think. The British, unlike most other nations, never refer to 'Ambassador This or That', or even to 'the Ambassador' except when he is actually *en poste*. But perhaps most worrying of all, I feared that when the time came to disembark the expectation by members of the crew of my tipping capacity would be inflated by a factor of anything up to fifty per cent.

The days passed pleasantly. Years ago I had been greatly impressed by

Gladwyn Jebb, when he left New York, having taken the trouble to write charming letters of appreciation to every member of his staff. Mine had seemed to me a model of its kind. I resolved to follow his example and wrote to my former colleagues in terms which perhaps now would seem pompous but which reflected sincere tributes and gratitude. We both also wrote to our friends, letters full of promises to keep in touch and of invitations to visit us in London and 'elsewhere'.

In those first days of separation, we felt curiously homesick for New York. We were objects of some interest on board, probably because the passenger list happened not to contain any very glamorous names. So we found that our shipmates began to play the same games as the New Yorkers, and I developed the same neurotic fear of being unmasked as a Grade 3 Ambassador when everyone had politely been assuming that I would end up in Rome or Madrid at the least.

The over-riding advantage of those sea crossings was the time which they afforded for thought. I had quite enough to be getting on with for a five day voyage, given that I found it difficult to concentrate and shipboard life provided plenty of distractions. I paced the deck (eight times round was one mile) and thought hard about the future, in particular about what kind of Ambassador I would try to be. I had plenty of models to choose from, some I had served under, some known from hearsay. Would I be remote, Olympian, sitting elegantly behind an unlittered desk with the tips of my fingers together contemplating human folly?; Would I be fussy, pernickety, driving my staff mad by obsession with detail? Would I be cheerful, back-slapping, bluff, common-sensical, popular on golf links and tennis court (neither of which game I had played for years) and a useful fourth at bridge? Would I cultivate a reputation for honesty (essential) or deviousness (unwise)? Would I argue with the Foreign Office about policy or be difficult about administration, or would I acquiesce in all but their silliest instructions? Would I be loyal to my staff or, most unattractive of qualities, be jealous of them if they seemed to be doing too well? Would I be able to preserve the right balance between friendship and authority in my relations with them? Would I be lonely at the top? I had seen or heard of all these qualities in action separately or in combination and believed that I knew some of the pitfalls they concealed. Then there were deeper, more personal questions to be answered. Africa was a violent continent in political turmoil; how would I stand up to any physical danger that I might have to face? I was not at all sure, my physical courage never having been really put to the test. Would I be able to get it right with the Africans? I liked them, or thought I did anyway.

On the whole I have admired my seniors and, with one or two

exceptions, received from them that loyalty and support which I, in turn, hoped to give to my staff. One quality, however, much to be desired, was now dying out – that of eccentricity. Civilized societies have always been enriched by their eccentrics. In the past the Foreign Service had attracted a spectacular number of unusual men. Legends still abound of Ambassadors who dictated seated cross-legged on their desks or even, in moments of acute stress, on the tops of bookshelves; who walked barefoot in public gardens reciting poetry to themselves; who spoke a private language compounded of schoolboy slang and Latin tags; who would only enter a car backwards; who wrote exclusively in bright green ink; who, though jolly and avuncular outside the office, were so forbidding inside it that you had to fight your way to their desk against waves of hostility. Such, alas, were now rare birds and such qualities can, in any case, never be acquired artificially, needing a more leisured, proconsular climate in which to blossom. It seemed clear to me that I would not be able to match the best or entirely avoid the worst. The safest course of action, I concluded, was to be myself, take advice where it was available and try to remember that I had not acquired overnight a crown or a halo.

With these rather undistinguished thoughts I stopped worrying about the future and devoted the rest of the voyage to amusing myself. We trans-shipped our luggage at Southampton and negotiated a suspicious Customs Officer who resented the fact that we were technically non-residents and became almost hostile at the mere mention of the Diplomatic Service. However, we were at last on our way to London, through a landscape beautiful, intimate and soft, looking like a child's garden after the great sweeps and slabs of American scenery. When we finally crossed the Thames, I could not believe how small it was, so used was I to the majestic Hudson River which had rolled by us for the past four years. How small, but how beautiful, and how old and wise! London wrapped us in her familiar arms like the mother she was, and it was not long before it seemed that I had hardly ever been away from her.

We had been lent a tiny mews flat by kind friends for the London months, and into this Babs moved with a speed and efficiency typical of the practised traveller. Our things were unpacked, sorted, redistributed; our London life organised, as it had to be, with time for children, grand-children and friends. She even managed to install a small upright piano so that I would not feel deprived. We decided not to try to take any leave in England. We were rested by the voyage and the English winter has few charms for those who do not live in it. We aimed at getting through all our preparatory work by the end of the year and leaving early in January for East Africa and a holiday in Kenya, before flying across to Kinshasa at the end of the month, when I was due to arrive. We both had a lot to do.

Those who believe that Heads of Mission spring, Minerva-like, fully armed from the head of Whitehall and, moreover, walk unprepared into the Elysian Palaces which are to be their future dwellings, are sadly mistaken. The Ambassador has, perforce, to prepare and be prepared for the special political, economic and administrative problems which his future post will present; and the chances are these days that long, intensive briefing will find him out of date when he arrives. His wife's task is equally complex, though less well defined; the role of Ambassadress is governed largely by legend, by cautionary tales of what *not* to do, and by oral tradition which, being handed down by feminine lips, is not notable for accuracy nor devoid of malice. In any case, her preoccupations are primarily domestic and tend to concentrate on the safe disposal of children, the reputedly inadequate way in which her predecessor has managed the domestic scene, her wardrobe, and such renovations and improvements in the house in which she is to live as can be cajoled from a reluctant Whitehall department. Our home-to-be in Kinshasa was referred to by the rather grand name of The Residence. It was, in fact, a rather superior bungalow and was said to be in need of a facelift in the shape of new curtains in some of the rooms. This, and other similar problems, meant numerous journeys for Babs to an obscure office somewhere near Southwark Cathedral in which those particular powers presided over the requirements of the Ambassadorial environment. Her wardrobe was a source of constant discussion, trial and error, and of lengthy consultation with colleagues who knew the place and happened to be available. Being a deeply inquisitive person, she also read everything she could lay her hands on about Africa in general and the Congo in particular.

By this time the *Agrément* had been received, the Queen had given her formal approval, and a one-line announcement had appeared in *The Times*, appropriately placed immediately below a notice of someone's Memorial Service. There was no ugly rush by Press, Radio and TV to interview me. At that time I could afford, as a non-resident, to belong to several London clubs. These institutions symbolised for me London, England, civilisation; and I would think about them in deserts and make a dash for one or other of their secure and friendly thresholds as soon as possible after arriving in London on leave or duty. But even their members seemed unaware, and certainly uninterested, in my change of status. All, that is, except the Colonel who unwittingly provided one more example of what I was beginning to think of as 'status magic'. He was a retired Army officer who had persistently treated me as a subaltern from an inferior social background ever since we first met. This visit was no exception, and as I walked up to the bar there was the Colonel, as if lying in wait.

'Hello,' he barked, 'you on leave again?' His most simple utterances seemed to have a kind of suppressed rage about them.

'Well, yes and no,' I replied cautiously. 'Actually, I'm on my way to a new post.'

'Ah,' said the Colonel, 'and where are they sending you this time?' He managed to convey by this question the conviction that all my previous postings had been disastrous for me and the Service alike.

'As a matter of fact, it's the Congo,' I said, trying not to sound too apologetic. 'You know, the big one – ex-Belgian,' I added by way of mitigation of this obviously unsatisfactory news.

'Christ, what have you done to be sent there?' said the Colonel, his nostrils a-quiver with the scent of some possible scandal. I chose to ignore his implications.

'Actually,' I said, 'it's rather an important country; very big, you know, and very rich.' He grunted, then switched his line of attack: 'Well, what are you going as? Commercial Secretary, something like that I suppose?'

Here I was presented with a first chance to make an entrance in my new role; I tried to sound as off-hand as possible, having of course privately rehearsed this particular moment. 'Well, I'm going to be the next Ambassador,' I said, looking modestly into my glass.

'Really?' said the Colonel, quick as a flash. 'Have a drink.'

His tone had not altered but his attitude had, and so rapidly that I was caught off-guard and failed to realise that the lack of any pause whatsoever combined with an offer only rarely made was indicative of a milestone, not only in my career but in my relations with the Colonels of this world which the mere mention of the magic word had brought about.

My return to London resulted in my now belonging to another, very exclusive 'club' that of H.M. Heads of Mission. Its 'clubhouse' was a small suite of offices tucked away in what used to be the Commonwealth Office in which an invaluable institution called the Heads of Mission Section lived and worked. The devoted and capable ladies in this unit were in charge of us and, like kindly aunts or competent nannies, did everything from arranging Audiences with the Queen and providing our Letters of Credence to fixing up our day-to-day programmes, acting as a message centre and finally booking our flights or berths back to duty with, if we were lucky or grand enough, a car to take us to the airport. The first person plural that creeps into my syntax at this stage is another indication of the separateness which I was beginning to feel; the Foreign Office had recognised this by the provision of this special facility to which all Heads of Mission on appointment and thereafter, but only they, had recourse. It was one of those privileges so typical of the laddered structure of British public life – like being able to run in the cloisters or walk through a certain door with your hands in your pockets when you became a prefect at school. The ladies were veritable encyclopaedias about conditions abroad, and if they could not answer a question they would telegraph imperiously to the post to find out. Life would have been very difficult without them; countless harassed and overworked Ambassadors and High Commissioners running out of time at the end of a leave or duty visit, have had, and no doubt still have, cause to be grateful. I certainly was, as they tactfully steered me through a myriad of engagements – Whitehall meetings, lunches with bankers and businesses with interests in the Congo; briefings with FO departments; with Ministers and members of the Opposition; with the Ministry of Defence and Armed Forces; and with representatives of Missionary Societies and charities operating in or near the Congo. Throughout all this, I was treated with a degree of deference which, to my alarm, I found myself beginning to enjoy, although I was deeply embarrassed when erroneously accorded by my hosts or their servants that Knighthood which, no doubt, they believed was an automatic and indispensable adjunct of my rank.

Coming over on the boat I had decided that my French needed a good deal of polishing, since I would have to live and work in that language. The ladies arranged this too, with the Foreign Office Language Centre, who agreed to provide exactly what I wanted, namely an hour's conversation a day, mainly on economic subjects. No problem, they said, come tomorrow and we will have one of our instructors available. I had not bargained for what was waiting for me when I duly turned up on a foggy November morning. Sitting in a room furnished in what was no doubt Whitehall's idea of tasteful intimacy was one of the prettiest girls I had seen for a very long time. I remember thinking as we shook hands that it would only be a matter of time before I became tongue-tied or bi-lingual. Needless to say, the circumstances were frustratingly prim; when not actually chaperoned, the dead hand of Civil Service propriety lay heavy upon us. Three mornings a week, and always at half-past nine, I discussed the falling pound, copper prices and the lack of racialism in metropolitan France with this ravishing and, to make it more difficult, highly intelligent creature. I never managed to discover her surname, the use of which paradoxically would have implied greater intimacy than the Christian name terms on which we were; and when I looked in just before Christmas to thank her and propose a farewell lunch, she had already skipped off on her *vacances*.

Christmas was soon upon us, a festival of which we have always made much as a family. Our children, all by now married with their own families, created as faithful a copy as possible of the Christmases we used to have in Sussex before we became fragmented by diplomacy. They were rightly determined to do their bit in preventing me from becoming pompous, and there was a good deal of ribald joking at the expense of His Excellency. Beneath all this, however, I think there was a genuine feeling of satisfaction that the old man had made it thus far 'without being found out', as they so delicately put it. Perhaps too they felt reluctant at seeing us off to so distant and seemingly inaccessible a post. The familiar, yet always unexpectedly hectic flurry of last minute packing and farewells claimed us immediately after the New Year. I paid my last calls on Ministers who were polite but hardly interested; I could already see that battling for Ministerial attention against the claims of other, more dramatic or politically sensitive posts was going to be a major occupational nightmare. We had not been to see the Queen. This was not unusual, despite the fact that an Audience for an Ambassador was usually referred to as having taken place for the purpose of 'kissing hands on Appointment', thus placing a seal of authenticity on his mission for the benefit of the receiving country. The ladies explained, tactfully in case we should be disappointed, that HM's programme was already too full; and that in any case, she preferred to see her Ambassadors after they had been some time in a post, because there would be more to talk about.

There is something remorseless about the tug of familiar places and faces as the days accelerate towards a departure date. We exhausted ourselves trying to see everyone, often not for their sakes but for our own, to satisfy ourselves that they were still there and would remember us when we were not. Africa seemed a very long way away; unfamiliar, vaguely hostile, demanding, unyielding and impersonal, a cemetery of European hopes and ideals. I was not without hope and purpose myself, far from it; but in those last days I wrapped London round me like a child unwilling to take the last, first plunge from the womb. I do not like travel. I like arriving and, better, having arrived. I dread most of all the moment of departure. The last acts are always the most painful, perhaps because they are unconsciously put off as long as possible; mine was to visit my sister in hospital where she was recovering from an operation, a parting which left us both with a sense of forlorn unreality.

It was a cold wet night when we finally drove off to Heathrow to catch the plane to Entebbe, the point of departure for our short African holiday. An Ambassador leaving to take up his post is treated with respect by the airport authorities, and on arrival we were ushered in to the Alcock and Brown Suite, a private lounge set aside for the reception and despatch of VIPs. No sooner were we through the door than it became clear that if I had counted on a few, quiet moments of nostalgia, a final tearful farewell to the country in whose Service I was bound, and other spiritual malpractices suggested, no doubt, only by fatigue, I was in for a big disappointment.

The lounge was awash with Africans. Even at the United Nations I had hardly ever seen so many in one place, nor heard so concentrated a babble of strange tongues and laughter. I suspected that they must be travelling on the same plane as we were, and this was soon confirmed by a Foreign Office official who materialised, it seemed from nowhere, to tell me that this was President Obote of Uganda, and his entourage, who had just decided to return home from a visit to the UK several days earlier than expected. It was my first lesson in the African way of official life – an absence of planning, of timetables, of forethought. No explanation of this abrupt change of plan had been given, since none was thought necessary.

The immediate effect on my circumstances, however, was considerable and, on balance, in my favour as so often turned out to be the case in that unpredictable continent. A harassed and deeply apologetic British Airways official drew me to one side and explained that, since President Obote's party had taken over the entire first class space in the aircraft, would I mind (indeed there was no alternative) travelling Economy class? Although I might have tried to remonstrate had I been going direct to Kinshasa – for HM Ambassador to arrive travelling Economy might well be noted as yet another sign of Britain's financial decline – I agreed with an alacrity that was born of quite different considerations.

As usual, we had a lot of luggage, and I anticipated having to pay a large amount of excess and then fighting a long, and probably losing, battle with the FO for a refund. What were called in the regulations 'our effects' had been sent direct from New York to Kinshasa, and were no doubt at the moment being battered into unrecognisable fragments in the Bay of Biscay. We had been living with what could reasonably be carried about in suitcases, and would have to continue to do so until the highly unpredictable arrival of our stuff on the Equator. So we needed to travel with rather more than the Foreign Office could bring themselves to recognise as essential – they seemed at times to have difficulty in distinguishing between journeys such as ours, and a fortnight's package tour to Broadstairs.

Nor was this entirely for our personal comfort. The odds were that I would have to present my credentials, a very formal ceremony, soon after arrival. This would entail wearing Uniform, complete with sword, and it would have been very risky not to have all the necessary equipment with me on the plane. Those accustomed to travelling with a sword will know that it is difficult, if not impossible, to fit one into an ordinary suitcase.

Thus, in addition to the rest of our things, I carried this curious object, looking decidedly sinister in its protective black oilskin sheath, in my hand like a wand of office which, no doubt, some of the Africans thought it was, being accustomed to this form of ritualistic dignity. There emerged the basis for a satisfactory deal; I was relieved of any excess baggage charges in view of the refund on my first class fares. I never confessed this to the Office, believing that the consequent mathematical inquest would last long and exhaust us all.

During the final stages of these negotiations, I caught sight of the FO official hovering with intent to speak; as soon as I was free, he sidled up to my ear and whispered that President Obote had heard that I was to be on the plane and was asking to see me. Thrusting my sword into Babs' hands for safe keeping, I followed him into a section of the lounge partitioned off from mere Ambassadorial travellers like ourselves. A charming Ugandan introduced himself as the Minister for Foreign Affairs and took me up to the President, who was sitting by himself drinking a cup of tea. Those around him were fortified for their journey with stronger stuff, indeed some of them seemed ready to take off. Obote, despite his somewhat sinister appearance, was pleasant and, apart from a dig at his fellow African Head of State, President Mobutu, to whose Government I was to be accredited, he talked of uncontentious things such as the preservation of wild life in Africa and the appalling state of the traffic in London.

I withdrew as soon as I decently could to find that a situation of near chaos was developing in the next room, the shock waves of which had not yet penetrated to the Presidential enclosure. A bomb scare! Something had been suspected at the last minute which necessitated all the baggage already aboard being unloaded and identified personally by each owner. Things had gone quite far enough in the VIP lounge, and many of the Presidential suite were already feeling no pain. All might have been well, but for this last minute hitch. There was much laughing and joking at British Airways' expense as we all trooped out to a point somewhere in the dark on the airport and wandered about looking for our bags.

To make matters worse, some officious but obstinate British Airways official began insisting that President Obote himself, in person, should come out to identify his own luggage. This naturally provoked a near explosion among the Africans, who suspected in any case the whole bomb scare business was somehow a manifestation of racial discrimination, and understandably resented their Head of State being subjected to what they regarded as an indignity. At this stage I intervened and, mobilising the FO official, who by this time was little short of punch drunk, made a frontal assault on British Airways and succeeded in convincing the official concerned that it was unlikely that President Obote would wish to blow up the plane in which he himself was travelling, and that in any case, one of his staff could surely be trusted to identify his bags. If there was any doubt, they could be brought in to him for a personal check. Reluctantly this was agreed, and I regained possession of my sword with the feeling of having avoided my first crisis in Anglo-African relations.

We were now faced with a considerable wait while the baggage was reloaded, and this period was used by our African fellow travellers for further fortification and celebration, so that, when we did eventually get on board, some two hours late, there was a distinct absence of that serious approach to travel which might have been expected after an official visit to the UK. To tell the truth, I was relieved that I was not travelling First Class, since the sounds of rejoicing emanating from that quarter were not encouraging for those who hoped to snatch a little sleep on the journey. By this time we were so tired that I doubt whether anything would have prevented our sleeping, but just to make sure I took a mild sleeping pill, persuading Babs to do the same, which was much against her New England upbringing. We both lapsed into the kind of nervous doze which is the only possible form of sleep in an Economy class seat in a crowded aircraft with half the Establishment of Africa living it up next door.

When we woke the great Continent lay beneath us. The sun was streaming into the cabin and the engines had made that change of tone which denotes the beginning of the descent. I heard the pilot's voice saying something over the intercom. In my still very dopey state, I looked out of the window, and was startled to see flying alongside us, so close that I could detect a slightly malevolent gleam in the pilot's eye as he peered into our cabin, a fighter plane; one of four, as it subsequently turned out, sent up as a ceremonial escort for the President on his return home. I was reassured by the calmness with which the crew seemed to be taking this, and was pulling myself together when our imminent arrival at Entebbe was announced.

Arrivals and departures are made much of in Africa, and the more important the person the bigger the fuss. When the ruler of an African country makes a journey or returns from one, a large part of the population shares in his farewell or welcome, seeing in him a continuation of their tribal past and simultaneous celebration of their newly found independence. They are not particularly interested in where he is going or has been, nor in what he has been doing; the fact of the journey itself is sufficient cause for celebration. Large crowds congregate or, more accurately, are brought to the airport and form a living perimeter of singing and dancing men and women dressed in their tribal best. They arrive in lorries and are reputed to be paid substantial sums for the privilege of greeting their leader. In many cases, the enthusiasm is genuine, but no very great excuse is needed for Africans to enjoy themselves; and payment is often less a bribe than compensation for lost earnings. The manifestation is highly organised; indeed, it is usually one of the few public occasions that can be counted on to be well produced. As we came in to land, I could see these great crowds assembled, a red carpet laid ready, and a group of anxious VIPs, no doubt Ministers, high-ranking officers and the like, waiting to greet their President and account for their behaviour during his absence.

All this was quite new to me, and I gazed on the scene in wonder, not realising that it was the normal procedure and one that would become only too familiar in the years ahead. As the plane came to a halt, the engines were switched off and the doors opened, I got the first whiff of Africa; the warm, slightly perfumed air and the sound of drums, rhythmic hand-clapping and brass bands, slightly out of tune but with a marvellous beat. President Obote descended to a frenzy of colour and movement and began to walk slowly along the line of greeters. By this time we were standing in the doorway of the plane but not allowed, as yet, to disembark. I could see our host, David Scott, the British High Commissioner, standing in a line of Europeans and realised with a start that he had not come to meet us but that the entire Diplomatic Corps was on parade, a habit which accounted for many hours in a hot sun, frequently on a Saturday or Sunday. The President then proceeded round the airfield, a father returning to the bosom of his family. It was fully three quarters of an hour before we could go down the gangway and mingle with the crowds who by then, the Great Man having departed, had themselves taken possession of the apron and airport buildings. Fortunately, David was an old hand at situations of this kind; by skilful manoeuvring and the right word to the right person, he caused our baggage to appear like magic and we were soon settled in his car on our way to Kampala through villages still thronged with celebrating crowds, who waved delightedly at us without, I am sure, realising who we were in spite of the Union Jack flying from the bonnet. David waved back and encouraged us to do so, but we were both a little shy of responding to this undeserved and unsought public acclaim.

We reached the Residence – a charming, modest house with a swimming pool set in a tropical garden, and with cool tiled floors inside – to find David's wife, Vera, waiting with all the kindness and concern for the traveller that Africa breeds. We were served a delicious breakfast of coffee, scrambled eggs and pawpaw, and told firmly to disappear into our room to unpack and rest until lunch time. The servants materialised silently; quiet dignified Africans, some of whom had been long years in the service of the British Crown.

As they gently helped us unpack and made sure that we were comfortable, they seemed to hold out the promise of a new way of looking at human relations. I was later to be convinced of a truth whose existence I had always suspected; that colour and class-consciousness are inventions of the white man, exported by him, like physical diseases, into cultures which had not acquired the immunity of so-called civilisation and consequently were ravaged by the effect of their exaggerated impact.

We went to bed early that night and slept the sleep of those who have arrived, too tired to think of either past or future. The next two days were spent in and around Kampala with the Scotts. We looked at the city, trying hard to Europeanise itself; we shopped in the market and bought souvenirs as pretty as they were useless; we went to see the source of the Nile at Jinja – or at least that source claimed by Speke in one of those spectacular bust-ups in the aggressive, competitive world of Victorian exploration. I became excited by the thought that a cork or bottle dropped in at this point might, with luck, eventually float past the balcony of Shepheards Hotel in Cairo where I had stood, years before, open-mouthed at my first sight of the Pyramids in the pink and gold twilight. It somehow made Africa less remote, more real. We stood on the Equator and took giggling pictures of each other in shamelessly tourist poses, standing in the upright circle, like the cross-section of a huge drainpipe, which some forgotten but imaginative Colonial Director of Works had set up in the old days to mark the actual position of the line.

David and Vera were ideal hosts under any circumstances, but especially for us at this particularly early stage in our transition from Europe to Africa. They understood very well the strain imposed by these sudden switches from the familiar to the exotic. We met some of their colleagues to whom we were presented with the full fanfare of Ambassadorial honours, and who responded with volleys of 'Excellencies' and 'Ambassador Wrights'. It would be gratifying to be able to say that we were aware of a sense of impending doom in these first meetings with Ugandans, but it would not, alas, be true. Certainly no-one would have predicted a rosy future for Uganda, with its searing poverty and already top-heavy bureaucracy, but the horrors of the future were mercifully veiled; indeed, it seemed hard to imagine, when we talked to Ugandans in David's hospitable house in early 1969 and saw their bewildered but friendly faces as we drove through the clean little villages, that Idi Amin's monstrous tyranny was crouched ready to spring and dominate them with such apparent ease. Obote's first regime was hardly a shining example of Whitehall democracy, but the violence, which later experience taught me was never far below the surface of African life, was certainly not in evidence at that time.

After three days of life in this generous and protected world, we moved on to Nairobi, leaving most of our luggage, including of course my sword, in the care of the hospitable Scotts. We travelled by East African Airlines, the most public symbol of the Economic Union between Uganda, Kenya and Tanzania which was, even then, beginning to crumble. It deposited us efficiently enough at the airport of this, one of the most up-to-date and sympathetic of African cities. Our High Commissioner, Sir Eric Norris asked us to lunch and spent much time and trouble giving me a picture of East African politics and introducing the senior members of his staff.

Nairobi, even more than Kampala, seemed to be suspended between the Imperial past and an African future which, one sensed, had not quite arrived. The Kenyans were unquestionably in control, but the streets, shops and bars were crowded with British for whom time had remained relatively static. On the surface, of course, they recognised the changes which had taken place; and many, to their credit, had become Kenyan citizens in what was a genuine desire to make Independence work and preserve as much as possible of the beautiful country they had known and helped to create. Their relationship with the Africans was courteous, correct and, in many cases, warm and friendly. But underneath it they managed to convey the impression that the whole thing was a kind of game, played seriously enough but likely, in the end, to be called off and be replaced by the real world. Whether this would turn out to be a return to the good old days or – as most believed, especially those who had lived and suffered through the past Mau Mau horror – a decline into something ultimately too hostile to live with, was a question most preferred not to discuss. There was a sense of waiting, of judgement deferred, of the day being sufficient unto itself. We stored up as many impressions as we could, convinced that West Africa would look and feel different and that this difference would, in some way, be important in terms of Africa's future.

To visit Nairobi was also instructive for those whose interest in the British Empire and its administrators is more than mere nostalgia. It was salutary to witness the sunset of the Raj from this viewpoint, so much less familiar than the India which gave it a name and a legendary flavour imbibed, by my generation at least, with our first cup of Bengers. I guessed that Nairobi might have changed less than most former Colonial capitals despite the gloomy prophecies, the sighs and mutterings of white hunters, which had accompanied the arrival of Independence. Here was still the paternalistic society, the solicitude and condescension, the sense of duty, the courage, the blinkered disdain of all things non-British, which characterised the latter stages of the British Raj. When I revealed, un-prompted by any great interest in who I was or whither bound, that I was on my way to West Africa, one man remarked, between puffs of Three Nuns, 'Oh, don't they speak French over there?', as if this alone disqualified them from being taken seriously.

We hired a car and set out down the long hot road to Mombasa and the coast. The Indian Ocean sounds very romantic but it is not, in fact, noticeably different from any other stretch of salt water. Indeed, it struck me as being less sea-like, so to speak, than the Caribbean or the Mediterranean; I doubt whether Homer would have conjured up a convincing Poseidon from it. Nevertheless, we spent a happy and relaxed week at a beach club near Malindi. We lived in grass-roofed huts with the inside beams exposed in intricate patterns. The food was good but plain, and despite the exotic surroundings, relentlessly called to mind the sensible fare of the English boarding house. We searched in vain for the advertised golden beaches – perhaps they are really there waiting to be discovered by travellers less in shock than ourselves – and contented ourselves with swimming in an estuary, beautifully buoyant at high tide but otherwise muddy and draughty.

In deciding to spend this week by the sea we had, subconsciously I suppose, expected a Mediterranean-type holiday complete with delicious shellfish and wine in a café-surrounded piazza. By such standards, our little beach-club honeymoon was a flop; it is a great mistake to imagine that the joys of one continent can be repeated in another. But it did provide us with rest and a break from the headlong rush of events which seemed to have taken charge of us ever since we left New York. Greatly refreshed and feeling once more in control of events, we set off back to Nairobi via the Tsavo National Park in which we had arranged to spend one night and hopefully catch our first sight of big game.

We reached the gate of the eastern part of the park and decided to drive through this before crossing into the Western Park where we had a room booked in one of the tourist lodges. The track was thick with red dust and the landscape of small hillocks and scrubby trees was shimmering under the unsubtle African sunlight. We became at once aware of that mysterious quality which gives African landscapes an extra dimension, removes them from time and space and sets them, throbbing with unseen life, into some other, earlier world. As we drove slowly along we felt ourselves slipping back to a time when man's relationship with the animals who surrounded him would have been more personal, at once hostile and friendly, but never the indifference bred by an urban civilisation. We were, of course, also breathless with excitement and had been laying bets with each other long before we reached the park about what we would see first. Our initial encounter proved something of an anticlimax. Babs, always the more observant, let out a yell and I was just able to catch a glimpse of a rabbit-like creature darting across the road and into the scrub, leaving a puff of red dust behind it. We stopped, switched off the engine and listened. Silence; at least, that absence of identifiable noise that in Africa passes for silence – a kind of buzzing, throbbing background like audible wallpaper. We started up again and went cautiously on, arguing about whether rabbits were indigenous to Africa. We were so pre-occupied with this zoological research that we almost missed our first elephant.

She – and I may say I have hardly ever since seen an animal more unquestionably female in the coquettish way in which she looked at us over her shoulder – was browsing about fifty yards off the track; although browsing is too tame a word for an elephant whose idea of *hors d'oeuvres* is to tear small branches off trees and stuff them in her mouth. We stopped again and switched off. The noise of her meal was prodigious. Fortunately, she had no calf with her or she might have tried to frighten us away, as was to happen to me on a much later visit to the Serengeti Park in Tanzania. So we looked at each other; and after another sly glance, she returned to the important business of stuffing herself with fodder, supremely indifferent to these wisps of humanity, and clearly unimpressed by the fact that one of them was an Ambassador. This first meeting – it can hardly be called a confrontation – was a moving experience for us, fulfilling in some curious way a search which we had not realised we were undertaking. No subsequent encounter, however dramatic, would have quite the same quality: an instant recognition of the kinship of all creation. Africa does this to you; it transmutes the commonplace into the elemental, and the temporal to the eternal. I put the car into first gear with a gesture approaching reverence, and we moved slowly on down the track.

The game became more plentiful, although we were not rewarded with anything more spectacular than some galloping giraffe; no lion or leopard, and no rhino. Nevertheless, by the time we had crossed into the Western Park and arrived, dusty and thirsty, at the Lodge, we were feeling quite professional. We had a late tea on the veranda and watched the animals gathering at a water hole conveniently, perhaps artificially, placed for the benefit of tourists. It was not a spectacular sight, consisting mostly of various types of antelope and other small game; we saw neither lion nor lamb, but the evening calm was such that it was difficult not to believe that somewhere they were lying together. Dawn is the time of danger; dusk of peace.

That night we lay surrounded by the mysterious noises that betray the unseen, unceasing life of forest and bush. In spite of a long day, I could not sleep and, tiptoeing out of our bungalow, stood silent and wondering beneath the great jewelled sky. Something coughed in the distance, a lion perhaps. There was a rustling of dry leaves nearer at hand and the constant frenetic scratching of insects which made one think of some huge, unoiled machine driving purposelessly into the night. It has always been like this, I thought, and it probably always will be. Africa is too big and too tough for man to ravage except on a time scale mercifully unimaginable. There came to me that eerie feeling, which Africa alone can arouse, of standing at one of the crossroads of evolution; the beginning of man's long journey from the primeval forests to the concrete jungles of Western civilization and on upward to the stars. It was here, perhaps on such a night in such a place, that the first, decisive steps were taken and that my ancestor, with a grunt and a malign grimace, shuffled awkwardly off towards love, peace and beauty, never suspecting the price he would have to pay for them.

The next day, fortified by this communion with nature we drove slowly back to Nairobi. We arrived feeling and looking like veteran white hunters just returned from safari, and hoping that we would be taken as such by the pale-faced visitors newly arrived from London who thronged the hotel lobby. Trailing red dust over the polished floors, we were soon back to the reality of hot baths, drinks and the mental arithmetic necessary to settle our outstanding bills. The following day we flew back to Uganda in order to catch the weekly plane from Entebbe to Kinshasa that evening. We hired a hotel room for the day, which we spent writing letters and sprucing ourselves up. I was beginning to be a little nervous of the impending first impact of the Ambassador on his staff and vice versa; in particular, I got into a most uncharacteristic fuss about the length of my hair which, after some argument, Babs proceeded to cut with a huge pair of scissors produced in some magical way by the hotel – from its kitchens, for all I know. The result, as always with Babs, was a great success in spite of my conservative forebodings. We set off in plenty of time for the airport, waved goodbye by the Scotts with promises of a return visit in the near future and accompanied by all our luggage and a capable young man from David's staff, who had been detailed to see us off.

On arrival at Entebbe we were informed, with the utmost gravity and conviction, that the Kinshasa plane had already left, although we were an hour before its advertised time. So great was my chagrin at the thought of arriving one week late at my new post that I seriously considered resigning on the spot; indeed, I was already mentally drafting my telegram – ('It is with deep regret and after much anxious thought . . .') – when the young man, who had learned never to take anything in Africa at face value, returned from an enterprising tour of the airport offices to say that, no, the plane had *not* yet left but was about to do so (no reason for the advance in timing was given). They were nevertheless awaiting His Excellency, Madame l'Ambassadrice, His Excellency's luggage and children if any. We raced across the tarmac, bade an unceremonious but grateful farewell to our young saviour and boarded the Air Congo Caravelle with the engines already turning. I dared not stop to check whether all our luggage was on board. But as we were ushered into the empty First Class cabin, I realised to my relief that at least my sword and briefcase were safely in my hands, as well as Babs' bottle bag without which her whole personality tends to disintegrate.

The abrupt African night fell as we took off and a soft-spoken stewardess prefaced all the usual welcome aboard announcements with 'Excellencies, Mesdames, Messieurs . . .' We were airborne. Below us, the great continent disappeared into the night as we headed west. The captain came back to see us; he was Belgian and, like all continental monarchists, brought up with a proper mixture of respect and irreverence for the representatives of Royal Houses. He seemed to know all about us, due no doubt to the operation of the African bush telegraph which the age of electronics had failed to improve upon, or even explain. I asked a few, regal-sounding questions about the weather, our route, our ETA, the plane, the airline, and so on, which he answered in bored but impeccable French. I suggested a drink; the pretty Congolese stewardess, by this time almost paralysed with giggles, produced a bottle of warm champagne whose cork, when released, nearly brought the plane down. Toasts were drunk – to the Queen, the King of the Belgians, President Mobutu, my future mission, Air Congo – until the bottle was finished and I settled back to compose myself for that climactic event which now lay only about an hour ahead, my arrival at Kinshasa.

I knew that certain ceremonies awaited us, although I was still ignorant of their precise nature, customs in this respect varying so widely. The Embassy staff had wisely made clear from the start the unpredictable nature of African welcomes and advised me, in effect, to be ready for anything. The one thing about which I was apprehensive was being faced with TV cameras on arrival and having to speak, or answer questions, in French. Those cosy chats by the gas fire in Whitehall suddenly seemed a long way away and hardly relevant.

I was halfway through the composition of a brilliant and witty speech in reply to the extravagant words of welcome which I felt sure would greet us, when Their Excellencies were asked to fasten their seat belts and prepare for landing at Kinshasa. I looked out of the window. We appeared to be flying over dense jungle, broken here and there by some flickering lights in the blackness. Of the great city of Kinshasa, the third largest in Africa, there was no sign other than a faint glow on the horizon. Suddenly the runway lights were rushing beneath us. We touched down and began to taxi towards the airport building, now brightly lit and expectant. 'O Trusty and Well Beloved, you have arrived at the Capital of the Country to which you are accredited; may you perform all manner of acts, duties and things as befitting Her Majesty's Ambassador Extraordinary and Plenipotentiary.'

'Don't forget your sword,' said Babs as the aircraft came to a halt.

CHAPTER SIX

My experience of the arrivals of new Ambassadors at their posts had hitherto been limited to one occasion; that of Sir Harold Beeley in Cairo in 1961. The circumstances preceding his appointment had been so unusual that his arrival could hardly be cited as a prototype for such ceremonies. Moreover, I was new to Africa but not so new as to believe that any particular precedents would apply; all too often you make it up as you go along. Of one thing, however, I *was* sure. Peter Mennell, the Embassy's Counsellor and Number Two man, in charge during the interregnum, would be there, not only at the airport but by my side throughout the first weeks – a sort of official Nanny to help me say and do the right things.

Although we had not served together before, we were old acquaintances and I felt I had already got to know him quite well from the marvellously detailed letters of advice which he had been sending me ever since my appointment. He was a widely experienced professional who liked to see things properly done and the thought of him waiting there was immensely reassuring. His wife, Prudie, was an equally comforting figure. She was born a Vansittart and had carried this distinction with grace and ease throughout a career to which they had both contributed much and which, when the time came to leave me, ought to blossom into an Ambassadorship of their own. (In due course it did; at Quito and, later, Nassau. He retired at the statutory age and had embarked on a distinguished second career as Director of the Thompson Foundation when he died, tragically and suddenly.

As the doors opened, Peter came bounding up the steps.

'Welcome to Kinshasa, Sir,' he said, shaking my hand and, at the same time, laying hold of my sword and initiating a little tussle with the other items of hand luggage. He greeted Babs with less deference but more warmth and we descended the aircraft steps preceded by Peter carrying my sword rather like a Mace. No TV cameras; no arclights; no reporters. It was quite late in the evening – nine o'clock, perhaps, and I could sense the African night beyond the immediate circle of the airport lights. There was one shadowy figure darting about with a hand camera taking pot shots of our descent. 'That's your Information Officer, Sir,' said Peter, apologetically, 'we thought we had better make sure of having a proper record of your arrival.'

In my nervous state, I regarded this remark as slightly sinister. But I was, on the whole, relieved as well as slightly disappointed at the obvious lack of interest in my arrival by the Kinshasa media. However, quite another preoccupation was, by this time, entering my mind. Sir? *Your* Information Officer? What the hell is going on here, I thought; all this is very unlike Peter. A feature of the Service had always been the almost universal use of Christian names, regardless of rank, to which Peter and I had probably conformed the first time we met, many years before. Ah yes, but with one exception; an Ambassador, *en poste*, is always addressed as 'Sir'. I knew this perfectly well, of course, having for years conformed to the same rule when serving in other posts in junior capacities; but on this occasion some mental blockage prevented me from realising that it was happening to me; that the Ambassador, the 'Sir', the remote but fatherlike figure behind his desk or in his Library or Rolls Royce, had suddenly turned out to be me – Paul Wright – and that I was being taken seriously and treated accordingly.

This ritualistic element in British life dies hard, however deeply social barriers are eroded by political economic forces. It's the uniform, not the man, that you salute; you may have been at school with the Bishop and seen him naked and defenceless in the showers; but clothe him in Cope and Mitre and he becomes the successor to Saint Peter, with power to bind and to loose; or, as a Dutch diplomat of the old school used to say, 'You see, when I put on my white satin breeches, I am the Queen of Holland.'

Now we were entering the VIP room where the senior staff of the Embassy, about ten in number, and their wives were standing in a self-conscious semi-circle waiting to be introduced. Prudie greeted Babs with a formal kiss of the kind which Royalty bestow upon each other in public, and we were led round the line, shaking hands, murmuring appropriate greetings and responding to equally vacuous enquiries about our journey. It was all very low-key and British, and once over, the formal line broke up and general conversation ensued rather like a garden party, everyone glancing nervously about to make sure that they were not missing anything. This was my first experience of power; not the exercise of it – that would come later – but its existence which I, at that moment, embodied. It was an odd sensation and it took me a few minutes to realise why all these decent, able men and women, whom in other circumstances I would have regarded as colleagues and friends, were making such efforts to create a good impression, being extravagantly polite and solicitous. It was, of course, because they recognised power; contained by law and endless regulations if you like, subject always to appeal, never absolute and not likely to be abused; but authentic power nevertheless.

I did not think the less of them for this. On the contrary, they were being sensible enough to take out the same kind of insurance for which I had paid many premiums in the past, not only in the Diplomatic Service itself but in business, the Army and at school. I was more concerned about myself for I sniffed the heady incense which had so impressed Lord Acton, although I prefer the well-known parody as being more descriptive of the real dangers: 'All power is delightful; absolute power is absolutely delightful.' I knew full well that a Head of Mission, often far removed from the restraining influence of his superiors in Whitehall, could suddenly begin to behave like an autocrat, making life miserable for his staff and sometimes affecting adversely their careers or driving them to actions which would have that effect. I had every intention of guarding against these dangers; perhaps I was over-impressed by them, for the necessary exercise of such power as was inherent in my post was a constant anxiety about which I agonised far more than the shortcomings and limitations of British foreign policy.

At this point the Congolese suddenly materialised. Whether they had mistaken the time of arrival or, out of an excess of politeness, were allowing our domestic greetings to take precedence; or whether, quite simply, they were late, we never discovered. I suppose that some of my older colleagues might think that I was wrong not to make a mountain out of this molehill of discourtesy, but I had a feeling that I had better save up my dignity for standing on in situations which might really warrant it. In any case, the Congolese were charming. We were welcomed by the Assistant Chief of Protocol and an official from the Foreign Ministry. They clasped me warmly by the arms and led me to a large sofa where, seated between them, we discussed such general topics as the Queen's health and my previous career and knowledge, if any, of Africa. Although I was now even further from foggy Whitehall, I thought that my pretty French instructress would have been proud of me, failing to realise at that first encounter how easy it is to talk to Africans especially in French; they have none of that linguistic snobbery with which the real French will freeze any conversation that does not reach the accepted standards of fluency and wit.

In due course, champagne was produced and toasts were drunk. We sat on, the conversation gradually slowing down like a train running into a terminus. There seemed no certainty, however, that this particular train would ever arrive, that the conversation would end and movement and action be restored. I looked anxiously at Peter who, with the rest of the staff, was shifting from foot to foot in a relaxed way now that the first impact had been achieved. Eventually, after what seemed several hours, my Congolese hosts rose to their feet and, with the utmost politeness, said goodnight, renewing their expressions of welcome and goodwill as they made a dignified withdrawal.

'Well done, Sir,' said Peter, for no apparent reason; he was fond of the expression which made me feel like the captain of the village cricket eleven. 'Would you care to make a move?' he added. The statement was hardly a question, and we were only too willing. The British semi-circle reformed, goodnights were said with many a 'thank you so much for coming – not at all, Sir, great pleasure' – and we moved off towards the door.

'How about the luggage?' I asked Peter. He gave me a withering look which said plainly: don't you know who you are?

'That's all being taken care of, Sir,' he said and, still clutching my sword, led us out into the courtyard. There waiting was the car, complete with flag flying; and beside it, Gabriel ('your chauffeur, Sir') with an anxious, toothy grin under a uniform cap which was plainly several sizes too large. It transpired that he had only been drafted into this responsible and elevated post on the previous day, my impending arrival having proved too great an emotional strain for the regular chauffeur who had been summarily dismissed for drunken and disorderly behaviour. We shook hands. '*Bonsoir, Excellences,*' said Gabriel in a voice like a tired disc-jockey, the grin now at maximum stretch. We were waved off politely by the rest of the staff, who were no doubt relieved that this close encounter of the first kind had passed off without incident; and eager to get back to the privacy of their own cars so that immediate first impressions of Their Excellencies' physical attributes and characters could be exchanged, and the delicious process of speculation about their probable behaviour and its effect on the Mission's life could begin in peace and earnest.

It is no use pretending that by this time I was not enjoying myself. Our arrival, anticipated with much stomach fluttering, had gone off far better than I had dared hope. Peter and Prudie had relaxed now that the parade, so to speak, was over, and were contentedly gossiping about mutual friends. Above all, waving on the car's bonnet was The Flag, symbol of this personal climacteric towards which my whole career had been moving. Babs sensed this moment too, for she gave my hand a squeeze and, as I turned towards her, she looked at the flag and then gave me one of her secret, coded looks which meant roughly, 'It's a great moment for you darling, and I'm thrilled to be with you', and then in the same glance, 'but you wouldn't be letting it go to your head, would you?' Well, of course it is heady stuff; the flag is not only a personal symbol but a distant extension of that Standard floating above Buckingham Palace at which people look up and say, with a certain satisfaction, 'Ah, She's there.' Its presence on the car meant that the Ambassador – Her Representative – was actually, physically there and that was me! I had naturally ridden before in beflagged motorcars, but always in an attendant capacity, being careful not to sit in the Ambassador's place and ready, like a good courtier, to open doors, smooth paths, perform introductions and facilitate withdrawals. All this is part of the stock in trade of diplomacy, the public exaltation of an Ambassador as the Representative of his country and, in our case, of his Sovereign. But now the moment had come for me to play the principal role in this pageant and for others to do the exalting.

We sped along the impressive four-lane highway – then the only major stretch of road of its kind in the whole vast country – towards the city. The outskirts were ill-lit and, despite the advent of social and racial equality among the enforced blessings of Independence, exclusively African and very poor. We were soon, however, driving through better-looking streets with the unexotic air of Belgian suburbia; and then the centre of the city, better lit and rather more spacious but still looking (and, as I was later to discover, feeling) as if suspended between the Colonial past and a utopian but ill-defined future. I hate arriving anywhere by night; it takes me days to become properly orientated and Peter's gallant attempts to answer my basic questions about where we were, where was the Embassy, how far to the Residence, given with dogged patience left me none the wiser. I was just deciding to give up the struggle and leave any further efforts at topography until daylight when we suddenly turned into a pair of modest gates, down a short driveway, and were at the front door of the Residence. It all happened so quickly that I had no time to check my first impressions against the often-imagined size, shape and colour of this, our home for the next few years. A blur of colour in the headlights, the soft, damp air coming off the Congo River which rolled majestically, but as yet unseen, past the bottom of our garden; the low, white house covered in bougainvillea – these immediate sensations were sufficiently sharp and accurate to be easily recalled as I write now, over ten years later.

There was little time to record, let alone savour, these first moments of arrival because, standing by the door, resplendent in white uniforms with gold buttons, were our household staff. Sebastien, the head man, very short and very strong, with a great natural dignity, imperturbable in an un-African way, and only rarely put off his stride; Pierre, the cook, also on the small side but thicker-set, heavier than Sebastien, endowed with all the temperament of the artist, which he was; Petit-Jean, well-named since he was smaller even than Sebastien and, being slightly mentally retarded and thus fearful and hesitant about life, was the constant butt of the rest of the household, a situation which he and they accepted as being part of the natural order; and Paul, who did everything the others did not do, including the laundry, and who was the eccentric of the family, tall, handsome and ambitious but completely devoid of the ability to co-ordinate thought, word and deed. They become like children for whose lives we felt responsible and whose actions and sayings provided us with endless, and sometimes moving, examples of the African thought-process.

They were essential to the efficient functioning of the Residence, a place of work at least as much as it was a home, and we depended on them as much as they on us. It was a partnership in which the terms were accepted with goodwill and dignity by all. Later Babs was to give each a code name, partly from affection, partly to avoid embarrassing or puzzling them when our discussions and planning made the mention of their names inevitable. Sebastien, of course, became the Elder Statesman; Pierre, the Prima Donna (not very apt in one way, for he was the most masculine of them all); Petit-Jean was always known as the Little One; and Paul became the Archbishop, owing to the grace and ritualistic style of his simple movements.

There they stood, their smiling faces shining with the effort of this first act of welcome and the imperative need to ensure that the right words were spoken, the right gestures made, that the ceremony should, by its rightness, provide favourable auspices for the future. We descended, there is no other word, from the car and the greetings duly took place, masterminded by the Elder Statesman who made the presentations and then proceeded to induct us into our Residence.

It was spacious, with wide verandas and furnished in approved Ministry of Works style befitting the grade of its occupant and with moderately good taste which, we hoped, would be more in keeping with our own when the results of Babs' refurnishing efforts in London arrived. What we could see of the garden revealed a smooth lawn surrounded by lush, unfamiliar shrubs and trees. The Elder Statesman, still the host, showed us the large living room, small study and gloomy dining room, the latter uncomfort-ably out of place, like St John's Wood in a jungle clearing. We made a mental note to use it as little as possible, and also to banish to a less conspicuous but still honourable place the unflattering official portrait of the Queen which brooded over the large mahogany table. We visited the bedrooms, and I could see Babs' eye busily rearranging the furniture throughout. Our own room was large and airy, and the spare rooms delightful; the Ministry of Works, no doubt for some Freudian reason, always appeared at their best in bedrooms.

This periodic rearrangement of Residencies, not just of the furniture but frequently of the actual use of particular rooms, has been responsible for creating more bad blood in the Diplomatic Service than almost any other single factor. People become attached to the way they live in a certain house and find it inconceivable that their successors should be so stupid, not to say insulting, as to alter arrangements which were obviously the only possible solution arrived at after a lifetime's experience of shuffling other peoples' furniture. 'God, have you seen (or heard) what she has done to the house!' distraught ladies will cry when the name of their successor crops up. Their husbands, knowing that it is often easier to move a foreign government than a sofa, remain silent, nodding sagely and hoping to convey the impression that a grave mistake has been made in the appointment of his successor.

It was now nearly midnight, and as we sat and gossiped over a final drink, the staff reappeared in their ordinary clothes to say goodnight, as if by this reversion to normality they would emphasise the solemnity of the original welcome. They did not sleep in and when working late had to be transported to their homes by the Embassy bus. But one final ceremony remained; locking up. It is a depressing fact that hardly anywhere in the world, certainly hardly a single city, can be said to be safe in the sense of an absence of danger of robbery, with or without violence; not to speak of terrorism, hostile demonstrations and other anti-social phenomena of the twentieth century. Thus the end of each day entailed a retreat into a kind of prison, with heavy steel grills drawn across doors and windows and locked on the inside. The Elder Statesman performed this act as if it were the ceremony of the Keys at the Tower of London, and they all withdrew bidding 'Bonsoir, Patron' – the endearing name by which, I had by now realised, I should always be addressed by the domestic staff.

Peter and Prudie finally said goodnight and were let out of Fortress Wright with admonishments to us to lock up afterwards, with which I was glad to comply, both of us by this time being slightly jittery and suffering from mild claustrophobia. We were at last alone, save for a night watchman about whose theoretical presence we had been told, but for whom the only evidence was the pale glow of a small charcoal brazier somewhere behind the garage, and a faint smell of what we afterwards discovered was his nightly joint of cheap hashish, after which he dozed off. We unpacked the minimum amount and, resisting the temptation to talk over the day's momentous events, fell into an exhausted but uneasy sleep. It somehow seemed an anticlimax, this being locked up, alone, at night in the middle of a strange African city; a reminder, perhaps salutary, that the gilt on the Ambassadorial gingerbread was only wafer thin and that the same ugly old world lay beneath it, a common threat to all humanity against which no letters Patent, no cocked hat, not even my sword, now finally at rest in my new study, were any real defence.

We awoke at half past six next morning to creation transformed. When you live on the equator (Kinshasa is less than five hundred miles south of it) sunset and sunrise both happen without warning and at about the same time all year round; the long cool dawns and gentle twilights of the north are unknown, indeed, disturbing to the Central African for whom nature is an anthology of fierce, positive statements of divine origin, brooking no contradiction or discussion. At one moment we lay in the dark listening to the exotic African birds chatter their good-mornings to each other; at the next, the sun blazed up to give us a first clear sight of our garden, lush, tropical, altogether bewitching. The Elder Statesman, having mysteriously arrived by bicycle, knocked at our door, refusing to believe that any Englishman, let alone an Ambassador, did not drink quantities of early morning tea before he was properly awake. He and the Little One gave us our breakfast on the terrace and from it we watched for the first time the slow, majestic waters of the Congo River relentlessly flowing from unimaginable distances and darknesses towards the thundering rapids and beyond them to the hot, treacherous Atlantic coast. The river is nearly a mile across at this point, and great islands of floating vegetation sailed past on their way to destruction by the pounding waters.

It is foolish, and perhaps unfair, to expect diplomats to give an accurate description of their post; the life they lead is too artificial and protected. At times the environment itself appears to treat them as a race apart; the local inhabitants almost always do, except on those occasions, all too rare in most countries, when the diplomat and his family escape to play at normality and try to melt inconspicuously into the background. Even when the physical and social environment is implacably hostile, there is usually someone to stand between it and one of Her Majesty's representatives, mitigating its harsher effects and sweeping the evidence of its intransigence, often literally, under the carpet. The joys, too, remain partially veiled, the smells and sounds filtered by the screens of discretion; even the scenic beauties are sometimes denied by artificially imposed restrictions of movement. The degree of removal from real life differed, of course, from country to country. In the so-called grand embassies, such as the capitals of Western Europe where a certain wistful desire to prolong the sunset of Britain's Imperial past can often be detected, and a style and standard of life now only to be found in the households of Royalty, Republican Heads of State or the very rich is still tenuously maintained. In posts like the Congo, the differential is not so marked. Our house would not have seemed out of place in any prosperous European suburb and, moreover, was constructed by architects well aware of hazards not normally encountered in Purley, Neuilly or Bronxville – for example, tropical storms of Old Testament intensity and blindly furious hordes of predatory insects.

Our garden was perhaps more unusual; I never took for granted the simple fact of being able to pick avocado pears and bananas off our own trees, nor reconciled myself to the speed with which things grew – spit on the ground, they used to say, and you'll have a tree by morning.

But from many of these natural phenomena, as well as from other problems caused by man himself, we in the Embassy were moderately well protected. The Elder Statesman and his team waged an unceasing war of vigilance and attrition against the animal kingdom, all representatives of which, irrespective of species, were contemptuously referred to by Sebastien as '*les bêtes*'. Gabriel was on hand, not only to whisk me to and fro in the great world of State affairs, but to run errands of a humbler kind, delivering letters, the postal services sharing with other public utilities that element of fantasy so marked a feature of African life.

Babs drove our own car on shopping expeditions, for she soon realised the essential need to do her own marketing and brushed aside any suggestion that the British Ambassadress would lose face by poking about in the market. Indeed, it was due to her energy, and to some sixth sense which warned her of impending shortages that made it possible for us to entertain at all. The supply of provisions was never stable enough to make planning of menus a safe practice – exciting for the guests, but nerve-wracking for the hostesses. From the numerous material obstacles that littered the Ambassadorial way, we were also partially protected by the Embassy Administration Officer, with his willing but disorganised band of Congolese helpers, his local contacts and the edge he maintained over them by methods of which I pretended to be unaware. Breakdowns in the plumbing system, failures of electricity or gas, peeling plaster and disintegrating wood-work could all be patched up given patience. But such hazards were frequent and often beyond our own control, arising from natural causes or deep-rooted flaws in the city's administrative structure.

Telephones were a particular bugbear. They were perpetually in short supply and reputedly only available for installation on payment of a substantial '*prix supplémentaire*'. I remember a period of some months when only three out of the Embassy's fifteen houses had a working telephone – the Head of Chancery's, the Commercial Secretary's and mine; which led to much extra night and weekend activity if some unexpected crisis arose. Once installed, however, connection with the outside world was not necessarily improved; at certain times of the day it could take up to fifteen minutes to get a dialling tone, let alone, of course, a ringing tone. Babs got through several novels in this way, cradling the phone between her shoulder and neck while she turned the pages.

Our day begins peacefully enough, breakfasting on the terrace in the cool clear early morning light, with Simba, our Alsatian guard-dog, lying sprawled but watchful while he pretends not to notice that there is food about. We listen to the seven o'clock (our time) news on the BBC World Service, its martial signature tune reminding us that the Foreign Office windows overlooking the Horse Guards might be catching a glint of the same rising sun, its precise accents recounting the flat, but awful truths of our world. But soon after, skirmishes break out in the constant war waged against man by nature and by the machines he has created. Gas leaks, cisterns overflow, a snake is seen in the garden, cars break down, telephones go dead; an unexpected traveller arrives or, perhaps, is rumoured to be in distress at the airport; appointments are made and cancelled; the market is besieged and soon capitulates, having sold its meagre stocks of the day's special offer; the heat rises, and by two o'clock the world is stunned into a comatose silence. Later a titanic storm breaks without warning, felling trees, washing away pavements and flooding the garden; five minutes later a reluctant guilty sun drenches the world with evening light before plunging, red with shame, abruptly into the river, leaving the streets and gardens dry as if no rain had fallen for months, but with a warm damp fragrance in the air that was not there before, and which is gone again in half an hour.

In spite of the defences, however, not every battle was won. I do not know what noun of assembly applies to cockroaches – a crawl, perhaps? – but I often needed one to describe the scene in my bathroom late at night or early in the morning. These stupid loathsome creatures would be found exploring the bath, washbasin, and loo, even my various bits of washing and shaving equipment came in for inspection before I found places of comparative safety for them. The questioning antennae would hover doubtfully, sensing my presence, but I was usually quick enough to catch and drown the majority of any one assault, providing, of course, that there was some water in which to drown them. Other, unseen creatures affected our lives out of all proportion to their size. Mosquitoes somehow found ways through the smallest mesh screens, and would frequently stage a kind of Farnborough Air Show of their own over our bed. In spite of heavy aerial spraying, Kinshasa was still malaria-prone. The effects of their bites could be counteracted by regular doses of any of a variety of anti-malarial drugs with medieval-sounding names. Opinion varied between those favouring daily or weekly doses; we adopted the latter course, performing a ritual on Sundays at breakfast for which, however, we had to remind ourselves by the prominent display of notices at various strategic points in the house, bearing the slogan 'Remember Daraprim', as if it were the place name of the scene of some ghastly historic horror. These drugs were alleged to have no side effects, but after about six months I began to suffer from loss of memory. I thought that it must be the heat, until my doctor assured me that it was our old friend Daraprim, and that my chances of winning Mastermind would return once I had stopped the weekly dose. All this, I may say, did not prevent me from contracting a mild attack of malaria about six months before I left – a not altogether unpleasant sensation, like floating in warm soup with a swarm of reasonably quiet insects humming round my enlarged-feeling head.

But with all these problems, life nevertheless had many attractions in addition to the main interest of my work. We quickly made friends amongst our colleagues, the Congolese and the British community; a lively social life was conducted largely round swimming pools or cool verandas in the evening. Bridge and gossip were the main ingredients of entertainment, but the more adventurous organised play readings and even a little music. There was tennis for those determined to increase their chances of an early coronary, and even a nine-hole golf course round which my Indian colleague endlessly and devotedly plodded, now and then giving vent to some spectacularly idiomatic obscenity which he had no doubt picked up as a boy at Harrow.

On this morning, the first of my Ambassadorial life, Peter collected me at about eight o'clock and together we drove off, the flag flying, Gabriel tearing along at great speed from sheer nerves until restrained. The Embassy offices were on the three upper floors of a centrally-located building owned by Barclay's Bank. My own office was on the top floor within what was known as the secure area, to which access was restricted, and to and from which outside visitors had to be escorted. My secretary, Ailsa Mackintosh was reintroduced (she had been at the airport the night before) and Peter then took me on a tour of the offices and staff. I am good on faces but bad on names and it was a long time before I was confident of getting the right combination and fitting it to the right job; I was sometimes saved by Babs or Prudie from marrying off the wrong couples. We were a largish group – about thirty UK-based, including wives and other dependants, and another twenty or so Congolese. There was nothing particularly unorthodox about the Kinshasa Embassy, and I had no difficulty getting my mind round its structure, being similar to those I had worked in before. This constancy of official environment is a comfort to the diplomat overseas, but one which his wife cannot share.

After this stately progress round my new fief – a little too formal for my liking, but correct, I suppose, for HE's first visit – I went back to my own office and began to wrestle with the considerable amount of paper which was lying in wait. First and most important was a document known as the 'charge telegram', which Peter asked me to initial, thus authorising its despatch. 'I arrived last night and have assumed charge. WRIGHT.' I was, of course, familiar with this stock wording, and had once launched a similar telegram from Cairo when I became *Chargé d'Affaires* there in 1960. But it had never occurred to me how imperial and romantic it sounded, especially coming from Africa; as if, after a hazardous journey up river in a gunboat, I had reached an outpost besieged by native hordes and was about to put new heart into the dispirited garrison. Indeed, the whole system of telegraphic communication, although as efficient as modern electronic gadgetry can make it, has retained something of the Imperial past. In theory, all telegrams pass between the Head of Mission and the Secretary of State personally, all being signed with their respective names. In fact, only those drafted in the first person singular can safely be assumed to have been seen and sent on their personal authority. But they carry personal responsibility for each word of each message, as for every other aspect of the Service's work. Moreover, telegrams, whether in cypher or *en clair*, are not written in the kind of language in which one used to be informed of the death of an aunt or a missed train, but in a style which the writer hopes will stand the test of history. The constant need for economy of language in order to save time and money makes for a certain austerity and clarity of expression.

As well as being speedily transmitted to the addressee – usually, but not invariably, the Secretary of State in the Foreign Office (who reads personally a surprising number of the day's haul) – telegrams are also repeated for information to those other posts with a need to be kept informed either from geographical proximity or political interest. Good communications confer a sense of power and when they are as efficient and rapid as those of the British Foreign Office, that power can corrupt both sender and receiver. It is exciting to be able to flash your views round the world in a matter of minutes or, in the case of those working in Whitehall, to despatch instructions to a dozen Ambassadors and High Commissioners setting in train a diplomatic manoeuvre. I have often contemplated the paradox that this superb machinery, essential and effective though it is, may by its very existence do us all (Ministers and officials alike) a disservice in suggesting that the subject matter of all these messages is more important than is often the case, and in giving a slightly distorted reflection of our real importance in the scale of world politics.

I quickly found Ailsa to be a treasure. Besides being a very efficient secretary, she had an Honours degree in French and was able to correct not only the spelling but the dreaded grammar of that much bruised language when I had to write it. During that first morning I also began a series of talks with the Heads of each Section of the Embassy in order to get to know them and their problems. That evening we invited all the staff and their wives for a drink. The garden was floodlit and looked enchanting. I made a little speech, probably of toe-curling embarrassment, about how we were all part of a team, Babs and I were both always available for any problem, however personal or minimal; things at home were OK, the Embassy's reputation was high, let's keep it that way; and so forth. It seemed to go down well, at least according to Peter whose extreme correctness of attitude and liking for protocol was never remotely tempered with sycophancy.

Later that evening he and Prudie gave a small dinner for some of the senior staff and one or two of their close friends among the British residents in Kinshasa of whom there were a surprisingly large number. Their presence gave me a first experience of that slightly grudging respect for the office, but deep suspicion of its holder, which characterises the British attitude to authority in general and Ambassadors in particular. We all sniffed round each other like strange dogs on a frosty morning; but those present were destined to become close friends and helpful colleagues; a Head of Mission needs the support of his resident compatriots as much, or more, than they do his.

This was the only kind of social function that I could attend until I had presented my credentials; as day succeeded day and I became more familiar with my new role, the question of when this essential ceremony could or would be arranged began to dominate my life. An Ambassador cannot be said to exist officially until he has been received by the Head of State and has presented the letters recalling his predecessor and those, signed by his own Head of State introducing him, so to speak, and enshrining the confidence with which he is entrusted with his Mission. This ceremony is preceded, usually by a day or two but sometimes longer, by a less formal call on the Minister for Foreign Affairs when copies of the documents are handed over, the forthcoming meeting with the Head of State is discussed, and the acquaintance made of the one person with whom more than any other Minister or official an Ambassador is likely to do most of his business. Without fulfilling these time-honoured rituals I was a non-person, unable officially to meet my colleagues or to transact any business with the Congolese Government, but at the same time remaining fully responsible to London for everything that went on.

It was frustrating, to say the least; as day followed day, I busied myself with the internal affairs of the Embassy, lived an incestuous kind of social life, and began to feel a little sorry for myself. Was it for this, I wondered, that my sword had made its uncomfortable journey in my hand, my uniform urgently fitted, made and transported, the timing of my arrival, the preceding journey and London preparations, had been worked out? If the Congolese were aware of this unsatisfactory state of affairs, they showed no sign of it in the face of Peter's polite but insistent and almost daily enquiries about 'a date for my Ambassador'. My only solace was that one or two other Ambassadors were waiting in the same limbo, having arrived about the same time as I; and I was, in one sense, thankful for this extra time to rehearse my part before I was forced into the limelight.

Then one day what seemed to be a break occurred. Babs had asked me to collect some ice-cream from a shop near the Embassy on my way home. Gabriel thoroughly disapproved of Le Patron being asked to perform so domestic a task, but as he had also quickly developed a healthy respect for Madame l'Ambassadrice, we set off without much grumbling. My arrival at the little ice-cream parlour caused a minor sensation and attracted a group of wide-eyed African children such as materialise from nowhere, even in the most remote parts of the bush or desert, drawn by their infallible instinct that something which ought not to be missed is about to take place. They watched solemnly, hopping from one leg to the other, while I crossed the pavement and went in to collect and pay for my order. I had just accomplished this with many polite smiles and good wishes from the owner, (who appeared as if from a trap door to serve personally his unusual customer), when a handsome, well-dressed Congolese gentleman came up to me and, with a wide, confident smile, introduced himself as a high functionary in the President's Office.

'What a coincidence, Mr Ambassador,' he said, waving a hand to indicate his familiarity with the bizarre. 'I was just on my way to your office to see you.' He laughed as if we were accomplices in some project of doubtful propriety.

'How delightful,' I replied cautiously, 'would you like to come back now with me?' I was beginning to wonder how I could establish his *bona fides* without causing offence; and also if, in some mysterious way, he could be the bearer of good tidings on the crucial question of my credentials.

'Oh no, we can easily talk here,' he said, pointing to a not very clean table with two empty chairs by the wall. We sat down opposite each other and there was a pause during which I debated whether or not to offer him an ice-cream. It somehow did not seem an entirely appropriate gesture, so I said nothing but gave him a friendly look of encouragement. He leant across the table and put his hand on my arm; Africans are very tactile and often feel more at ease with strangers when some physical contact has taken place. He then launched into what was obviously a prepared speech.

'Mr Ambassador, what I have to say is very painful.' Goodness, I thought, *persona non grata* already? And what an eccentric way of conveying the information! 'It's my wife, you see,' he went on. 'She has had to have this operation which was very costly. I thought you might be able to help, seeing that my position is bound to be helpful to you sooner or later.'

I was busy adjusting my mind to this quite unexpected and disappointing development when he added, 'It wouldn't be more than two hundred Zaires, and I could pay you back, say fifty a month.'

I dismissed the immediate and irresistible vision of Sir Burke Trend trying to touch the American Ambassador for a hundred bucks in a café in Regents Park, and thought quickly how to get myself out of a situation which, although awkward, somehow did not strike me as amounting to actual blackmail. I put on my most sympathetic smile and placed my hand on his which, since it was already resting on my other hand, must have made the onlookers believe that we were about to begin a game of Pattercake, Baker's Man.

'My dear friend, I am devastated,' I said, 'and only wish that I could help. But you know how strict our rules are about this kind of thing; and I know that you have much the same regulations.' He nodded vigorously in complete agreement. 'I am sure the President would not wish us to do anything irregular, and I personally would deplore causing him offence, especially' – here I gave him a challenging look – 'before I have even presented my credentials.' He sighed and all the resignation of Africa was there.

'Ah, how right, Mr Ambassador, how right. The President is particularly concerned over the morality of such situations.' With this bewildering observation he withdrew his hand and rose from the table. 'Goodnight, then,' he said with an intimate sort of half bow, 'it has been a great pleasure to know you; my compliments to Her Excellency. No doubt we shall meet again when the time comes for you to present your letters.' He gave me a look of new-found respect, walked with great dignity out of the café and, giving the goggle-eyed Gabriel a brotherly wave, disappeared from sight.

Neither then nor thereafter did he seem to hold my refusal against me, and I would have gone on thinking that I had been the target of a pretty jaunty con-trick had I not run into him, several months later, and discovered that he was, in truth, quite an important figure. He was charm itself and did, in fact, do me a small favour. He must have solved his financial problems for he was wearing a new suit, even flashier than the one in the ice-cream parlour.

Then, as if this strange episode had indeed been some kind of catalyst, things began to happen. I was summoned to my first meeting with the Minister for Foreign Affairs at precisely four hours' notice. Fortunately we were well prepared, Peter knowing from experience that time in Africa is elastic and that cause and effect can be either simultaneous or separated by months, perhaps years. However, my formal entry into Congolese diplomatic and political life turned out, as was often the case, to combine drama with farce. On arrival at the Ministry, Peter and I were informed that, oh no, there must be some mistake, it is arranged for the Minister to receive you at his house. Apologies, simultaneous disclaimers and acceptances of responsibility having been exchanged, we hurriedly re-activated Gabriel who, as usual, had dozed off in the shade, and were speeding on our way towards the Ministerial Residence when we spied Bomboko, the Minister, in his official black Mercedes going equally fast in the opposite direction, no doubt heading for the Ministry. I saw no reason why this situation, which was not one for which my experience had prepared me, should not be prolonged indefinitely, Bomboko and I passing each other at approximately ten minute intervals without ever being able to exchange a friendly wave since we had not been properly introduced.

It says much for the effect of the African climate and customs that all thought becomes paralysed in the face of these frequent mix-ups about time and place; even the most dynamic of Europeans becomes resigned to waiting for nature or luck, or both, to impose a solution of the problem. Nevertheless, we turned round, gave chase and arrived back at the Ministry a few minutes after Bomboko. We were greeted as if for the first time and informed that the Minister had just arrived and would receive us immediately. An enormous face-saving operation, in which we were expected to take part, was clearly in progress, so we smiled back and said that we hoped we had not kept him waiting. Within seconds we were ushered into Bomboko's office.

I made my carefully prepared little speech and handed over the documents in a large white envelope marked in huge black letters 'OHMS' and, underneath them, a long and complicated set of numerals which was, in fact, the Stationery Office code number for re-ordering but which must have considerably puzzled the Congolese. Bomboko replied in a graceful little speech full of idiomatic expressions of great felicity and charming sentiments about our two countries and their relationship. His performance made me feel that mine, of which I had been quite proud, had been a little amateurish by comparison. These formalities, for which we remained standing face to face and rather uncomfortably close, being complete we all sat down and began to talk informally.

Justin Bomboko was a great charmer, and far from being the light-weight figure which the ludicrous events preceding our meeting might suggest. He was an old crony of Mobutu and a member of the famous Binza group which had helped to engineer his seizure of power in 1963. He was intelligent and articulate and less interested, I thought, in the formulation of foreign policy than in its expression and execution. He knew a lot about contemporary African affairs, and was a powerful and sophisticated spokesman for the moderate, and relatively conservative views which at that time characterised the Mobutu regime.

He was also, however, a compulsive and determined playboy, his handsome face and well-dressed, tubby figure being a familiar sight in all Kinshasa night clubs, so much so that he was credited by his enemies with the supernatural power of being able to be in two places (and, no doubt, two beds) at the same time. He was frequently missing when most needed, and the Kinshasa one-channel, government-controlled TV would inter-rupt its programmes from time to time to demand that any viewer knowing his whereabouts should tell him to report immediately to his office or to the Presidency, or give him some other urgent message of State. His ready sense of humour was a great help, and he appeared to enjoy my jokes, always essential equipment in any African dealings. I became very fond of him and missed him when, as I suppose was inevitable, he fell from grace and disappeared into the complicated and dangerous world on the dark side of Presidential favour.

At this meeting a date was at last set for the presentation of my credentials. Although still ten days ahead, it appeared definite and likely to stick; the other waiting Ambassadors, we found, had also been alerted. It was going to be an assembly-line production, each being received in turn in order of arrival in Kinshasa (the normal way of establishing precedence) at hourly intervals. I was to be the second among four and again, thanks to Peter, we were well prepared. Indeed, the speech which I would make had already been written and a copy given to Bomboko so that the President could prepare a suitable reply. It was important to get this particular speech absolutely right since it would set the tone for the future and would be regarded by the Congolese as a declaration of intent, rather like the manifesto of a political party. We discussed it at length in the office, and I got all senior members of the staff to contribute their ideas before drafting it. I received no specific guidance from the Foreign Office; indeed, it would have embarrassed me if I had done so.

I knew full well the broad lines of our African policy and those elements which were likely to please or displease the Congolese. It would have been dangerous to avoid contentious issues, such as our attitude to Smith and UDI, and to South Africa, or to give the impression that I was in a position to change the British Government's attitude on any major question. At the same time, I wanted to convince Mobutu that there were areas of co-operation, notably economic, in which I could and would do my best to persuade HMG to play a more active role in our relationship. Phrases and words had to be carefully chosen, for I knew that the Congolese would scrutinise each in order to squeeze out such nuances as would be useful to them in the future. Peter had also worked out the protocol and procedure for the ceremony in a series of meetings with the Congolese, and had produced a masterpiece of ceremonial prose.

When the great day arrived, my principal preoccupation, as the sun rose on what was going to be a very hot day, was with my uniform. I had not had the foresight to stage a dress rehearsal; sure enough, we found that the London tailor, whose air of immense superiority and centuries' experience had lulled me into a false sense of security, had put all hooks and no eyes on my collar, which consequently could not be fastened. Babs came to the rescue, as always, with needle and thread and literally sewed me in. Peter and the other senior staff, who were to accompany me, arrived also in their uniforms. We stood about like the cast of some Ruritanian musical comedy, swords clanking and medals flashing, to await the arrival of Mr Kallimazi, the Chef de Protocole. He came about twenty minutes late, which is punctuality itself in those parts, resplendent in morning coat, top hat and gloves, already feeling and showing the heat, and accompanied by an escort troop of motor cyclists from the Presidential Guard. They wore powder blue breeches, white coats and red crash helmets, the whole encrusted with gold braid and buttons. They kept their engines revving, no doubt for fear of the awful loss of face from stalling, and cavorted around on my lawn, forming and re-forming in readiness for our departure.

All conversation at once became impossible and the Ruritanian musical turned into a silent movie as I wordlessly introduced Mr Kallimazi to my wife and colleagues and he, in turn, motioned me to take my place in the open Presidential car. With a final crescendo we roared out of the gate, waved goodbye by Babs and the Elder Statesman, and watched by a crowd of appreciative onlookers. Peter and the Defence Attaché followed in a second car. Mr. Kallimazi chatted amiably with me; he was a career diplomat who took great pride in his work, regarding it, as do many Chefs de Protocole, as an art form rather than a function of government. He used

110

to complain constantly about the hopeless inefficiency of his staff and the slap-dash way in which things were done – 'Not like you British, my dear Ambassador, from whose ceremonial we have so much to learn.'

The Presidential Offices were, fortunately, not far from my house; I was already suffering from stage fright and was glad not to have to continue to exchange small talk with Mr Kallimazi, charming though he was, at the top of my voice. The last half mile of the route was lined by more Presidential guards whose salutes I acknowledged with my own brand of gesture – half military, half political – rather like a general hitch-hiking in full dress. We arrived to be greeted by a large guard of honour and a band whose conductor kept his eyes fixed on me, ready to burst into our National Anthem as soon as I had alighted. It was at this point that my sword decided to pay me back for the indignities it had suffered throughout our journey by getting itself stuck underneath the driver's seat. It looked as if I should have to abandon it altogether, or undergo the whole ceremony seated in the car, like Queen Victoria at the steps of St Paul's on her Diamond Jubilee. Fortunately Mr Kallimazi was equal to this, as to most things, and by a deft gesture, too fast to be seen with the naked eye, freed the offending weapon and bundled me out of the car in time to stiffen with appropriate solemnity to the strains of what Peter afterwards assured me was *God Save the Queen*. It was, in fact, a gallant musical effort, all the more touching for the obvious certainty that I, if no-one else, would be bound to recognise and accept the compliment. The tune of our National Anthem is not, unfortunately, one which has its listeners dancing after the first few bars. But in spite of this, the Congolese managed to give it a touch of those exotic rhythms which permeate their martial music.

Thereafter the ceremony progressed exactly as laid down in Peter's memorandum. Mobutu, an impressive figure wearing the uniform of a Lieutenant-General in the Congolese Army, and surrounded by Bomboko and other Ministers, listened attentively to my speech. His reply, formal but by no means platitudinous, was in markedly friendly terms and contained only a brief, and mildly-worded mention of Rhodesia, at that time the main issue of contention between Britain and the black African states. In diplomacy, what is *not* said is often more significant than what *is*. I had not ducked the issue of Rhodesia in my speech, but had not dwelt on it at any length since I had nothing to say of which the Congolese were not well aware. Nevertheless, I had rejected advice from some quarters that I should omit any reference to it, precisely because I wanted to see whether Mobutu would take the opportunity thus offered to launch a full-scale tirade on the iniquities of British policy. A lesser man might have done so; but Mobutu had, at that time, a budding sense of statesmanship which I was encouraged to see him exercise by saying the minimum on this matter, consistent with the demands of his own internal public opinion.

The formal part of the ceremony having been completed, Mobutu led me into an ante-room with Bomboko. We were served the obligatory champagne in which we toasted each other and, in a charming gesture by Mobutu, the Queen, while eyeing each other warily. The conversation which followed was not easy. Mobutu was far more critical in private than in public, complaining about Rhodesia; about the size of our aid programme to the Congo, so much smaller than those of some other Western European countries; and about the alleged activities of British so-called mercenaries, always an obsession with Mobutu and his Governments. Their recurrent nightmare was an attempted secession of the Katanga Province, with its vast mineral wealth, inspired by the once powerful, now exiled Tshombe acting in the interests of Western big business and backed by European mercenaries. I answered him fully and frankly (as the communiqués always say) on all these points. Then, feeling that the atmosphere needed lightening a little, I asked him how he had enjoyed a recent visit to Scotland. I struck a lucky chord; he had loved it and immediately launched into traveller's tales about Edinburgh and Braemar. I risked a joke, by saying that his was not the only country with tribal problems, as he must have observed. This had him and Bomboko in stitches, and we ended what had become quite a jolly party trying unsuccessfully to remember the French word for bagpipes, which even defeated Mr Kallimazi, who was specially summoned as the nearest authority on foreign customs.

I was genuinely sorry when the time came to leave. We returned to the main audience hall where Peter and the others had been chatting to the Congolese Ministers and officials, all no doubt baffled by the sounds of hearty laughter coming from the inner sanctum. Mobutu came with me to the door and when I signed the visitors' book, he and Bomboko stood over me, watching as if I were putting my name to a treaty or major commercial contract. The guard saluted. I saluted. The convoy with its deafening escort sped away, Mr Kallimazi well pleased and looking at his watch in readiness for the next round. When we arrived back at the house, Babs had gathered the other wives and we persuaded Mr Kallimazi, now beaming with pleasure, to have a drink and to pose for a picture, with us all. There is nothing that Africans like more than group photos; I have seen chiefs of small tribes in remote areas of the bush produce fading scraps of sepia coloured paper on which groups of mutton-sleeved, straw-hatted missionaries can just be discerned. With a final flash of his magnificent teeth and profuse congratulations, Mr Kallimazi and the powder blue escort roared off to repeat the process with the new Indian Ambassador.

We all exchanged congratulations, like children after the first perform-ance of the school play. Peter, never at a loss for a few well-chosen words, proposed Babs' and my health, adding that although we were now flying solo, co-pilot Mennell would always be in the cockpit when needed. He was justified in feeling pleased for this first phase would have been impossibly difficult without him and Prudie. When they had all left, Babs gave me one of her secret looks of complicity.

'Come on, you must be roasted,' she said, 'let me cut you out of that uniform.'

CHAPTER SEVEN

Having at last become legitimate, I was able to launch myself whole-heartedly into the role of Her Majesty's Ambassador. But was exactly *was* that role? What were the priorities and how was I to divide each day between them? Working outwards, so to speak, I had to be responsible for the overall administration of the Embassy, including the considerable amounts of taxpayer's money that passed through its accounts; and for the welfare and morale of the staff, a constant preoccupation in Central Africa, where infection and boredom are ever present hazards. Then there was the British Community for whom I was expected to act as a kind of resident Saint George, protecting their rights and furthering their affairs. I needed to be literally a Jack-of-all-Trades in order to promote British exports and steer visiting businessmen or delegations through the shoals and rapids of the Congolese establishment. I was also expected to be the embodiment of British culture, part scholar, part impresario, part travel agent. I had to do most of this in French while at the same time advocating the teaching of English, long regarded as Britain's secret weapon, especially by the French who rightly considered themselves threatened in a vital interest. Such duties were the fabric of my daily life. Of course, I had willing and able helpers in all fields. But the world is a very snobbish place, especially the developing world; a surprising number of people could be expected to insist on seeing the Ambassador rather than a First or Second Secretary, who probably knew more about the details of the subject in question than I did.

The Diplomatic Service has changed enormously since World War II, but its pre-1939 image of a patrician élite has lingered on in the public mind. The world of diplomacy is so specialised and seemingly artificial that those who inhabit it are likely, at best, to be misunderstood if not to incur active hostility or secret envy. The national and international post-war climate provided fertile ground in which these seeds of mistrust could bring forth a luxurious growth. The long, deepening economic crisis whose shadow lay over successive post-war governments demanded that

114

above all we should 'export or die', as the official slogan-making machine so aptly put it in the mid-fifties.

British diplomats of the old school had not concerned themselves greatly with trade; indeed, there was no reason for them to do so, since the flag was still omnipresent for the trade to follow. It was time that the businessman was shown in through the front door of the Embassy rather than the tradesman's entrance, that Ambassador and export director should speak to each other in roughly the same language, and that a posting as a Commercial Secretary should be regarded as an important step towards promotion rather than, as in the past, as a kind of punishment or vote of no confidence. The Service was not slow to respond to the resulting pressures for reform, recognising the validity of some of the criticism and conscious, as always, of the advantages of flexibility. But in my view the flexibility went a little too far, the emphasis on our commercial role tending, by the mid-sixties, to obscure those other, more classical functions for which diplomacy has been known and respected since the days of the Greek city states, to whose language we owe that much abused word.

A diplomat's proper business remains the promotion and maintenance of good relations between sovereign states, a political task to which trade often, but by no means invariably, contributes. Anyone who has witnessed the scramble for contracts which takes place in rich developing countries like Zaire, and knows some of the methods employed to secure them, must have his doubts about the degree of international harmony which they promote; although it must be admitted that trade is not in the same class as international sport for creating really bad feeling between nations. A diplomat is not his own political master and has to support and implement policies which he does not formulate himself, and over which he can exercise only a limited degree of influence. But he must, nevertheless, explain them to the government to which he is accredited, and try to make them as acceptable as possible. He must also do much the same in reverse, explaining that Government's policies and attitudes to Whitehall, and trying to minimise their negative or damaging aspects.

He can achieve little, however, unless he retains the absolute trust of both parties. No more foolish aphorism has ever been coined than that which describes a diplomat as being sent abroad to lie for his country. Lie, if you must, to your employer, your tax inspector, your lawyer, your priest, your wife or mistress; but never lie to the Government to which you are accredited. A diplomat must also tell the truth to his own Government, however unwelcome he may judge that truth to be. Unlike Matilda, he must be believed if danger of fire is to be recognised in time.

These thoughts resulted from many years of imagining myself in the position of my superiors, setting my own solutions to the problems they faced against those they actually adopted. Naturally, I often preferred mine, but the cosy complacency of the back-seat driver or armchair strategist disappears uncomfortably rapidly when you have to do your own driving. It is lonely at the top, and especially so for a diplomat by virtue of the need to be perpetually on show, never a private person, forever alert for the repercussions of a chance word or gesture. Since it is impossible to rehearse the role of Head of Mission, just as you cannot practise being Prime Minister, King or any other public figure – observing others or standing in for them when absent is not the same thing at all – it was not surprising that I should feel diffident and uncertain during these first months.

I could not escape the feeling that I was playing a part for which I had been inadequately rehearsed; or that I was, in some way, not the real thing, a kind of impostor. I would overhear members of the staff discussing a problem and one of them say, 'Well, I think that we ought to put that up to H.E.' Quite right, I would think to myself automatically, for keeping Ambassadors in the picture had accounted for a large part of my official life. Then it would dawn on me that I, not some remote figure, would have to make any decision needed. When calling on my diplomatic colleagues, I would be met at the door, according to normal custom, by a junior member of the Embassy concerned, and ushered into the Ambassador's office, usually being announced, as if at a formal reception, '*Son Excellence l'Ambassadeur de la Grande Bretagne*'. Good God, that's me, I would think, still not quite believing it myself. It was proof, for me, of Shakespeare's distinction between those born to greatness and those having it thrust upon them. To be an Ambassador is a form of greatness, or must be if the job is to be done well; I had certainly not been born to it, and was not even as fully prepared as most of my colleagues, since I had come late into the Service. Nor did I feel able to share these thoughts, even with Peter, lest the trust given me by the rest of the staff, which I feared was at that time less than absolute, might be undermined. But there was Babs, as always, ready with soothing balm or douches of cold water, whichever the situation might need. So on one rare night when we had no engagement, I told her of my worries.

'I don't think I'm getting it quite right,' I said. 'A lot of the time I feel like an amateur, and sometimes like a fraud.' This brought forth a bracing cataract of cold water. Time would take care of all this, she told me, and added the prediction that within a year she would be trying to bring me down to earth to mix with ordinary mortals. She was very nearly right; it took me almost a year to feel really comfortable and to cease this vocational introspection, although I hope and believe that I was always able to keep one admittedly well-shod foot on the ground.

So with fewer and fewer backward looks, I pushed on with the task of building confidence, in myself and in others, and trying to play the variety of parts which the script of this particular drama demanded. I began, as custom dictated, by getting to know my fellow Ambassadors, who numbered at that time about fifty; a time-consuming formality which, nevertheless, pays dividends in the relationships thus established, smoothed by professional *esprit de corps*, however disagreeably the two nations concerned regard each other politically; and, of course, in the occasional nugget of information sieved out after hours of dusty small-talk. Every new Ambassador, as soon as he has presented his letters, pays formal calls on all the other Heads of Mission; and they, in turn, pay a return call on him. It is rather like knocking up by yourself on a squash court; the harder and quicker you hit the ball, the quicker it comes back, and it demands a very nice sense of timing. It is usual to call first on the doyen of the diplomatic corps. In Kinshasa this position was held *ex-officio* by the Papal Nuncio, as is customary in countries which consider themselves Roman Catholic. But in non-Catholic, or non-Christian countries, the most senior Head of Mission fulfils the role irrespective of the country which he represents. It is an honorific, but onerous dignity, usually bringing more complaints than compliments from the rest of the corps, as whose spokesman and protector he acts *vis-à-vis* the receiving Government. As longevity of appointment (and hence often of years) is usually the criterion, many strange episodes about doyens are recorded in the archives of the world's Foreign Ministries. When I was acting as Chargé d'Affaires in Cairo, I thought it prudent to call on the doyen, who happened at that time to be the Ambassador of Afghanistan, an elderly recluse who took little part in affairs, and whose habits and personality were matters of uninformed speculation. I was unprepared for his opening words of welcome when, with both hands clasping mine and a beatific smile on his wizened, bearded face, he drew me down beside him on to a sofa and said, in a voice full of emotion, and in perfect English, 'My dear boy, I am so glad you have come to see me; I so admire your Jesus Christ.' On the spot I could think of no better reply than, 'Oh, thank you so much', while I tried desperately to remember his own faith so that I could return the compliment. I subsequently learned that his only real interest in life was comparative religion, and earned some credit with my colleagues for disseminating this unlikely information.

The Afghan admirer of the Christian Messiah, however, had very little in common with Kinshasa's doyen, an Italian bishop steeped in the ways and by-ways of the Vatican, to whom comparative religion was probably a contradiction in terms. He worked tirelessly, as only a priest can, for the betterment of conditions for the diplomats as well as at his primary and difficult task of keeping the Congolese firmly within the arms of the Church. I once saw him standing in the middle of the road in purple cassock and biretta, flagging down all diplomatic cars on the way to the Presidential Palace to advise them that the Congolese, for no known reason, had cancelled the President's New Year party at so short a notice that no-one had been able to be informed. This apostolic gesture was much remarked on as being typical of him, combining diplomatic skill with Christian humility.

My enforced, pre-credentials limbo had not been devoid of informal contact with some of my colleagues; for example, the French Ambassador telephoned to welcome me on the first day after my arrival, thus endearing himself for ever and making me regret the unkind thoughts I had sometimes harboured about his nation and compatriots. A few others had done likewise; but no formal calls, no parties, nothing public until my official coming of age. I had also to pay calls on the principal Congolese figures – Ministers, senior officials, religious leaders, who included a Congolese cardinal and the rector of the impressive university of Louvain, himself a Congolese bishop, and so forth. This process was a good deal less smooth than calling on my diplomatic colleagues, who were used to it and some of whom, to be honest, had little else to do. But with the Congolese we made appointments which were cancelled and remade, with locations and times subject to last-minute alterations.

None of this really mattered, provided that the mental frustration and physical wear and tear could be kept within reasonable limits. It was part of the African way of life; they could no more be expected to share our concern with punctuality and efficiency than we could be asked to accept the practices of the witch doctor as effective medicine. I got there in the end and when I did, my reception was unfailingly friendly and interested. They would have found any complaint about the difficulty of arranging a rendezvous completely baffling. A colleague of mine told me that a Congolese Minister had once explained his last minute absence from a dinner party, which he had long before agreed to attend with every sign of pleasure, on the simple grounds that he had not been hungry on that particular evening – perfectly reasonable and not impolite, if the society in which you live happens to be organised in that way.

The trouble comes when the culture and habits of one kind of society begin to conflict with those of another which, for economic and political reasons, it is trying to imitate. Like most newly independent African people, the Congolese were painfully conscious of the technological gap which separated them from European economies, and of the immense human effort, in education, communications and the creation of a consumer society which closing it would demand. Moreover, in their case there was a lot to play for, since they were sitting on great wealth; not only gold mines, but copper, diamonds, cobalt and a host of other natural assets. They cherished the belief that they could somehow succeed in creating an industrialised society capable of developing and marketing these riches while at the same time preserving their own native, largely pastoral, culture; some even thought that they might avoid the grosser mistakes visible in the evolution of the West.

I had arrived in Africa with some illusions of this kind myself. Whilst I did not believe in the Noble Savage, I refused to subscribe to the theory of the African's innate mental inferiority; and on this last point I was soon vindicated by the mental agility and intellectual capacity of those Congolese who had managed to acquire a first class education – their paucity in numbers being more a commentary on the Belgian colonial past than African natural ability. But the African seizes on the vision of a consumer society with a greed no less ferocious than that which must have animated so many nineteenth century Europeans; and he finds it almost impossible to resist the opportunities for self-enrichment which development and gradual modernisation so abundantly provide. Hence, I soon came to the conclusion that the Congo would be lucky if it escaped the social and economic injustices which have flawed the Industrial Revolution in the West.

I cannot say that a pattern developed in my work: for those who like variety, the job is one of the most attractive. No two days are alike and the history which you hope you are in the process of making never repeats itself. Much of my work was undramatic, and there were few political issues which caused me more than momentary concern. I saw Mobutu infrequently, holding that it was not sensible to seek an audience (which would almost always have been granted) unless I had something definite and important to say. Occasionally he would summon me, sometimes to appeal for our help over some wider African problem; and sometimes to complain about some deed or attitude, real or imagined, of the British Government. The written and spoken word were constant sources of difficulty. Like many rulers in the third world, he found it impossible to believe that the British Government could not control the media, and that in particular the BBC and *The Times* were not actual instruments of government policy. He would argue, with baffled logic, that it must be so; the Government paid for the BBC and everyone knew that *The Times*' editorials were dictated from Downing Street. My long, patient and often repeated attempts to explain exactly how things worked fell upon ears as deaf as Nasser's when, so long ago in Cairo, I had tried to counter exactly the same arguments. Examples of these organs actually criticising the British Establishment were dismissed as propaganda to confuse the Africans.

Mobutu was sensible enough, however, not to worry this, and other bones of contention, unduly. It did not surprise me that he had come out on top, for he had a breadth of vision and sense of realism far superior to most of the leading Congolese. He recognised the task which he faced; that of creating a nation out of the diverse, fragmented tribal groupings which had become assembled but never unified under Belgian rule, and for whose political cohesion there was no natural reason. He was forced to employ methods, ruthless or extravagant by turns, to try to weld this amorphous mass into a nation, to give it a common language, ideology, and institutions through which it could express its nationhood. He ignored the criticism which they attracted. By 1970, he felt secure enough to hold elections, albeit for single-party candidates and for himself alone for President; and he was sophisticated enough to be publicly furious when one district was reported as having returned a majority vote in his favour of 106 per cent! Once, when I was deeply worried by the abduction and subsequent rape of one of the Embassy secretaries by five Congolese soldiers, he sent me a personal message of apology and spared no effort to ensure that the culprits were found and punished. The stories of his vast wealth are probably true; he was, after all, the great tribal Chief and Le Grand Patron, and as such was expected to be rich and to show it. No doubt many of these gains would have been regarded as ill-gotten by our standards. But, like a medieval king, there were some areas in which he regarded his private funds and the national exchequer as indistinguishable. His personal lifestyle had dignity and lacked the excesses of those of some of his fellow African Heads of State, notably the clown Emperor Bokassa, whose frequent unannounced state visits to his brother rulers were a source of much amusement to us all. Above all, Mobutu was a realist, knowing that what was good for him was good for the Congo, and having no truck with ideologies and political theories, whether from right or left, which did not extract and market the mineral wealth on which all depended.

I liked and respected Mobutu, but never felt really close to him. Indeed, getting to know the Congolese with any degree of intimacy was a major problem. It was difficult to penetrate beneath a surface relationship, admittedly very pleasant and not in itself hard to achieve, of polite social intercourse, light-hearted banter, or the necessary official dealings. We

My parents (*c.* 1910)

Vincent Square, Winter 1928–9. The author (*centre*) as Cheer Leader.

My Aunt Winifred with Queen
Mary at the opening of the new
Whitelands College in 1931.

Unsuccessful candidate Wright ...

... campaigning in the East End.

23 May 1942, our Wedding Day.

The three Pauls at my wedding:
left to right: me, Paul de Labillière, Dean of Westminster,
and Paul Hammond (Bab's uncle).

Babs with the first Parliamentary baby, our daughter Faith, 1943.

Three of Babs' reasons for not standing again for Parliament in 1945: Tim, Pauline and Faith.

With President Nasser in Cairo, 1961

With Prince William at the Kinshasa Trade Fair, 1971.

An elegant President Mobutu on the banks of the Congo.

Diplomacy has its rewards; receiving the Order of the Leopard (Second Class).

aeb Salaam, Prime Minister of the Lebanon before the tragedy.

fter presenting my credentials to President Frangieh.

David Rockefeller visits Beirut.

Getting the policy over, for once.

made an early decision to try to entertain as many Congolese in our house as possible. Much rubbish is written and talked about diplomatic entertainment; the alleged glamour of gold chairs, caviar, champagne and glittering jewels, and of state secrets falling from the pretty but careless lips of the Prime Minister's mistress. Much indignation is generated by the supposedly artificially high lifestyle necessarily adopted by our diplomats in order to suborn and seduce the foreigner, and the false picture of the so-called British Way of Life which this presents.

The reality is quite the contrary, as anyone will vouchsafe who has sat through innumerable meals, struggling to keep going conversations of stupendous dullness, or has hung about at cocktail parties clasping a sweaty glass and trying to avoid the Olympic-class bores of which the profession has its share. These are crosses which the diplomat willingly bears, because shared social occasions, however painful, do in the end produce familiarity and, in some cases, intimacy – qualities essential if the job is to be well done; and it is true that occasionally you can take the Foreign Minister aside at a cocktail party and have the kind of conversation that would be impossible in the more formal atmosphere of his office. In this way the ice gets broken or, more important, is prevented from forming. Moreover, indiscretions have been known to filter through the noise and smoke and to have been recognised as important when discreetly reported back; or if deliberately let slip, as I have done on more than one occasion, have been picked up and acted upon in exactly the way hoped for. Much of this is possible on a social occasion, little of it elsewhere. Those who ridicule these frequently dreadful parties as merely unique opportunities for oiling the working parts of international diplomacy have hit upon a more telling metaphor than they imagine. Moreover, the scale of entertainment is grossly exaggerated in the popular mind, very few posts being able, or needing, to indulge in the kind of Edwardian splendour so beloved by romantic novelists and gossip writers; and where the scale does perhaps appear ornate, it is in order to keep up with others who tend to make material judgements about British credit, and whose sterling balances and general commercial confidence we wish to maintain.

As for the lifestyle, I can only say that living in most Embassies is rather like permanent residence in a three, sometimes, perhaps, four-star hotel; not a bad description in view of the numerous visitors who feel they have a right to stay with the Ambassador, and are not above complaining if the standard of comfort is not to their liking. Guests of surprising eminence arrive with piles of dirty laundry, demand a diet either difficult and expensive, or impossible to produce, and leave a tip for the servants so derisively small that I have on occasions been compelled to supplement it from my own pocket on some invented excuse, such as a last minute shortage of local currency, to save face all round. Others, it is fair to say, seemed to understand that an Ambassador's Residence was also his home, and to behave accordingly.

Entertaining the Congolese, however, turned out to be something to which the ordinary rules clearly could not be applied; certainly not British rules. When we had begun to get to know a few Congolese, and had made friends with many of our colleagues, we tried our hand at a dinner party. Arranged on conventional lines, with a seating plan, the Ministry of Works candlesticks and the Elder Statesman behaving as if he was Hudson in *Upstairs, Downstairs*, it was a disaster. All the Congolese, save one, either refused or accepted and did not turn up; the one that did arrive came an hour late without his wife. There was chaos and temperament in the kitchen, and Babs and I were nervous wrecks with the uncertainty of it all. Never again, we swore. Thereafter, except on very rare occasions, we had buffet suppers at small tables in the garden, and our Congolese guests came and went with delightful informality, sometimes bringing a child or two to be put to sleep in one of the spare rooms. They loved it, and consequently came in greater numbers than to many other Embassies who tried to reproduce European formality and rigidity on the Equator. It called for a certain agility since, in spite of their seeming vagueness about time and place, Africans have their own strict etiquette; rank is important to them. Hence we had to try to seat people in the right order, irrespective of when they arrived. We usually managed, sometimes at the expense of being ourselves starved by the need to move from one table to another during the evening.

What intrigued us both, and had done so since we first heard of our posting, was the possibility of travel in Central Africa. One of my favourite games as a small boy had been to turn Richmond Park or Barnes Common into the African jungle, and march determinedly through it with staff and imaginary pith helmet, taking very small, quick steps because I was reproducing the part of Dr Livingstone which had deeply impressed me in an early silent film. Our journeys now were to be mainly accomplished by Air Congo, more rapid but not necessarily more reliable than trekking up the Zambesi on foot. We usually travelled together in Africa, Babs' presence with me being deemed necessary for the job, and hence a justifiable expense on the public purse. This worried us in one way. The wives of other members of the staff were not allowed to travel at public expense and, since air fares were prohibitive and there was nowhere much to go in the environs of Kinshasa, they were confined to the claustrophobic and monotonous life within the city and the circle of their fellow diplomats or British residents, even if their husbands were travelling on duty. I fought a long battle with the Foreign Office to get this situation improved, and after two years of continuous bombardment was able to secure some relaxation of the rule.

The demands of the job and the needs of our family, plus the bonus that Kinshasa, being classified as a hardship post, entitled us to paid home leave once a year, meant that we were both absent more frequently, and for longer periods, than in any other post of my experience. But we were not always absent together. I tried never to leave Babs alone, and she did not like the idea of my being left behind. But occasionally one or the other was unavoidable. We tried to work out an arrangement for one of the servants to sleep in, but the idea was foreign and unwelcome to them and, in the African way, a number of unsuspected difficulties mysteriously appeared which, in the end, disheartened us. In most respects, I did not much mind being left alone; the house was secure enough by night, and even if the sentinel was a minus quantity as regards security, the Residence of the British Ambassador was thought to have the invisible defence of mystique which discouraged criminal attempts by all but the most foolhardy. The era of kidnapping, hijacks and other hazards of an otherwise peaceful career lay ahead, or at any rate had not yet dawned in Central Africa.

The house at night, however, was more than a little eerie; there is a ghost or spirit, usually assumed to be evil, round every corner in Africa, and there were times when I did not much like looking over my shoulder. All my life I have suffered from fear of the supernatural. I have never seen a ghost and I am fairly certain – not quite certain, perhaps – that I have never sensed the presence of one. But I have been, and often still am, haunted by the thought that one might appear. Nor is it the idea of an evil apparition that so appals me; I dread equally a benign manifestation, and have never quite got over those nursery fears which Nannie unwittingly conjured up in the name of Christianity.

* * * * * * * * *

Central Africa is still remote enough to intrigue, and the Congo offered many opportunities for travel. It was clearly important to see as much as possible of so large and varied a country; each region had a capital city of some size which could be reached without much difficulty by air. At one of them, Lumumbashi (the former Elizabethville) we maintained a Consul-General and a small staff. It was the second most important city in the country, being in the centre of the rich copper and mineral belt, and the capital of the Katanga Province about which the Congolese were hypersensitive. On our first visit we spent four days inspecting the offices, meeting the staff and trying to raise morale in what was a lonely, occasionally dangerous and certainly unstable post. There was the British community to be met and calls to be paid on the local Congolese Provincial authorities and the Management of Gecomin, the state body which had taken over the running of the mines. We also visited outlying mission stations. On a subsequent trip we motored down across the border to neighbouring Zambia, a journey said to be fraught with danger on account of the bandits who were alleged to infest the frontier region, but of whom we saw no sign. We were struck by the contrast between our smiling, friendly Congolese, and the sullen, ungracious Zambians who, however much they may have cherished their connection with the Commonwealth, gave little sign of caring much about its representatives. However, it is usually a mistake to judge a country by its frontier officials, and when we reached Lusaka, to stay with our High Commissioner there, Laurie Pumfrey, we met some very congenial Zambians. There was, even so, a certain dourness from which our jazzy old Congo did not suffer, and which reminded me a little of East Africa, so much so that I began to wonder if this were not part of the British legacy; had we, perhaps, taught these people, among other things, to take their pleasures sadly, or at least seriously in the way so familiar to those who have risked play with the British? Malcolm MacDonald was also staying at the High Commission (he was at that time HMG's Special Representative for Africa). He had that rare quality of being able to listen, and of appearing to be impressed with what he heard. After half an hour with him, my ego was dangerously inflated and I hoped that I had enlisted his support in my battle for greater recognition of the importance of the Congo. He did, in fact, help enormously and I shall always be grateful for the support and encouragement he gave me.

During the two and a half years of our posting, we visited Lumumbashi several times, twice presiding over the celebration of the Queen's Birthday there. It was a provincial town with little entertainment or interest for the staff outside their work, and those who persist in believing in the glamour of the Foreign Service should pay it a visit. Each of the Consuls-General who served there in my time made the best of a difficult and lonely job, and provided the kind of presence and service which the taxpayer expects, but complains about when the bill comes in. Sitting in the garden of the small, suburban house that served as the Consul-General's residence, I understood the loneliness and frustration which must often overtake those in such posts. We would be foolish to allow arguments about the size and structure of the Diplomatic Service to blind us to the dedication which such men display in these far-flung places, or to dismiss purely on grounds of financial or managerial expediency the benefits to Britain's political and economic reputation and interest.

Of the other provincial capitals, only Kisengani (formerly Stanleyville) needs a mention. This northern city saw some of the fiercest fighting and worst atrocities of the period of turmoil which followed Independence. It was here rather than in Kinshasa that Mobutu, with his flair for political manoeuvring, decided to stage the annual conference of the country's single political party in 1969. The result was a colossal face-lift for this much-damaged, little-repaired city, although not quite enough to house the thousands who descended on it for the conference. All the diplomatic corps were invited, but only a handful accepted. As it was, we slept in barely furnished rooms in the half-completed hotel, and spent a good deal of our time waiting for events advertised in the elaborate and fully-charged programme to take place. There were some historic moments; a parade – a form of celebration and entertainment much beloved by the Congolese – which lasted six hours and which included not only contingents from all over the country and of the armed forces, but representatives of all the municipal services of the city, brought up in the rear by the staff of our very hotel; needless to say, the barman got a standing ovation from the entire diplomatic corps; and a public meeting in the football stadium which Mobutu addressed for over an hour.

This occasion was especially memorable for me. Over the previous two years, the British Government, as the only substantial part of its aid programme for the Congo, had maintained a team of Royal Engineers at Kisengani to rebuild the bridges, vital for the life and commerce of the city, with the still ubiquitous and indispensable Bailey Bridges. At the beginning of his speech, Mobutu introduced all the VIPs sitting beside him in the grandstand to the crowd, including, one by one, those Ambassadors present. When he came to me, he added something which, as he was speaking in Lingala, one of the four main languages of the Congo, I did not understand. Fortunately, I was near the end of a row and close to a Congolese minster who obliged by translating. 'He wants you to remain standing,' he hissed. On such occasions I am inclined to view the immediate future with pessimism, and I had immediate visions of Mobutu taking the opportunity to say something critical about me or my Government, something perhaps which might compel me to walk out on the meeting, always a very difficult decision for a diplomat to have to take on the spur of the moment and one which, as it turned out, I am thankful to say, I was never to be faced with myself. My mind was racing on to wonder how, if I did have to make such a gesture, I would get away from the stadium – none of us had our cars with us, the Heads of Mission being transported from one place to another in a bus labelled 'Numéro 4: Ambassadeurs'. Even if I made it to the hotel, what then?

Before I could relax from my self-imposed nightmare he was speaking again, and my kind friend was supplying a simultaneous translation. The gist was that the crowd saw standing before them the Representative of a Power which had made possible the reconstruction of their bridges and the provision of new ones where necessary; would they please show their appreciation in the usual way? For the next few minutes I experienced something akin to what a pop star must feel when he makes his entry at Earls Court or Wembley in front of ten thousand fans. They went mad; they cheered, throwing their hands in the air and, as always, began dancing. I was moved by this, my first sight of what can be done by careful and intelligent use of aid; how the lives of simple people can be transformed if only someone will take the trouble.

I was told afterwards that about five thousand people had been saved a daily journey of over two miles by the repair of the main bridge in the town, a long distance for those who carry everything, from their babies to their bedding and cooking utensils, øn their backs. I wished that some of my colleagues in London, particularly those who had questioned the value of this and similar schemes, could see me now, the target of so much enthusiastic goodwill from the football pitch, and so many envious glances from my colleagues sitting round me who, as professionals, did not underestimate the impact of this extraordinary demonstration.

Although my travels were, in a sense, official, not all of them were as formal as those to the provincial centres. We spent three days in the Congo's principal game reserve, the huge Parc Albert in the eastern province of the Kivu. At that time, arrangements for visitors were primitive, but the management of the park itself was in expert hands, a mixture of Congolese and Belgian personnel who had maintained the levels of game throughout the vast area by scientific conservation and fighting a merciless war against the poacher, still a major menace to embattled species. Its remoteness, and the lack of adequate tourist facilities, meant that the park did not attract the camera-clicking, dust-raising convoys of packaged tours such as were to be found in Kenya, where it was more a case of the animals watching the behaviour of the tourists, and the lions sitting by the side of the track with their paws out waiting for a tip before obliging with a roar.

Here, on great rolling plains, with the Mountains of the Moon in the northern distance and the still active volcanoes of the northern Kivu to the south, huge herds of buffalo, antelope and elephant roamed as they must have done before man had found his feet; we had a strong feeling that we might well have been the first human beings glimpsed by some of these creatures, browsing peacefully, unaware of their small place in history. We would set off just before dawn with one of the guides, and within half an hour could count on finding a pride of lions with whom to have breakfast. It was a landscape on a grand scale, not unlike some parts of the west of the United States – except that in America one is always conscious of a certain emptiness, a sense that nothing much of human significance has happened in those great open spaces, whatever the future may hold, whereas in the Parc Albert I had the same eerie feeling which I had experienced on that first night in Kenya, that everything of human importance had begun here, and that the idea of man was not strange to these animals, however unexpected was their first sight of an example in the flesh.

It was during a subsequent visit to the Kivu Province that we undertook our most ambitious journey, penetrating right up into the Ituri Forest in the north-east corner of the country and spending a day with a tribe of Pygmies. My step-son Tim Rathbone had managed to free himself from his London life long enough to spend a holiday with us, and came on this trip. He turned himself into the perfect ADC, rescuing our luggage from over-enthusiastic officials, chatting up the local notables, and making sure that the friendly chaos which invariably accompanied our journeyings was kept in check. I doubt whether the Congolese ever discovered our relationship, or that he was not a fully-fledged diplomat; he enjoyed it immensely and our visible status was considerably enhanced at no expense to Her Majesty.

We flew first in a private plane to a small town in the foothills of the Ruwenzori Mountains. As we came in to land, I was startled to see a large crowd assembled on the airfield, together with a guard of honour and all the trappings of an official welcome. Although our visit was supposed to be private, we were given a welcome which could only be described as Royal – which would not have surprised me had I known then what I afterwards discovered, namely that this particular town had been scheduled for a visit by the King and Queen of the Belgians during their highly successful tour of the whole country earlier in the year but, by the mysterious process which passes for planning in the Congo, had been subsequently deleted from the programme without any explanation, leaving a head of steam which the local authorities wisely thought could be dispersed by switching their attentions to the next best thing, which happened to be the British Ambassador. Our arrival was, therefore, most opportune and we inspected the Guard of Honour, shook innumerable hands, and generally tried to behave like the Royalty for which we were the unsuspecting surrogates.

We were housed in the Town Guest House, which boasted running water but no electricity. Over it was flying a puce and Cambridge blue flag which I fortunately recognised at the last minute as the local version of the Union Jack, run up by the town tailor, who must have been working to an oral description only. This moved us greatly, and I asked the Mayor if I could keep it. Yes, he said, but it must fly while we were in residence. So it did, only to be taken down and handed over to me in the pitch dark at five o'clock the next morning, a ceremony which I felt rather than saw, and which made me slightly nervous since I knew that the Gendarmes concerned were armed – and probably with one up the spout.

We set forth at half past six in a Landrover, accompanied by a Congolese District Commissioner and another local official whose precise functions were never made clear. We drove for about three hours, the forest edging nearer to the track as we left the familiar world behind. Then we stopped abruptly. Standing by the roadside was a small figure who, on sighting us, gave a cry which might have signified surprise, joy, anger or fear, so strange was it, and then ran off into the forest which by then had crept to the road's edge. He was the harbinger, we were told, sent to greet us and to warn of our arrival. He would now speed back ahead of us to prepare a suitable welcome. We were soon following him at a more sedate pace, walking along a forest path made uneven by the roots of huge trees, but cleared of the thick undergrowth which lay around us. After we had been going for about an hour, we suddenly became aware that we were hearing music; a strange, beautiful piping, with a faint metallic, rhythmic background and an insidious theme full of repeated phrases. We stopped to listen to these haunting sounds which, our guides explained, signified that the little messenger had arrived and that our approach was known and welcome. As we pressed on down the path, the music seemed everywhere, tumbling down the shafts of sunlight through the thick trees and laughing at us, Pan-like, in the damp fragrant air. Suddenly we had arrived; a small clearing, some grass huts, a smoking fire and a group of shy, smiling people all less than five feet in height, all naked except for a *cache-sexe* made, as we afterwards were told, of tree bark.

It did not take long to reach across the barriers of language and culture which separated us, for our hosts and hostesses were tremendously excited by our arrival to which they had been looking forward for several days. Soon we were being shown their huts, their weapons, their cooking arrangements and methods, and their simple ornaments. The imagery of their language came strongly through the double sieve of Swahili and French, and they seemed anxious to impress us with their way of life. During a demonstration of hunting, clearly a compulsive and collective occupation, one of them spied a monkey sitting on a tree branch not far away. Now they would show us true hunting, they cried, and while Babs became frantic with conservationist zeal, they fitted arrows to their bows and let fly.

The monkey watched them with a sardonic expression born, no doubt, of experience and the virtual certainty that they would miss; as they did, much to our relief, but with enormous loss of face. After this debâcle, they switched to a dramatic portrayal of an elephant hunt in which, there being no real elephant available, the part of the quarry was brilliantly played by one of the tribal elders, a born actor, which proved much more satisfactory to all concerned. We ate a meal with them, hardly appetising, consisting mostly of a paste made from Manioc (Cassava) roots and some dried fruit; and we learnt how they made such clothes as they wore, and about their method of building. Thus passed an unusual but enchanting day with these small people, so earnest and so welcoming, whose physique was perfectly proportioned to their diminutive size, and whose minds had not yet become contaminated by the world beyond the forest. It would not be long, we thought sadly, before their forest clearing would be invaded by the exploiters, who would teach them that sex meant cash, not *cache*, and how to take off their clothes for the tourist rather than to put on their G-strings in modest deference to their visitors. In spite of the dirt, discomfort and perhaps disease, we had seen something of that quality which the outside world had missed or forgotten; the calls of farewell and the fading music as we retraced our steps through the forest in the evening light seemed to come from a great distance, and to have about them a message of finality, telling us that another epoch was ending.

* * * * * * * * *

These journeys did us both a great deal of good. We not only escaped briefly from the claustrophobic atmosphere of Kinshasa, but never failed to find our morale higher on our return to the familiarity of Embassy work and life. The process of coming and going somehow made me feel more professional and gave me greater confidence in dealing with my colleagues, with the Congolese, and above all, with London. But as the months wore on, it became clear that I was failing to raise the level of Whitehall's interest in the Congo, and far from making a dent in the established thinking about Africa, the door against which I was hurling myself, with however greatly increased accuracy of aim, remained all but closed. Indeed, quite soon after my arrival in Kinshasa I developed an obsession about this lack of interest. It was a constant theme in my Despatches and less formal correspondence. I suppose that every Ambassador, except for a few in major posts, feels this way, like an anxious parent who is baffled by the world's indifference to the talent and beauty of its child. I marshalled arguments of extreme ingenuity and intensity when trying to attract the attention of my harassed colleagues in Whitehall. However exaggerated they may have appeared if applied to the Third World, in the case of the Congo they were valid, or so I thought, and capable of standing up to critical examination at the highest level. A vast country in the centre of a huge continent; great riches, actual and potential, in mineral wealth and agricultural products; a relatively stable pro-western Government; an infrastructure crying out for major redevelopment; what were we waiting for? These exhortations fell on deaf ears, and my irritating capacity for seeing both sides of an argument convinced me that the degree of priority for which I had hoped and argued could not reasonably be expected, in the face of critical situations in the Near and Far East affecting our vital interests; the superior (although, in my view, sentimental) claims of the Commonwealth; and other pet Whitehall preoccupations, to say nothing of arguments predicting the recurrence of serious trouble in the Congo itself and, consequently, in favour of leaving it all to the Belgians (whose baby it originally was) and to the Americans who, fortunately for us, seemed prepared to underwrite the Mobutu regime to an impressive extent. Wise men with pipes sent me cliché-ridden letters about not spreading our efforts too thinly, about the concentric circles of British policy in which Africa had no place, and even offered the monstrously flattering, and hopefully placating suggestion that my own presence and efforts were, in themselves, a contribution to the stability of the Congolese state.

I enjoyed reading this rubbish but was not taken in by it. I therefore decided to try to bring a few Mahomets to this mountain, in the shape of visitors distinguished enough to flatter the Congolese and to gain the ear and respect of those with influence at home when, as I hoped, they returned duly impressed by what they had seen and done.

My first visitor was Maurice Foley, then Parliamentary Under-Secretary of State in the FCO, and the Minister responsible for African affairs. With him came Donald Tebbit, an old friend and the senior official in the Office on African matters; and a very pretty private secretary called Lucy. It did not represent much of a triumph on my part, since Kinshasa was included as one stop in a tour of several African posts. But the great thing was that a British Minister came, and I did my best to represent his visit to the Congolese as a special mark of favour and interest. They received him with the utmost politeness, Mobutu and Bomboko giving us long meetings in which a good deal of quite hard-hitting sense was talked on both sides. The

British Community and the Embassy staff were glad to see him. That the visit did not produce a revolution in Whitehall thinking about the Congo could not be blamed on Maurice Foley. He took a great deal of trouble and remained a good friend and supporter while in Office. Although the Congolese liked him as a person they were not taken in by my sales talk and held to the view that anything short of a special visit by the Secretary of State himself was second best and not in accordance with their own estimate of their position and importance in the African scene.

The next visit was more ambitious, consisting of a special trade mission, led by the late Sir Peter Runge, and composed of senior executives of British companies mainly concerned with construction, heavy engineering and other capital goods. This shoal of big fishes had been eventually netted by my patiently dangling the bait of the enormous construction contracts likely to be placed by the Congolese Government in a long overdue, but now imminent, effort to rebuild their infrastructure, and particularly the transport system. I had pestered my friends in Whitehall and the city with oily letters of special pleading, and had devoted days of my leave to knocking on their doors. At last, probably as a result of exhaustion or in an effort to get rid of me, factors not to be ignored when you are trying to get your way as every properly brought up child knows, those responsible agreed to mount and despatch an outward mission. It was typical of Sir Peter Runge to accept its leadership despite ill health; it was an arduous task which this charming and public-spirited man carried out with his accustomed skill and grace. There were endless discussions about composition, programme and timing, this latter turning out to be of some importance to me since it emerged that the only possible dates clashed with a journey which Babs was forced to take for family reasons. Her absence was a great drawback, and turned out to have one particular consequence of extra-mural significance.

The mission duly arrived and was given a splendid welcome by the Congolese who appreciated this practical evidence of Britain's growing interest much more, it must be said, than a Ministerial visit. They were housed in handsome accommodation provided by the Government, and lavishly entertained between and after meetings with Ministers and Officials. Mobutu received Sir Peter Runge and the Government gave a banquet on the final night of their stay in Kinshasa after which the Mission split up to visit various parts of the country. Not much business was actually concluded at the time; obtaining the kind of contracts in which we were interested – construction work, renovation of the infrastructure, particularly the railway system – is a slow process in Africa. But hosts and guests were astonished and pleased to find that they had more in common than they thought; whatever suspicions and doubts the former may have had were dispelled by the latter's serious and practical approach to their problems. Mutual compliments were exchanged in an atmosphere of genuine warmth and the Mission returned to base with at least a corrected and more constructive view of the commercial prospects for us.

I have never subscribed to the puritan Anglo-Saxon view that work, to be effective, must be solemn and, if possible, unpleasant. Needless to say, the Congolese tended to share this view and indeed to project it beyond the bounds of good clean fun to something difficult not to brand as frivolity. There was, therefore, a good deal of merriment generated during the visit, encouraged by myself and my staff in the belief that once an African has laughed with you he is your friend. My visitors played up manfully and not only endured, but eventually began to be amused by, the uncertainties and surprises of Congolese entertainment. The last night provided a classic example of this delightful but unpredictable way of life. The Government banquet was a formal affair and finished quite early, in spite of lengthy speeches and toasts. As we were saying goodnight the senior Congolese Foreign Official present, a very bright young man whom we will call Mr N'Gumba, came up to me in a conspiratorial way.

'Rather a pity to break up so soon,' he whispered. 'Would you all like to come on to a night club?' I was computing the pros and cons of this unexpected invitation, when he added, 'I own one, you know,' (thus confirming one of my favourite pieces of gossip) 'and I would be delighted if you would all be my guests.'

Why not, I thought, and rapid consultation with Peter Runge and the others confirmed that they, too, saw the point of falling in with the plan. So off we drove in convoy, led by Mr N'Gumba in a large black official Mercedes through the dimly lit streets to a quarter of the city I had never before visited. On arrival there was more champagne, music and pretty Congolese girls, one of whom, with the not entirely unsuitable name of Magdalena, proceeded, no doubt on Mr N'Gumba's instructions, to identify Sir Peter Runge as the top VIP and make herself exceedingly pleasant. As the evening wore on with dancing and drinking, Peter was obviously tired, so I spirited him away and sent him home in my car with strict instructions to Gabriel to return immediately.

On his departure, Magdalena transferred her attention to me, doubtless unable to resist the Ambassadorial glamour, at least I thought so, sensing that euphoria which creeps up like mist at the end of a perfect summer's day. But enough was enough, and as soon as Gabriel's safe return had been confirmed, I set in motion the complicated rituals of farewells and the logistic exercise of getting the right people into the right cars for the right destination. The girls seemed sorry to see us leave, and Mr N'Gumba tried in vain to detain us. But everyone had an early start the next morning, and the Anglo-Saxon upper lip was maintained in the face of these final temptations. I was the last to leave, but just as I was about to drive off, having said a third and final farewell all round, Mr N'Gumba came running out to the car hand in hand with Magdalena. With a deft, not to say graceful, movement he thrust her into the car beside me with the unambiguous exhortation 'Have a good time, Mr Ambassador'. Gabriel remained motionless, only his gently heaving shoulders betraying the fact that he was enjoying the scene immensely. There wasn't a moment to lose. Aiming a chaste kiss at Magdalena's right ear, I opened the door of the car again and, with an equally chaste pat on her spectacularly shapely behind, tumbled her back into the arms of a crestfallen Mr N'Gumba and drove off waving fatuously and shouting vaguely about early starts, another time, what a lovely evening. '*À la Résidence, Patron?*' lisped Gabriel at his most maddeningly innocent.

As we drove home, I speculated on Mr N'Gumba's motive in making, for him, so generous but unmistakable a gesture. Magdalena, though clearly not actually repelled by me, was complacent rather than passionate, and probably regarded whatever might have followed during the night as being part of such contract as bound her to her employer. Was it payment for services rendered, my having been instrumental in introducing so many VIPs to patronise his night club – a kind of expense account claim for a valuable gesture in a highly competitive field? Was it an extreme example of African hospitality? Or, since it was undoubtedly known that Babs was away, was it perhaps more sinister; a security trap as a result of which Magdalena would wheedle British secrets from me, or that I should become vulnerable to blackmail, or a combination of both?

As usual in Africa, any of these might be the truth, or any mixture of them. But the most likely seemed the simplest; an unpremeditated action whose consequences were not thought important. If I had taken Magdalena home, no Congolese would have thought much about it, miscegenetic adultery being accepted as a necessary part of the blessings of European civilisation. I suspect that I would have been more embarrassed than the Elder Statesman who would certainly have found out the next morning. Mr N'Gumba would have been pleased and perhaps flattered. But all my training, not to speak of my views on matrimony, flashed computer-like reflexes against such behaviour; its irresponsibility goes without saying, and part of my thinking had been to wonder what attitude I would have adopted towards a member of my staff who did the same thing. A part of me resented my enforced public and restrictive life of which this incident was a reminder; that even if I had wanted to choose that moment for a once-in-a-lifetime derailment, the very letters before my name, the knowledge that I could, even then, hardly go anywhere in Kinshasa without being recognised, prevented me from giving the whole idea a moment's serious thought at the time. A small price to pay, you will think, and in an obscure currency at that. Very well; but public life has a habit of levying innumerable small charges which, when added up on sleepless crisis-tossed nights, represent a formidable sum to set against the receipts of privilege and power.

CHAPTER EIGHT

One of the strongest strands in the ties binding the diplomat to his Service is leave. The allowances are generous, especially in places like Kinshasa, classified as a 'hardship' post and thus qualifying for more leave at more frequent intervals. I long ago came to believe that leave quotas were fixed in the certain knowledge that most, if not all officers, would be lucky if they were able to take up their full entitlement in any given posting. Nearly everyone accumulated a considerable backlog, not all of which could be carried over indefinitely; I suspect that when I retired I must have been considerably in credit. It was home leave, of course, which counted, for most people could not afford to return often, if at all, to the UK at their own expense, except from very nearby posts. But by whatever calculation, October 1970 found us in London when the first date and time became available for our Audience with the Queen.

A rare privilege accorded to Ambassadors, but not to most other dignitaries, is that their wives are received with them on these occasions, a recognition I suppose of the connubial nature of the Diplomatic Service, and the important role which the wife can, and usually does, play. The principle which governs all contact with the Royal Family is that nothing is left to chance. You are told exactly what to do, where to go and when, and what to wear. This is most relaxing, for people tend to approach a meeting with their Sovereign determined to behave in the right and accepted way.

As we drove up to the main entrance of Buckingham Palace, Babs looked frightfully smart in unaccustomed gloves and hat, I in my morning coat with black waistcoat as prescribed, I could not help thinking of the equivalent situations in the Congo or, indeed, in many other countries where the proceedings, however ceremonial and public, were generally conducted by inspired guesswork. There is always a small crowd at the Palace gates, some of whom, as we drove in, waved as if on principle, just in case we were someone important enough to include in the day's sight-seeing bag. They did not seem disappointed by our blank, unfamiliar faces, nor the lack of an acknowledging bow which we felt it would be

135

somehow fraudulent to give. Their probable attitude was that coming and going is proper to a Palace, and it does not matter greatly who comes and goes; if you were lucky you might catch a Princess or a Prime Minister, or even the Queen herself; otherwise a diplomat would do. Our car deposited us at the Grand Entrance, which has seen three Kings and two Queens leave for Westminster Abbey and return as anointed Sovereigns. We were met by an imposing gentleman who, although he was wearing an ordinary lounge suit, managed to convey the impression that he was in full dress uniform. He led us through a series of corridors each narrowing into the next, increasingly less imposing and more intimate; then, in a small but ornate lift, to the first floor where we came to rest in a late Victorian room overcrowded by stuffed furniture, and with highland landscapes and portraits of lesser members of Queen Victoria's vast family on the walls. We were early for the time of our appointment, although right on planned schedule, and were invited to wait by our handsome guide, who then withdrew.

By this time we had somehow lost our sense of direction and were a little vague as to exactly where in the Palace we were. The muffled sounds of traffic reminded us that there was a world outside where ordinary people got on with their daily lives, wearing ordinary clothes unaware, most of the time, of the quiet but intense life which went on behind the Palace façade and of which we were, briefly, a part. It was all unreal, the essence of fairyland complete with the certainty that the clock would strike twelve. This is the secret of successful monarchy, unshared by those other Royal Houses, the bicycling Kings and Queens, who are mistakenly advised that people prefer their royalty to be as accessible as the folks next door – supermarket products designed for the tourist trade. The British have an instinctive understanding of the human need for mysteries and for the pageantry with which they must be surrounded. From it derives our love of theatre, the joy of dressing up, the need to play the part and to play it well; and our pleasure in the sight and sound of a good performance.

In due course we were summoned by a member of the Household, this time paradoxically wearing uniform with an ease which made it look like a tweed suit. He came to the door and said, in a matter-of-fact way, 'The Queen will receive Mr and Mrs Wright'. We followed him to an ordinary-looking door which he opened, allowing us to pass through into a medium-sized, airy room with a bow window looking over the garden and furnished in simple taste, comfortable and homely. In the middle stood the Queen, a small figure, quite alone. She seemed at once domestic and regal, startlingly like her pictures and appearing genuinely pleased to see us. She looked not exactly frail, but vulnerable; the modest centre of this immense, gilded labyrinth through which we had been so skilfully led so that the simplicity of this, the innermost core was all the more impressive; but there was present also the bright and mysterious aura of Monarchy, a living reminder of so much that had happened on this spot and before that at Westminster, Windsor, Greenwich, Richmond, Winchester, perhaps at Glastonbury and amid the cold barbaric splendour of Stonehenge.

I was deeply moved but find it, even now, very hard to convey the exact quality of my emotions. Some time afterwards some younger friends tried to suggest that the Queen was an unremarkable, though pleasant lady, out of touch with the world and whom, if she were not the Queen, one would find rather uninteresting. This is nonsense. For one thing, it is quite impossible to imagine her other than as the Queen, so deeply is her image engraved on the national subconscious – a symbol which produces an instant reflex. The question therefore does not arise in the first place. But when it is possible to think of her objectively, away from the emotive atmosphere of her physical presence and the trappings with which she is usually surrounded, there are qualities discernible which transcend the popular, public image. Although not exactly beautiful in the classic sense, she is much more than pretty; her spontaneous smile lights up her face in a way which is both charming and infectious. I do not know whether or not she is clever in the academic sense, but she clearly has great intelligence, a much more valuable quality, and she knows exactly how and when to use her unrivalled experience gained over twenty-five years at the centre of our national life.

During this thirty minutes she kept up a lively conversation, firing off extremely pertinent questions and making shrewd and often downright comments on the answers. It was a polished performance which contrived simultaneously to put us at our ease and have us on our toes. Prime Ministers have spoken in awed tones of her formidable memory and powers of concentration; and of the imperative need to 'do your homework', as Harold Wilson put it. They were right. As we left her – a process which I had been dreading, believing that it would entail walking backwards out of the room, but in practice made infinitely easy by her simple courtesy in coming with us to the door – we both felt as if we had run a mile in a time which equalled some record or other; and we experienced that simultaneous elation and fatigue which is said to be the aftermath of a good sporting performance. Our departure was as ceremonial as our arrival, and conducted with the same punctilious attention to detail which characterises all the doings of the Royal Household. Our car, which fortunately had not turned into a pumpkin although by now the clock had certainly struck, appeared as if summoned by spirit. We drove across the courtyard and out of the gates, where the same crowd, perhaps a little swollen by lunchtime gapers, gave us a perfunctory wave to which this time we felt entitled to respond in the belief that a glint or two of the Royal radiance might still surround us and be visible to the bystanders. It had been an experience illuminated by the unusual light, difficult to depict but instantly recognisable, which irradiates a throne and has done since the first hallowing of a tribal chief. It does not change, however much its reflections are distorted by the societies on which it shines.

We returned to Kinshasa refreshed, as always, by our leave and fortified by our experience at the Palace. I found that the Congolese Press had made quite a fuss about our having been received by the Queen, building up the whole affair into something unusual and dramatic. But opinion was divided when it came to interpreting it, some claiming that it was an indication of the esteem in which Her Majesty held the Congo, others that I had been hauled over the coals for not sufficiently promoting Congolese interests. The Congolese media reflected the Africans' total absorption with their own affairs; the one thing they refused to accept was the truth, that there was no particular significance in what was a normal, although in my case slightly delayed, event. Congolese journalism was not highly developed; the Press printed what came to it from a variety of sources, few of them reliable, without bothering too much about such tiresome details as accuracy, provided the so-called news was about Black Africa, and preferably the Congo itself. Mobutu's activities and speeches were fully covered, the latter usually verbatim; even my own public appearances were accorded an attention as flattering as it was meaningless. I had been impressed by the fact that the TV carried a forty-five minute item on the presentation of my credentials, giving my speech and Mobutu's reply *in toto*; and I was not unduly deflated when I discovered that they had done much the same for the other Ambassadors, the only consolation for any wounds my ego may have suffered being that at least they put me on first. The truth was that, apart from a few sleazy French films of about 1960 vintage, they had nothing much else to show. However, I will admit that the Press, never having mastered the spelling or pronunciation of my name (which has always baffled the Franco-phones) produced some deeply imaginative variations: Writh, Wrigt, Rygth, Ritg, Wrate, and so on.

By now, after nearly two years, we had come to terms with our life and were feeling as at home in the Congo as we were ever likely to be. The political atmosphere remained relatively calm, with Mobutu seemingly in control and his rivals for power either dead – both Tshombe and the former Premier, Kasavubu, had died during our time, the former suspiciously in Algiers allegedly on his way back to lead a revolt in the Katanga – or, like

Bomboko and others, politically neutralised. Copper prices were high and while prosperity had not visibly affected the massive, wide-spread poverty, there was an air of optimism about and, in the towns at least, the good things of life seemed to be available on a slightly wider basis than before. This was not a bad record for a huge country whose unity itself was artificial and fragile and which, in addition, had to contend with the geo-political vulnerability of having nine independent states on its borders, by no means all of them friendly, and only twenty-five miles of coastline.

These facts reinforced one main conclusion I was reaching about the best way to understand Black Africa at this stage of its development. The concept of nationhood was, in fact, European and so often cut across tribal boundaries, physical and mental, that it invariably failed to produce patterns of behaviour consistent with European ideas of international intercourse; and there was little point in expecting it to do so.

I was also becoming accustomed to the Congolese way of life and had begun to develop that flexibility of stance which, combined with ex-perience, prevents a goal-keeper from being wrong-footed no matter from what angle the ball comes at him. Moreover, I had overcome my initial exaggerated sense of esteem for the Congolese big shots, maintaining, however, a healthy respect for Mobutu himself. It is at first a little unnerving to be operating exclusively with, and at, the top; until it becomes evident that the men who occupy the higher reaches are not necessarily superior to, or more difficult to deal with, than the rest; in a surprising number of cases they are simply lucky. In truth, the Congo was being run by a group of gifted amateurs whose attitude to the task of governing and the demands of everyday life was summed up in a delightful phrase by the Senegalese Ambassador, one of the wittiest and most polished diplomats I have ever known: '*Ici on pratique le culte de l'improvisation.*' It sometimes takes an African to see the truth about Africa and to have the courage to say it.

These first two years had seen many changes in personalities, always testing for diplomats who depend so greatly on personal contact. Bomboko had at last proved too great a luxury for any government to indulge in, let alone one headed by Mobutu, against whom he was said to be plotting. So he disappeared, to be replaced as Foreign Minister by Cyrille Adoula, a former Prime Minister and one of the best known, internationally, of the Congolese leaders. I was able to arrange for him to pay a useful visit to Britain before he was tragically struck down by a massive stroke and barely survived to eke out an invalid life in Switzerland. Less important Ministers changed more frequently, portfolios being shuffled with great dexterity by Mobutu who usually kept most of the court cards in his own hand. The

Embassy had also seen some changes. The Mennells had departed and been replaced by Ham and Sheila Whyte, old friends from New York where he had been attached to the UK Mission to the UN. He had a reputation for sartorial eccentricity and advanced views, and although both qualities were often in evidence, they added to rather than detracted from his solid professional ability as a modern diplomat. His pretty wife Sheila was a gifted painter, and together they produced a cheerful civilised atmosphere in the ghastly house, newly built by the Ministry of Works at considerable expense, in which they were compelled to live. It had been expressly constructed for the Counsellor with the exact measurements, number and type of fitments and sanitary appliances appropriate to his grade. By what can best be described as dogged imagination, they made a charming, studio-like house out of this unpromising material, and gave wonderfully relaxed parties for their Congolese friends. But to say that I welcomed the Whytes is not to imply that we were glad to see the Mennells go. I missed Peter very much; his departure was like losing Nanny and replacing the nursery, where a gentle firm hand was always available at the first faltering, by the slippery corridors of power where there are no excuses and few second chances. The relationship between a newly-appointed Ambassador at his first post and the second-in-command who receives and inducts him is crucial. I remember an Ambassador under whom I had served in a similar capacity saying, in his speech at a farewell dinner he gave for us when we were transferred, that I had taught him how to be an Ambassador. At the time I had thought this an exaggerated compliment, but I now see that it might well have been true. It was certainly what Peter had done for me, and often in the years ahead I found myself looking back to those early days and measuring my performance by the standards he set. My relationship with Ham was, of course, quite different; he was then the new boy, I the old hand, showing him the ropes rather than the other way round. Fortunately, he refused to accept all that I said and did as infallible, and we had some lively arguments out of which there often emerged something more sensible than my original *ex-cathedra* proposals. It is rare for me to be so convinced of the rightness of my judgement as to be impervious to contrary arguments; indeed, the ability to see the force of the opposite point of view, although sometimes useful in negotiation, has been a great nuisance to me and has, I suspect, earned me the reputation of not sometimes knowing my own mind. A watchword of British Foreign Policy throughout the fifties and sixties was flexibility. I suppose that in a storm it is better to bend than to break; hence a nickname with which I was not altogether displeased – Pliable Paul.

We worked hard at carrying out properly our roles as the British

Ambassador and his wife; each day was full of activity and interest, although I would have been hard put to it to give an exact profit and loss account of my time. Those whose mentality craves 'results', by which they usually mean some beneficial effect derived from a cause which they themselves have initiated, need not contemplate diplomacy as a satisfactory career. It is rare to be able to say 'I did that and this happened.' The most that I, at any rate, could feel was that, over a period, a relationship between Britain and the Congo was building up which might be beneficial to us both and in which some of the grosser misunderstandings and hostilities were being ironed out. Each gesture, each casual word, counted; the clothes you wore, the games you played, the company you kept, all contributed; and, in Africa, the acceptance or rejection of life on African terms, the ability to transcend the barriers of race and culture; from these emerged the picture by which a diplomat, and through him, for want of a better or more visible yardstick, his country was judged.

It might be thought that all this was enough for one man in one country. But political realism combined with growing demands for economy in public expenditure decreed that I should be simultaneously accredited to two other, neighbouring African countries: Congo (Brazzaville) which faced us across the Congo river; and the Republic of Burundi, a very small country formerly part of the Belgian Colonial Territory of Ruanda-Urundi which lay along the eastern borders of the Congo proper. My accreditation to Brazzaville was theoretical and destined never to be consummated. The Brazza Congolese, so-called to distinguish them from their Kinshasa cousins – they mostly came from the same tribal grouping – had thrown the British out in 1967 after a violent quarrel over our attitude in the Middle East, and although tentative approaches about restoring our relations had been made from time to time through third parties, it seemed unlikely that we should get to the church door, let alone up the aisle, while I was *en poste*. The situation was a text-book example of twentieth century diplomacy at its most peevish. We felt we could no longer afford to maintain a full-scale Embassy in Brazzaville where our interests were minimal and that the task of representing Britain could as easily, and far more cheaply, be done from Kinshasa, less than a mile away on the opposite shore. This did not suit the Brazza Congolese at all. They held that it was a slight to their national dignity to be fobbed off with occasional visits from a Representative who, to make matters worse, lived and spent most of his time with the other, richer, altogether more powerful Congolese across the river of whom they were intensely jealous. They were convinced that such an official must have long since been recruited by their rivals as a kind of super-spy. That sort of second-best might be all right for smaller powers, but not in the case of the British, if only because no-one wished to be deprived of London as a juicy post to which deserving friends of the regime and cousins of the ruling family, who might otherwise be a nuisance, could be sent. In diplomacy, reciprocity is all; we were deadlocked. To complicate matters, we still owned a couple of Embassy houses in the town of Brazzaville, and with the uncertain communications it was difficult to be sure they were being properly looked after. I was, in fact, quite content to keep watch as best we could from across the river, having quite enough to do in Kinshasa and knowing that if the Brazza log-jam were to break and result in my being accredited over there, the Kinshasa Congolese would, in turn, become suspicious and touchy.

However, I could not avoid a degree of responsibility, for one day I received instructions from London to send the Embassy Administration Officer over the river to inspect and report on our property. This meant long, roundabout communications through the Power (the Swiss, I believe it was) who looked after our interests, as was normal in cases of ruptured relations. By the time that we had satisfied ourselves that the visit was acceptable to the Brazza Congolese and could take place without undue political, and perhaps even physical, risk, relations between the two Congos had deteriorated for some trivial and temporary reason to the point where no-one, not even diplomats on duty, unless actually accredited in both capitals, was allowed to cross the river in either direction. The trip would have to be circuitous to say the least, and involve a detour via several countries. After much research, we discovered that the quickest route, not by hours but by days, was to fly to Paris and back to Brazzaville! Nor would the overall expense be much greater than the protracted milk round on local airlines.

This tale is a sad commentary on the state of communications in Africa. To cross the continent by any means other than air was still a feat of adventure and endurance; even the available air transport was often primitive and unreliable. But our Kinshasa/Paris/Brazzaville route was indicative also of the still vertical nature of such communications as did exist, suggesting that in this respect, at any rate, the umbilical cord of colonialism had not yet been completely severed. The telephone also reflected this pattern; the recommended, indeed the only way of speaking from one African capital to another was via the former colonial capitals of Paris, London or Brussels. The power or powers that can make it possible for the Africans to establish genuine and effective lateral communications and who can finance and build the first railway or road from the Atlantic to the Indian Ocean will have contributed to a giant step forward in the development of Black Africa and written a page of history comparable, in

African terms, to that which records the driving in of the last, golden, spike in the trans-American railway system.

There were no accreditation problems in the case of Burundi. Although we had, until quite recently, maintained a resident Ambassador and a small staff at the capital, Bujumbura, the Burundis accepted without undue fuss the change of status to a non-resident representative. We retained the Embassy Residence and employed a full-time caretaker-cum-chauffeur. We also appointed a resident Honorary Consul, a post then traditionally the perk, or cross, however you look at it, of the manager of British Petroleum's operation in Burundi – a task, it may be said, always performed with diligence and skill. Our infrequent visits – I aimed at, and usually achieved, three a year – would have been impossibly difficult without this amateur but hard-working colleague. As it was, they always seemed to combine the amenities of a camping holiday with the drama of a staging post on the retreat from some great natural disaster. On arrival after a three-hour flight from Kinshasa by Air Congo jet, sometimes hours, and occasionally days late, we would be met by our faithful Consul and by Christophe, the chauffeur, with what passed for the Ambassadorial Rolls, a dilapidated but serviceable Land-Rover on which, nevertheless, the flag could be flown when needed. Our house was another bungalow much smaller and stuffier than our Kinshasa home, with a pokey little garden overshadowed by dusty trees. What little charm it had was dispelled by the need for it to serve also as an office. While we were there a constant stream of visitors, alerted to our arrival by the bush telegraph, would descend on us with problems ranging from difficulties over visas or British Government pensions to long-forgotten litigation over wills, taxation and death duties. When I was alone and had to cope with these unaided, it was difficult to find time for a meal, since the clients, as we called them, usually arrived before breakfast and camped out in the driveway until dealt with. Set hours of business were, of course, a theoretical possibility but in Africa every problem is *sui generis*, and everyone has a watertight case for special treatment, always as heartrending as a natural talent for the drama can make it.

The 'office' still possessed a safe, the combination number of which I was so nervous of losing that I wrote it down, strictly against the rules, in my pocket diary disguised as the telephone number of a fictitious girlfriend. In the safe were all manner of necessary forms, some smart, blue notepaper on which I wrote letters to confuse and amuse my friends, bank and accounts books, such liquor as had not been consumed on a previous visit (we had to bring all that, plus a good deal of what we ate with us from Kinshasa on each trip); and the Embassy silver, an incongruous collection of past splendour consisting of fake Georgian candlesticks, ashtrays, a cigarette box and other Ambassadorial impedimenta, all of which had to be cleaned, usually by Babs before each use. There was no-one much to entertain in Bujumbura, apart from the few resident Ambassadors. The American, French, Belgian and Soviet Governments were the only major powers who considered it in their interests to maintain Embassies, although it was difficult to detect any resulting benefit other than flattery and, perhaps, an extra post for an overcrowded service. There was a Papal Nuncio who divided his time between Burundi and the neighbouring Ruanda. He was one of the few non-Italian diplomats from the Vatican I had ever encountered, a spectacularly handsome Canadian bishop of great charm and ability who seemed type-cast for the lead in a successful TV serial. We did our best to entertain these in a manner to which they were accustomed, together with the few British residents of which the capital boasted. The Burundis themselves were shy and withdrawn, and did not often venture into European houses.

It was quite a strain attempting to behave as if I were a permanent resident, picking up the threads afresh on each visit and trying to convince people that I cared about the sad little issues which dominated their uneventful and limited horizons. Burundi at that time had sunk into a kind of torpor, characteristic of its tribally rigid society which later, however, erupted into a squalid and barbaric struggle for power. It was a desperately poor, severely overcrowded country, having the greatest density of population in the whole of Africa, and depending only on an inadequately-grown and inefficiently marketed coffee crop. It owed its economic survival to massive doses of aid and technical assistance from America and the European powers, much of which was given for genuinely humanitarian reasons, for Burundi has no known deposits of minerals, no agricultural potential, no real political significance other than its votes at the UN and in the OAU. I returned from each visit deeply depressed by the seemingly hopeless future of these poor people, barely able to keep afloat in the cross-currents of African development, and so pathetically anxious to enjoy the doubtful benefits of the twentieth century which someone had persuaded them was more civilised than its predecessors.

But, as always in Africa, there were contradictions and compensations. The country had an intimate, luminous beauty unlike anything I had seen elsewhere in the great plains and mountains of Central Africa. Amid its soft, green hills which looked oddly like English downland or Scottish moors – but a painting rather than a photograph of them – a simple, rural folk inhabited neat round huts in circular villages, their existence like a perpetual smiling afternoon, their livelihood a few acres of roots and some

144

drowsy cattle. We travelled a good deal in this tiny country, bumping over the rocky, rutted tracks which passed for main roads, with Christophe finding his way by ancestral instinct, since there were no reliable maps and if there had been he could not have read them. Our target on these expeditions, for which we set out equipped with rations, sleeping bags, extra petrol and spare parts, were the mission stations which, whether attracted by the density of population or an excessive paganism of the inhabitants, seemed to be present in greater numbers than elsewhere in Africa.

I have always had mixed feelings about the Missionary presence in Africa, and this first-hand experience did nothing to clear my mind. No-one can fail to be impressed by the courage of these dedicated Christians; by their faith and devotion to their cause; by the sheer goodness of many of them, toiling away in this lush wilderness to bring not only Christianity but health and practical knowledge to these half-forgotten people. And yet . . . something in me still recoils at the immodest assumption not only that Christianity provides the sole effective way of salvation, but that they have been personally chosen by God to jolly well prove it to the Blacks who couldn't be expected, poor dears, to find it out for themselves. The fact that marvellous, often heroic work is carried out in the process, hospitals and schools built and manned, standards of behaviour more acceptable to the majority of humanity inculcated; these are great and good benefits. But with them all too often goes a certain grimness, a joyless sense of duty and sacrifice, sometimes carried to extremes, especially in the more Protestant missions. Babs and I both drank and smoked in moderation; but we soon learned that if we were not to be faced with a choice between total abstinence and offence to our disapproving hosts, our travelling kit must include not only small quantities of liquor, but paper cups in which to drink it and peppermints to avoid subsequent detection. The trick of puffing smoke up a chimney, so necessary for Victorian Cabinet Ministers staying at Windsor or Balmoral, also came in handy when our bedroom happened to contain such a luxury; otherwise a long solitary walk was the price for a drag at the foul weed. The sanitary arrangements in some of the stations were such that even a modest house-holder in the Middle Ages would have felt obliged to apologise for them.

At the risk of sounding sectarian, I am bound to say that Roman Catholic Missions did not display the same devotion to austerity and joy-through-squalor; on our occasional visits to them – the majority of British Missionaries belonged to Protestant denominations – quite appetising food and wine was served without any detectable whiff of brimstone, and I never found evidence that the resultant Christianity was less effective than its Protestant counterpart. In truth, the Christian doctrines of original sin, sacrifice and redemption are difficult for the African to accept, although he likes the ideas of the virgin birth and the resurrection. But all too often the witch doctor reasserts his magic and the profession of faith becomes merely a passport to the school or infirmary. The fact that Missionaries continue to devote their lives to Africa in the face of what must be frequent and dreadful disappointments increases the respect in which they must be held by all civilised people; and the probability that an alien religious faith is not the only way to bring the civilising benefits of medicine and education to an apathetic Africa is no reason not to applaud those who do so; or to assume that, somehow or other, those remote and beautiful hills would necessarily have benefitted equally without the inspiration of the Christian Gospel.

* * * * * * * * *

In 1970 the Congolese organised for the first time an International Trade Fair. Needless to say, I and the Commercial Staff made a great nuisance of ourselves trying to persuade HMG to participate, if only on a scale comparable to Switzerland and the Ivory Coast who, together with most other nations' representatives in Kinshasa, had decided to take space. Once again I was destined to be orphaned by the claims of similar projects in Nairobi or Luxembourg, a sense of priority which we found baffling but apparently immutable. Two British firms, however, both strongly engaged in the Congolese economy, decided to go it alone and finance jointly a small stand, so there was at least a basis for flying the British flag. I set about my usual task of trying to make silk purses and argued vigorously for a VIP visitor to dress up the stand, so to speak, and to preside at our National Day, a somewhat ill-defined event which each participating nation was expected to celebrate. With a rare insight amounting almost to genius, someone in London hit upon exactly the right person; the Lord Mayor of a Midland manufacturing city who promised to come, complete with Lady Mayoress, robes and Mayoral chains, the latter being equipment on which I had insisted in the lengthy correspondence with His Worship preceding the visit. The Congolese had never received a Municipal visit as such, and the Governor of Kinshasa who, by protocol, was to be the host rather than the central Government, took a great deal of time and trouble studying the form for such occasions. What should he wear? How should he address his guest? Clothes presented little problem, since he had a uniform. But nomenclature was more difficult. Prefect, the literal translation of his own continental title, *Préfet*, was misleading since the two functions were not

146

comparable and to us the anglicised version smacked uncomfortably of the British Public School. So we settled for '*Le Lord Maire*' which inevitably became shortened to '*Le Lord*'. In spite of its Old Testament ring, it was near and grand enough we thought. My friend Mr Kallimazi was also very active in the planning, for although it was not strictly his affair, he could not resist the opportunity presented by this novel kind of visit to add to his colourful and wide knowledge of the ceremonial ways of the world.

The Lord Mayor and party duly arrived at eight o'clock on the appointed morning. He stepped from the plane wearing not only his chain, eagerly anticipated by Mr Kallimazi, but also morning coat, gloves and top hat. Behind him came his Lady Mayoress also be-chained and be-gloved, and wearing a flowered hat worthy of Ascot. I was greatly touched by the trouble they had taken, for they must have changed into their finery at a very early hour in the plane, unless they had left London in full rig the night before, which I could hardly believe. These two beaming but incongruous figures descended to be greeted by the Governor, in full uniform and, of course, by Mr Kallimazi who had found some excuse to muscle in on the proceedings much to the annoyance of the Governor who, like Municipal Authorities the world over, was prone to nasal dislocation. Greetings and small-talk were exchanged as we walked across the concrete apron, preceded by TV cameramen and photographers. I had to act as interpreter since the Governor spoke no English and the Lord Mayor no French. Sure enough this being Kinshasa, the curtain was about to rise on yet another local drama.

On my arrival at the airport at about half-past seven that morning, I had seen a large number of Congolese standing on the tarmac immediately in front of the VIP suite. They were members of a Christian sect known as Kimbanguists, a name derived from the fact that they believed the Word of God to have been uniquely revealed to one Simon Kimbangui whose mantle, on death, had descended on his nephew, now known as the Holy One and Prophet. I liked the Kimbanguists. They were sincere and humble people, rigid abstainers and determined champions of the deprived; moreover, they possessed one of the best brass bands in the Congo and belted out their versions of familiar hymn tunes with irresistible rhythmic force. This band was even now on parade and warming up against the arrival of the Holy One and Prophet who, I quickly established, was travelling on the same plane as the unsuspecting Lord Mayor.

As we made our way towards the VIP room, the band struck up and the Kimbanguists burst into song, dancing with that marvellous stationary step of which only Africans know the secret, and waving brightly coloured kerchiefs. It was indeed an inspiring sight, and the Lord Mayor was obviously impressed. 'Very kind, I must say,' he remarked as one well used to civic welcomes, although not perhaps of such intensity. It was now too late for explanations, which I was, in any case, unwilling to give in English in front of our hosts; and although I dared not look behind me, it was plain from the Kimbanguist crescendo that the Holy One and Prophet was close on our tail. The Lord Mayor and the Governor sailed on, each unaware, for reasons a continent apart, that anything unusual was taking place. The Kimbanguists separated, leaving a path through their ranks to the VIP room but, at the same time, falling to their knees, no doubt in anticipation of the passing of their spiritual leader. This almost stopped the Lord Mayor in his tracks.

'That's most kind, most hospitable indeed.' He beamed a municipal smile at the Governor. 'Should I acknowledge?' Fortunately, I had by this time a firm grip on the Mayoral elbow and hurried him into the VIP lounge, hissing out of the corner of mouth – 'will explain later'. It was indeed much later, after many ceremonies in the lounge, including the presentation of the Lord Mayor to the Holy One and Prophet, when we were on our way to my house, that I was at last able to give my guest a coherent explanation of the scenes at the airport. 'I thought t'were a bit excessive', he said with a chuckle.

His visit was a huge success, due to his practical, no-nonsense attitude and his patience and good nature in performing every task which the programme demanded. It is asking a lot of an Alderman to travel to Central Africa carrying with him the trappings and rituals of medieval England and behave as if he did it every day. The British businessman is often criticised for inflexible insularity; I could myself cite some cases to prove that. But our Lord Mayor's visit was the obverse of that coin, showing how the imperturbable temperament can rapidly adjust, like an automatic camera, to the most extreme variations of light, temperature and custom. The programme for our National Day was a heavy one, especially for the Lord Mayor who had gallantly agreed to wear his full ceremonial robes throughout the day, beginning with a morning call on the Governor at the City Hall at half past nine. Mr Kallimazi had excused himself on the grounds that some Presidential occasion required his guiding hand.

I was somewhat surprised, therefore, when he turned up at my house a little after nine o'clock. 'Just passing,' he said breathlessly, 'wanted to be sure everything was all right.' I offered him a cup of coffee, which he accepted with alacrity. Then, as he looked around, his face fell with disappointment. 'But where is the Lord?' he asked with a touch of petulance. I realised at once that what he had really come for was a close-up view of the full Mayoral splendour which was, even then, being assumed in the spare room with the assistance, no doubt, of the Lady Mayoress, Babs, the Little One, the Archbishop, and any other helpers available. The Elder Statesman was sent off to announce Mr Kallimazi's presence, and shortly after the Lord Mayor made his entrance; flowing robes of beaver-trimmed red velvet, buckle shoes, lace jabot, a huge chain, gloves and a black tricorn hat with feathers. A truly magnificent sight which, when viewed against the lush tropical garden and the majestic, jungle-born river, had more than a touch of the surrealist about it.

Mr Kallimazi was stunned. After several moments' silent admiration, he spread out his hands palm upwards and said 'Ah!' – a long, drawn out expression which needs no translation. A short conversation followed, during which I explained to Mr Kallimazi that the Lord's costume dated from the fifteenth century. 'Really?' said Mr Kallimazi, and stretched across with finger and thumb to feel the texture of this excellently preserved material. It was getting too hot to put right this and other little misunderstandings. Mr. Kallimazi took his leave, well satisfied with his private view. The Lord and I, riding in an open car with police escort, drove off to the City Hall. I had put on a morning coat in deference to the occasion, and we were already drenched in perspiration. As we drove along the crowded streets, I was startled to observe nervous groups of Africans on street corners turn away from our cortège as it passed and make the sign customarily used to ward off the evil eye. It was only some days later that I was enlightened by one of my staff who discovered that the cause of this departure from the normal gay Congolese welcome was the presence of black feathers in the Lord Mayor's hat, an infallible sign of the sorcerer. No-one takes risks like that in Africa. There were, however, no repercussions, natural or supernatural, and the visit came to a successful, if humid end with a banquet in my garden to which, after many conflicting and confusing indications, the Governor himself came. I shall always be grateful to the Lord and Lady Mayoress, who blazed a trail and performed a service which notched my Congo (as I was now beginning to think of it) a peg or two higher in the Establishment mind.

The International Fair had attracted its quota of prophecies of doom before it opened; but in the event it was a triumph for which much credit must be given to the organisers. It was well run, attracted visitors from all over Africa and even further afield, and provided a framework for those ceremonies so beloved by the Congolese and so necessary to their incipient nationhood. Mobutu went there frequently; each National Day was presided over by a Minister, many of them by Bomboko himself, whose impromptu speeches of welcome were prime examples of his virtuosity. It was a bold thing for them to have undertaken, and not surprisingly they decided to repeat it the following year. Much to my relief, London reluctantly agreed to participate, encouraged no doubt by tales from returning travellers such as the Lord Mayor, and perhaps also at long last believing that my arguments were slightly more respectable than the special pleading common to all proud parents.

Nevertheless, official support and encouragement did not go much further, and the British presence was noticeably less extensive and elaborate than those of our commercial rivals. In one respect, however, we attempted to cut a dash: the British stand was to include a British Pub, a touching example of the belief that this institution, together with the red double-decker bus, the Beefeater and the London Bobby are universally recognised symbols of British culture without which no overseas manifestation can be complete. These cherished illustrations of the British Way of Life were, in fact, quite difficult to explain in French to West Africans; in the event, Beefeaters, buses and Bobbies were either considered unsuitable, or were not available, so we were fortunately only called upon to explain the pub.

However, the project took on a new dimension when I was told that Prince William of Gloucester had agreed to visit the Fair and to preside over our National Day; indeed a visit lasting nearly a week was proposed. Although I had been pressing hard for a visitor at least as grand as the Lord Mayor, a Royal Prince was beyond anything I had hoped for, and when I told the Congolese they were delighted. Their love-hate relationship with their former colonists included respect and affection for the Belgian Royal Family personally, but they had no view of the Monarchical principle in general, and no member of any other Royal Family had ever visited them. My stock was therefore high as we plunged into the intricate and meticulous planning which always precedes a royal visit. We soon found that we were boxed in by dates which were extremely awkward but interrelated in such a way as to be unchangeable. We were reaching the end of my mission, and I had to leave Kinshasa by a certain date in July in order, as my last act, to attend a Conference of all African Heads of Mission in London which I was anxious not to miss. But this departure schedule coincided with the dates on which Prince William's visit had to take place to fit in with the timetable of the Fair, a collision course which would entail not only packing up our house (after two and a half years' occupancy) during a royal visit, but with the visitor actually staying with us. I expected Babs, for once, to revolt, but after several deep breaths and some uncomplimentary remarks about the way things were being run, and my incompetence in allowing us to be manoeuvred into such a position, she agreed. Planning went smoothly, with occasional misunderstandings. A last minute suggestion that Sunday's programme looked a little thin – perhaps HRH could have a picnic and a swim in the river? – had to be countered by a telegram pointing out that seven Europeans, including a West German diplomat, had been killed and eaten by crocodiles in the last year, and that I advised against the swim, although we were trying to organise a boat trip if the necessary support craft was available. The programme was at last complete – not the usual document with timings to the minute, since Congolese habits of imprecision had been explained to Kensington Palace and accepted; but a serviceable indication of what we hoped would happen, how and when.

The party arrived in good order on July 7th and there were no scenes comparable to those which had greeted the Lord Mayor. With Prince William was his Equerry, Lt Col Simon Bland, who had become an understanding friend during the planning stages; Inspector Mackintyre, one of those self-effacing policemen who accompany members of the Royal family everywhere and who, chameleon-like, fade into the background but are ever present and alert; and Sir John Colville, representing British business, who was a great asset having himself been both a diplomat and courtier, thus bringing long experience of more important occasions to our modest, but unusual, enterprise. We arrived at the Residence to be greeted by a whole platoon of Congolese soldiery drawn up in our garden which the Congolese, in a paroxysm of combined protocol and precaution, had provided for the protection of my Royal guest. They let off a deafening, and I thought rather dangerous, salute and the Elder Statesman hauled up the Prince's personal Standard which flew proudly over the house during the visit. Thereafter, the guard was not much in evidence except at meal times – they were fed, naturally, at our expense – but the fact that someone had even thought of them was vaguely comforting. We gave Prince William our own bedroom, with Simon in the dressing room next door; Jock Colville stayed with Ham and Sheila Whyte and the Inspector with the Embassy Administration Officer, who happened to live very near us. Babs and I moved into the other guest rooms and settled down to our last week, one of the most frantic that I can remember.

Besides the official Congolese programme of which the National Day at the Fair was the centrepiece, we had laid on a number of less formal engagements; an all-day visit to a Salvation Army outpost in the bush; the famous non-swimming trip on the river; and other diversions of which the most colourful was a visit to a Kinshasa nightclub. The band in this rather dubious haunt consisted of a group of young Congolese who had been rescued from petty crime and trained to use their natural musical talent by an enterprising and gifted young Englishman who ran the English

Language Centre. They were, of course, beside themselves with excitement and composed a special song in honour of HRH, which went on for a long time, calypso-like, extolling his virtues, with a refrain which sounded something like '*Prinz Villyahm de Glewsester*'.

I had secured permission to hold the Queen's birthday party during HRH's visit rather than on the official date in June. The presence of the Queen's cousin seemed so obvious a reason for changing the date that I could not understand the heavy weather made about it in London, where it was agreed only with the greatest reluctance and severely worded warnings that it was not to be regarded as a precedent. Nevertheless, this gigantic operation, at which we entertained over five hundred people, had to be superimposed on the full operation of a Royal visit and the preparations for our own departure. It was only with the devoted help of all our colleagues and their wives, for whom admittedly the excitement was a welcome change from the daily routine, that we got through it all.

Queen's Birthday Parties abroad are normally rather dull affairs. I had established a tradition of enlivening the proceedings by the introduction of some special happening. For the previous year I had discovered that the Elder Statesman, after twenty-five years service to the same employer, was entitled to a Congolese medal. I persuaded the retired Congolese General who acted in a capacity roughly equivalent to Garter King of Arms, to present the medal during the Queen's Birthday Party. Despite frantic appeals by the General's staff that no-one, least of all the great man himself (on grounds of propriety) should have a drink before the ceremony took place, liquor was flowing freely by the time the good General arrived, late and drunk. He was hardly able to stand when the time came for the ceremony, having eluded all attempts to keep him from the bar. The Elder Statesman, barely five feet in height, stood before his swaying compatriot who, after a couple of outers, managed to hit the bull's eye, causing the Elder Statesman to wince as the pin of the ribbon penetrated his uniform, his vest and finally his skin. Madame Elder Statesman, reluctantly present but consumed with secret pride, watched from a corner of the veranda while she suckled the latest in a long line of Younger Statesmen.

We had now reached the final hours, normally a time of measured preparations for departure, reflections on the past, formal and informal farewells to colleagues and friends. I had little time for such luxuries, many of which I had, in any case, cleared out of the way before Prince William's arrival. Babs and I had attended the customary farewell meeting of the Diplomatic Corps, at which the Nuncio, as Dean, had extolled our virtues and deplored our leaving in terms which differed little from those he habitually employed for all at whose similar departures I myself had been present; I replied on behalf of us both, after which he handed over a suitably engraved silver salver, a handsome article for which we have still not found an appropriate use. I had written my valedictory despatch - a mandatory document in which one tries not to grumble about real or imagined shortcomings in the attitude of one's superiors in London, to emphasise how valuable the experience has been and how important the post, and to drop a few hints for one's successor whom one is privately convinced will be a disaster. I took Prince William to call on Mobutu, as protocol demanded. I had not expected this to be more than a brief, formal exchange of compliments and gifts – there was no reason why it should. But it turned out to be a lively and friendly meeting which lasted nearly an hour. Prince William had served in an African post when he was, for a short while, a member of the Diplomatic Service; he knew and liked Africans, a fact which always communicates itself across any number of cultural and linguistic barriers. He and Mobutu got on famously, although I was exhausted with the extra burden of interpretation, Mobutu apparently preferring the meeting to take place *à trois*. The President was obviously not satisfied with the gift selected for him to give to Prince William and so sent off his ADC, who returned with an extra one, a handsome book about African Art which he inscribed in warm terms. Mobutu's comment after it was all over, relayed to me by a close member of his staff, is worth recording. 'That's a very nice young man,' he is reported to have observed, 'so intelligent, so relaxed, but at the same time, he is every inch a Prince; and he likes us. But tell me one thing, isn't he rather young to be a member of the Royal Family?'

Our last day dawned in an atmosphere of brooding chaos. The packers had already been working surreptitiously for two days. Babs had devised a plan rivalling Overlord in complexity, to ensure that as far as possible our guests should not notice anything unusual. Occasionally, HRH found a picture missing in his bedroom, and was once asked by Babs to get off a certain chair as it had to be preloaded. By what miracle our clothes and personal things got packed I shall never know. That last morning I went off alone for my final meeting with Mobutu. He was charming and, thanking me for what I had done, gave me the same book as he had given to Prince William, and a signed photograph of the two of us together. We joked about old times and, a little gingerly, about the disagreements which had been forced on us by politics. I then told him that I, in turn, had a present for him. 'Really? How kind,' he said, looking round hopefully. I explained that I had not brought it with me because it was an aeroplane. With a sense of timing which made me feel guilty about my past strictures, London had finally agreed to a proposal I had long been urging; the provision of a light aircraft for the medical services which Mobutu was trying to build up in the outlying districts along the River, and for which he had already built an impressive hospital boat. This little Islander was just what was needed, and would arrive, I told Mobutu, within the month, equipped as an ambulance. I hoped, of course, that its presence would stimulate further sales; but as a piece of aid, it was well timed and genuinely useful. Mobutu was delighted, and as we parted he introduced a final complication into my carefully organised programme.

'Since you are leaving tonight,' he said, 'and will have to pack' – no French word or phrase could be adequate for what was actually going on at my house, but he was not to know that; the thought was kind enough – 'I have arranged for the ceremony to take place at five o'clock this evening.'

Fortunately I had my man-of-the-world-nothing-could-be-more-natural-I-do-this-every-day expression ready on my face as I replied, 'How very thoughtful, Mr President. May I enquire the precise purpose of the ceremony?'

'Why, to give you your decoration, of course,' said Mobutu, 'I have asked the General to perform the ceremony in my name.'

I quailed at the thought of being punctured, like the Elder Statesman, by our unsteady friend the General, but since Mobutu seemed to treat this as a matter of course, I thought I had better do so too. My dilemma was the existence of a rigid rule that servants of the Crown are not permitted to accept foreign decorations without prior permission, which is hardly ever given except for acts of gallantry and on the occasion of a State visit by the Sovereign. 'My dog shall wear no collar but mine own', as Queen Elizabeth I's words put the matter in a nutshell, and thus it has always remained. Nevertheless, I did not hesitate for one second. The prospect of trying to explain the intricacies of British protocol to Mobutu at this stage in our last meeting was grotesque enough; but the idea of appearing to hesitate about receiving so important a distinction, offered personally by an African Head of State was unthinkable. So without so much as a backward glance at the Lord Chamberlain, the Central Chancery of Knighthoods, not to mention the awesome Garter King of Arms, and mentally preparing myself for a sojourn in the Tower at Her Majesty's pleasure, I told Mobutu I was honoured and touched at this signal favour, and would be on parade at five o'clock. We said goodbye and for the last time I received the powder blue and red salute as I drove through the gates, thinking not of my final talk with Mobutu or of the many which had preceded it, but whether I had time to telephone London and at least tell them about my impending elevation to the rank of Commander of the Order of the Leopard (Second Class). I decided that to do so would be undignified, even if I managed to get through, which was doubtful, Babs having handed out positively the last box of chocolates to our old friend the international operator the day before.

Not surprisingly, I found that Prince William not only fully agreed with my intention to receive the decoration, but offered to come with me to the ceremony, a generous, not to say sporting, offer which I accepted with alacrity. Together we set forth, the Queen's cousin and Her Representative, and stood side by side while the General, whose aim this time was worthy of Bisley, put the blue and red ribbon round my neck and the band played the National Anthems, their version of *God Save the Queen* not having noticeably improved since their first performance.

I reported this episode to Whitehall, making full use of Prince William's presence as a mitigating factor, and believing that it would one day be of minor historic interest. The reply, when it caught up with me, was a masterpiece of Foreign Office brevity.

'Dear Paul, Your letter of . . . All right, but don't let me catch you wearing it. Yours ever . . .'

The end was fast approaching. By some trick, the Elder Statesman and Pierre served up a meal that did final justice to their regard for Le Patron and his royal guest. Just before this, Prince William asked to see Babs and me alone, and thanked us with great warmth, giving us a signed photograph and, to me, a pair of gold cuff-links engraved with his personal monogram. He also received my friend the Indian Ambassador, a former Rajah of a small State and an Indian Cricket Cap, who had laid on a splendid party for HRH, combining the best food and entertainment, and giving a hint of where his affections, if not his professional loyalties lay.

The convoy of cars and vans arrived to take us all to the airport. We hunted through drawers and cupboards knowing that we must have left things behind. The Congolese guard turned up out of the night to give a final salute. Even the Sentinel shuffled round so as not to be left out. The Elder Statesman and his team gathered by the front door. The air was heavy with sadness, for our faithful household were not coming to the airport to say goodbye, since the house had to be tidied and locked up after our final whirlwind packing. We embraced in the warm African way, enough of the British having rubbed off on Sebastien to allow him to show his embarrassment. We did not try to hide our sorrow. We owed them so much, and there was so little we could do for them in return. They had now to face the slow, painful process of getting to know a new Ambassadorial family. But Sebastien was wearing his medal, as if to underline his feelings, and he sensibly broke the tension by going to stand by the flag pole in order to lower my flag – (the Royal Standard had had to be replaced at the packing stage) – for the last time. A final, furtive look at our home, and we were off, the rising dust behind us luminous with memories, redolent with things done and left undone, each speck an hour of grinding work or hard-earned play, of happiness and doubt, hope and despair. We were too tired to think except about the superficial details of the journey ahead.

We found virtually the whole Embassy at the airport, together with a number of Congolese many of whom, including my old friend Mr Kallimazi, had come out of friendship rather than for any official reason. We tried to maintain some sense of order, but for once even Mr Kallimazi's august presence failed to inhibit the spontaneous warmth of this im-promptu farewell scene. It was as much a tribute to Prince William, after his short visit, as to Babs and me at the end of our long mission. He had that rare gift of commanding respect and affection simultaneously, and we were lucky that our last days had been illuminated by his presence. We were still in the middle of our goodbyes when a minor panic hit the Sabena Airline's officials and we were hustled towards the doors of the VIP room. Prince William waved while I screwed up my face in an effort not to weep – how much energy our compatriots spend in trying not to cry in public when in reality, as Churchill proved, the world loves the tears of an Englishman!

We were hustled aboard and airborne almost before we could fasten our safety belts. I never discovered what the hurry was, but it certainly helped our parting from so many dear friends, and no doubt dispersed the emotional head of steam that had been building up inside. I sat in a daze while the doors were closed, we rolled down the runway and were quickly swallowed up in the low cloud which hung over the airport like a visible anaesthetic, blotting out the past and future. When the time came to sleep I realised that I had allowed Babs to pack my pills in her bag. She was already slumped across my shoulder, dead to the world; a Royal lump of blankets opposite indicated that Prince William had lost no time in settling down; of the others there was no sign or sound. I had not the heart or nerve to disturb any of them and so, in trying to compose myself to sleep without the aid of modern science, fell into the trap of attempting to assess the '*bilan*' of my mission.

It was an exercise that called for a degree of mental clarity and objectivity which, in my present state, I was most unlikely to achieve. Even on the personal level, instant history is one of the banes of the twentieth century. If the picture I saw that night as we sped northwards was blurred, I had only myself to blame. Nevertheless, there did emerge a sense, not exactly of success but of not having failed. Nothing dramatic had happened, although I suppose there was a secret corner of my mind which had hoped it might. But the Congolese had been helped to edge a little nearer an understanding of the limitations of British policy towards Black Africa; the British Government had, in turn, moved the Congo up a peg or two on its priority board. Our Aid Programme had been enlarged; investment had increased, and one large contract for railway reconstruction and re-equipment had been won under the noses of the Japanese who were bidding with all they had – a fine example of eighteen months' determined and relentless work by the company concerned; an English Language Centre had been established, and the Congolese were asking for more; useful visits had been exchanged in both directions; the few political clouds on the horizon had not grown bigger, and in one or two cases had been dispersed; all in all, nothing to boast about perhaps, but by no means a debit balance.

On the personal plane, I was already conscious of a double debt which I would always owe to Africa; first, the experience of living and working there had enriched my mind and spirit; second, in Kinshasa I had overcome the doubts and hesitations with which I had taken up this first Ambassadorial post. The experience had been highly specialised and I would not repeat it. But I was no longer an amateur and, like an actor after his first season of repertory, felt that I could tackle whatever future role might be demanded of me with a degree of professionalism which I could not have imagined two and a half years before.

I suppose I must have dozed between the phases of this silent soliloquy, because in a surprisingly short time we were preparing to land in Brussels. One of the many awkwardnesses about Kinshasa was that there was no direct flight to London, thus imposing a change of plane at a European capital. On this occasion, Prince William had been kind enough to invite us to travel on to London with him in an aircraft of the Queen's Flight, which had been sent to meet him. When we taxied in from the runway, it was standing close by – a bright red, twin-engined plane looking comfortable and slightly old fashioned, like a Royal car. Our luggage was transferred with amazing speed and we were soon heading for Heathrow. I had refrained from eating the not very appetising meal offered us on the Sabena plane, in the confident expectation that a Royal breakfast awaited us; I had visions of scrambled eggs, kidneys, lamb chops, who knows, perhaps a pint of claret. But the reality was a good deal less appetising – excellent coffee and biscuits but that was all. However, this marvellous organisation, to which the Royal Family and hence the country owes so much, deposited

157

us swiftly and courteously at Heathrow. If there was a Customs Officer lurking in the VIP suite, I did not see him, and one battle in the war of attrition between our two Services was postponed so that we could fight another day. The ladies in the Heads of Mission Section had, as usual, got everything buttoned up and a Foreign Office car was waiting to take us into London. We said goodbye to Prince William, who sped off, driving his own station wagon. I could not find the right words to thank him; it was still too early in the morning for all of us, and I vowed that I would do justice to him and his visit in the official account which I would still have to write. We said goodbye to the others and were soon part of the great throng of commuters which pours into the city every morning. I paused briefly at our flat to spruce up, and by eleven o'clock was in Downing Street with all the other Heads of African Missions.

Fatigue can dull the wits, but it can also sharpen them. I was very tired as I sat in the large Foreign Office conference room which smelt of old files and furniture polish, listening to my colleagues argue about the future of Africa and the role Britain should or could play; but I was alive to every nuance and fully aware of the passage of each moment, knowing that the African sands were running out for me, and that I would have to turn my back on that dark continent of dreams. It was here that my real farewell had to be said, rather than at the airport the night before. I had not faced, then, the near certainty that I should never again work in Africa, at any rate not as a Head of Mission, let alone the possibility that I might never return even as a tourist. Such relief as I felt at having no longer any responsibility for the conduct of affairs and the welfare of the staff in the unpredictable and alien atmosphere of Kinshasa was drowned in a great wave of nostalgia for the life I had left behind.

Just as realism and sentiment compete at the end of a love affair, so I recognised that I would not really relish having to do it all again, while at the same time being thankful that I had done it, and wishing it were not all over. When my turn came to speak I excused myself on grounds of fatigue and went off to lunch at my Club. There, my friends greeted me as if returning after a short summer holiday, and asked polite questions about my future plans until their immediate interests and concerns took over and I was suddenly a thousand miles and a million years from Africa. By the afternoon session of the Conference, I was sufficiently recovered to make what I was afterwards told was a sensible, balanced statement about the Congo and how I saw it fitting in with our African policy. Soon the past was fading so quickly before my fickle eyes that it was an effort to conjure up the sounds and smells which I had thought I could never forget. Thus it is for the diplomat, whose Casanova-like profession compels him to weep afresh at each parting while his heart races at the prospect of a new and ravishing conquest.

CHAPTER NINE

We had not expected to stay in Kinshasa more than the usual maximum of three years for posts of that kind; the question of our next and probably final appointment accordingly became active several months before we actually left. When I had been in London earlier in the year, the Personnel Department had told me, with their usual air of awarding a prize (Has done very well this term, grammar much improved) that they hoped to send us back to New York this time as Consul-General. Their assumption that this was exactly what we wanted was only partly true. From the banks of the Congo, the Hudson looked particularly inviting and the familiar, rich razzamatazz of New York life appeared, mirage-like, to have everything that Kinshasa lacked. Babs would have certainly welcomed another four years or so of life so close to her family, now depleted by the death of her mother. But the New York Consulate-General, although the largest and most important post of its kind in the world, is not a Mission in the same sense as an Embassy and the Consul-General has not the same degree of independence as an Ambassador. The post had become more and more commercial and had acquired a vast and, to my mind, unnecessary substructure to assist British exports to North America. I did not relish this and imagined that our life would contrast unfavourably with our previous New York existence.

A more secret hesitation was that the post carried the same rank as Kinshasa, whereas I had begun to hope for promotion. The urge for advancement in any profession springs from different sources in different people; the craving for success and the need to win; the proving of oneself, privately or to the world; the cocking of a snook at some disliked contemporary; power and the need to be at the centre; better pay, and hence a better pension. In my case, this last factor had begun to play an important part in my private career planning as the months and years sped on towards my inevitable retirement. Morever, I still had that uncomfortable urge to cut a dash, to participate centrally in major decisions, to be in the know.

160

Accordingly I indicated that we would, of course, be happy to return to New York, but did so with a lack of enthusiasm which I hoped would be noticed. We then settled down to await developments, nervously aware that any alternative to New York might well be worse rather than better. In conformity with the practice – amounting to something akin to filling in the football pools – adopted by all members of the Service, I had been doing my own calculations, poring over the lists and trying to work out which of those posts likely to be within my reach would naturally become vacant at about the right time. There was, as I gloomily told Babs, nothing much going unless we were to hang on in Kinshasa longer than we expected or wished. Then a peremptory note arrived shortly after I had returned from London, saying that the New York job had fallen through; no hint of explanation, still less of an alternative. I remained limp, the wisest posture in such circumstances, not even asking whether, in any case, a term had been set on our Kinshasa duty so that we could plan a little for the immediate future. I have never discovered the real reasons for this change of direction by the Office. Perhaps the Department of Trade, who had an increasing amount of clout in appointments of this kind, had decided that I did not possess, on paper at any rate, sufficient commercial experience; perhaps the Ambassador (by then Lord Cromer) had been warned about me by his predecessor, Sir Patrick Dean, who, although personally friendly, had probably disapproved of my methods and of the level at which I had operated in New York when Head of BIS.

I was half disappointed, half relieved. I felt that I could have done the job quite well and brought to it a knowledge of New York and the USA which, combined with Babs' native expertise, was probably unequalled at that time at my level in the Service. And although I disapproved of the current emphasis on commercial work, it challenged and intrigued me and I would have liked the opportunity of putting to the test my theories as to how the Service ought to respond to its new role. On the other hand I was glad not to be going back to old, well-chewed up pastures and to maintain for a little longer the doubtful pleasure of speculation and the dangerous joys of wishful thinking. Babs took all this with her usual philosophical optimism being convinced, after an initial disappointment, that all would be for the best.

I was not able immediately to share my thoughts with her for she had stayed behind in London for an extra week or two of leave and family business. Thus it was that for the second time she was absent when the real news came through. It arrived by telegram marked 'D-YOU', a particularly irritating form of communication which was encyphered by hand in a special code used only for matters of extreme sensitivity, usually personnel questions, and had to be laboriously unpicked by the Head of Mission himself. I never completely mastered this technique, since it involved juggling with random sets of figures quite beyond my limited mathematical powers; the results were looked up in a special book which gave a word or a phrase against each of a series of numbers. A single error could reduce whole sentences to gibberish, or produce alternative meanings either comic or, occasionally, obscene in their context. An hour's tongue-biting labour at the end of a hot morning eventually produced the unmistakeable message, marred only by a few corrupt groups (as the mistakes were engagingly called), which did not materially affect the sense, that we were to go to Beirut, to leave Kinshasa in July and take up our new duties at the end of October.

I was flabbergasted. The possibility of Beirut had not occurred to me, since the incumbent had only been there about a year. I subsequently learned that he had been unwell almost since arrival and had decided to retire. My first thought was, of course, to get the news to Babs before she left London so that, in spite of the usual obsessive secrecy, she could take advantage of it for any discreet preparations which might save time and trouble later. In any case, she was equally anxious to learn our fate and would not have taken kindly to being told only on her return to Africa. I could, I suppose, have simply told her to telephone someone in the Office who would probably have spilled the beans. But that seemed too easy. Besides we both had developed a horror of wives who tried to take too overt or active a part in their husband's careers. We had heard grisly stories of sobbing ladies being assured by Personnel Department that their husbands were, really and truly, thoroughly understood and appreciated, the fact of their still not having risen above the rank of First Secretary being due entirely to circumstances beyond anyone's control; or of irate and formidable would-be Dowagers demanding to know why their spouse's name had not appeared in the last two Honours Lists. So I sent her a message containing a private code which I knew she would understand. It read, 'We are on the move. You can now start looking for the Bishop's teeth.'

The origins of this cryptic instruction lay in a visit which we had paid to Beirut in 1960 whilst based in Cairo. The Ambassador, an old friend, Moore Crosthwaite, took pity on us when told that we needed a short break from the oppressive Cairo atmosphere. We occupied his principal spare room, little dreaming that it would one day be ours. When unpacking, Babs found in one of the drawers a set of dentures. I can imagine circumstances in which this might have proved a somewhat delicate fact with which to acquaint one's host; some might have been tempted to leave it to a future guest. But I felt certain that Moore would appreciate the joke – which he did. Being a bachelor he was always a little vague about the domestic arrangements of the embassies over which he presided (he was subsequently Ambassador in Stockholm). It took some time, and a call to his Social Secretary, to establish that the last guest to occupy that room had been an Anglican Bishop. This intelligence caused great merriment and a happy evening was spent drafting possible letters to the Episcopal Palace. 'I write to enquire whether the Bishop has recently experienced any noticeable difficulty at meal times? If so, may I respectfully point out . . .' – 'In respect of the Bishop's recent and most interesting sermon on the text ". . . *and there shall be wailing and gnashing of teeth*", it may be relevant to draw your attention to the fact that. . . .' An enjoyable parlour game for which the circumstances are unlikely, I fear, to recur.

★ ★ ★

Autumnal London was at its loveliest as I plodded round the familiar paths of pre-posting briefing; Ministers, Departments, Banks and businesses. Alec Douglas-Home, then Foreign Secretary, gave up half an hour of his time to tell me, in his urbane and deeply courteous manner, of his anxiety lest the precarious stability in the Lebanon should be disturbed with consequent repercussions through the area; a presentiment which, like so many of Sir Alec's, turned out to be all too justified. We lunched with Prince William and had, for once, enough time to renew old friendships and to spend time with our children and grandchildren.

I was delighted with this posting. I had always liked the idea of Beirut. Apart from the dental episode, I had been there on several other occasions for periods of about a week and had greatly enjoyed my visits. For years Beirut had served as a regional centre for our Information Services and for Development Aid. When in charge of the Information Policy Department of the Foreign Office in the late fifties, I had presided jointly with Philip Adams over a conference of Information Officers from a number of our Embassies in the Arab world and Beirut tended to be the beginning or end of my journeys to other parts of the region. So I knew the city superficially and had always rather envied the Head of Mission there – it was an absorbingly interesting, highly political post; a beautiful house; a lovely country with charming and civilised people; what more could one ask for?

Once again I was able to speculate on the disproportionate role which luck continued to play in my destinies. The odds against my predecessor becoming ill and deciding to quit coinciding exactly with my unplanned availability were obviously considerable. But there it was; I was bound once more for the Middle East, to play a part in the continuing tragi-comedy of Britain's relations with the Arabs.

The Middle East has always seemed to me to be like shot-silk or multi-coloured taffeta; the component colours appear to change as your angle of vision shifts, but the resulting overall hue remains the same. Certainly the last few years had done nothing to dispel the gloom with which the future of the area had to be viewed by any but the most optimistic of romantics. A recurring pattern of false dawns and broken promises had dominated the scene ever since the Arabs had been awakened from their centuries-old torpor by the impact of World War I, only to be confused and maddened by the Balfour Declaration, to them an inexplicable betrayal. The uneasy years between the Wars ended with the explosion of 1947, after which the entire energies of a major part of the Arab World have concentrated on an attempt to reject from their body politic the transplanted Israeli organ grafted on to them with such high hopes by those responsible in the West. The air had been thick with cries and counter-cries of justice, historic rights, Allah and Jehovah; the boil burst again in 1967 with a result so devastating that Israel could probably have had peace with honour and, perhaps more important, security without any significant sacrifice of her basic interests. Then another mirage arose, in the shape of UN Resolution 242, painstakingly and skilfully piloted through the Security Council by Lord Caradon – still known to the Arabs as 'Abou 242' – only to be undermined hours after its successful passage by a bitter, still unresolved, dispute about what it actually meant; the flames being fanned by small but crucial linguistic discrepancies between the French and English versions.

Since then the situation, at least in the immediate area of conflict – known to generations of frivolous young diplomats as the futile crescent – had remained uneasily poised on the brink of renewed hostilities, grumbling, sullen, liable to sudden outbreaks of localised violence, intractable and seemingly hopeless, but always invoking passionate loyalties on either side. The Russians and Americans championed their respective parties, sometimes becoming dangerously overcommitted and risking confrontation in the event of a renewal of major hostilities. The prospect was daunting for the representative of a Power such as Britain with long established political, economic and emotional ties with the Arab world but now lacking the power and, as some would say, the political will to exercise more than a marginal influence on the future of the region.

However, though sharing a common frontier with Israel, Lebanon could hardly be said then to be in the front line of any battle, past or future. Apart from making noises sufficient from time to time to convince the rest of the Arabs that, despite the Christian domination of their state, they were all true Arabs at heart, the Lebanese had in the early seventies, no real quarrel with the Israelis. Their own forebears had been hunted, persecuted and dispossessed, and had known the bitterness of rejection and ostracism by their more powerful, purer Arab neighbours. Most Lebanese, especially the Christians, wished in their hearts that somehow the Arab-Israeli conflict would disappear and that they would be left alone to pursue their age-old, sensible occupation, inherited from their Phoenician forebears – doing business and making money.

Indeed the precarious balance which they had so carefully, if cynically, created between the multitude of Christian and Moslem sects represented in the population might well have been left intact or, at best, only slightly wobbly, had it not been for the presence in the country, and in the very suburbs of Beirut itself, of over 300,000 Palestinian refugees. These proud, tragic people had been festering and multiplying in camps since the conflict in 1947-8 which had driven so many of them from their homes and lands. Having been originally spread among the various neighbouring Arab countries, Lebanon was now virtually their only refuge, the last expulsion being in 1970 from Jordan whence tens of thousands poured into the already overcrowded Lebanese refugee camps, creating administrative chaos from which the long-suffering UN Agency, UNRWA, never really recovered.

Lebanon thus became the unwilling host of the many Palestinian resistance groups who fought their private wars of revenge and attrition against their arch-enemy to the south, attracting instant and severe Israeli retaliation which did not always distinguish between the prime Palestinian targets and the relatively innocent Lebanese, whose political stability, already undermined by the influx of a disproportionate number of Palestinian Moslems, severely shaken by the mounting casualties which the Government seemed helpless to prevent or avenge. It was a recipe for civil strife, and the wonder is that the situation was kept in check for so long.

No element of British foreign policy has given rise to so much contentious passion as that concerned with the Middle East. Deeply involved in its affairs since the Crusades, British reliance on its stability as the gateway to India was hardly shed before a greater dependence on Arab oil took its place. It was more than symbolic that the last fling of Imperialism, the ill-conceived and ill-fated Suez operation, should have taken place in this troubled region; and perhaps equally significant for the future historian that it was in Bahrain, in 1972, that the Flag was finally

lowered over the last few square miles of the Imperial Raj; and that
Geoffrey Arthur who, as the last Political Resident in the (Persian) Gulf,
lowered it, should pause for a couple of days with me in Beirut, half way to
Europe to catch his breath.

The alleged pro-Arab bias of the Foreign Office has, in recent years,
replaced even that favourite plot, the Roman Catholic Infiltration syn-
drome, as the bogey with which those fearful, or jealous, of the Diplomatic
Service have attempted to make the appropriate flesh creep. Elaborate
sums are worked out to prove that the number of Arabists in the Service is
much larger than the posts available for them. Tales are told of the silent,
sinister mafia which twists and perverts British policy, against whose
network no Minister stands a chance, as they pace the corridors of
Whitehall in their figurative ghalabiyas and birnouses, planting well-timed
anti-Zionist stories and peppering their minutes with the flavour and
romance of the desert. Indeed, I can vividly recall the effort, increasing
with each month as the situation in Beirut worsened and Lebanese appeals
for our help multiplied, required to remain objective and emotionally
uninvolved in the classic conflict between Arab and Jew. Perhaps I did not
always succeed, as once when, in response to a particularly outrageous
telegram from my colleague in Tel Aviv, I commented that what he was
suggesting seemed to me to be going rather far, even by Old Testament
standards. I was rebuked for this . . . Ministers were in a particularly pro-
Israeli frame of mind . . . but privately told not to worry too much in an
encouraging personal letter from Denis Greenhill, then Permanent Under
Secretary. There is something about the Middle East which engages men's
passions and drives them into positions which reason or prudence can
seldom justify. Perhaps it is the thick, mystical air of a part of the world
which has given birth to three great religions; perhaps it is the superstition
that Armageddon must follow the Garden of Eden in space as well as time;
perhaps a more prosaic combination of strategic and economic factors is
responsible for heating the blood; whatever it is, intelligent men are prone
to be carried away and to become stubbornly committed to policies which
seem to be justified only on emotional grounds.

When, shortly after arriving in Beirut, I began to urge that the time had
come for British Middle Eastern policy to cease being conceived in pro-
Arab or pro-Israeli terms and begin to concentrate on being pro-British,
my attitude was regarded as eccentric by some, unsound and even
dishonourable by others, so deeply entrenched was the abstract notion of
'Britain's role in the Middle East' and the conviction that we still could
afford the luxury of power politics.

At that time the fiasco of Suez had still not completely driven home the lesson which, when I left Beirut, the oil embargo was painfully teaching. Such arguments require an assessment of exactly *where* British interests lie and how they can best be realised and protected. Not an easy task but one which could be, and ultimately was, carried out with honesty and realism. I certainly went to Beirut with the answer already fairly clear in my mind and everything that happened in the four eventful years which I spent there confirmed my view.

* * * * * * * *

Our departure for Beirut was in sharp contrast to that stormy January night nearly three years before when we had left for Africa. A warm, soft October day; a smooth, incident-free passage through Heathrow; a First Class flight with a minimum of luggage (no sword – uniform was not required, and Babs' impedimenta now professionally reduced to the basic necessities); and above all, a sense that we were remaining within the boundaries of our own familiar civilisation and that the mental and physical effort of returning to London and keeping in touch with our family would be nothing like so great as it had been from Kinshasa. Perhaps our own enhanced professionalism was also a factor in our comparatively relaxed state. Soon we were landing in Beirut, one of the world's most beautifully-placed airports, the Mediterranean living up to all its clichés on one side and the lush, olive-strewn mountains on the other. The arrival drill followed the same pattern as at Kinshasa, but the process was smoother and somehow grander; a Daimler on the tarmac, a large number of staff and welcoming Lebanese in the VIP room, an air of being the central figure in a drama of some consequence. In the very first hour we were wrapped in the warm, womb-like reassurance of sights and sounds long-remembered from past visits and, above all, by those elements in the life of the Embassy which I had most admired.

The first was Costi. It is hard to make believable a unique and extraordinary figure, for such indeed was Constantine Accad, to give him his full but seldom used name. As the Ambassador's personal Kevass, he was the first to greet us, having managed to give the impression that he had boarded the aircraft before it had come to a halt and the doors had opened. Costi was full of tricks like that, part showman, part magician, sentimental patriot (he was a British subject, although of Lebanese origin) and super-fixer in a land of fixers. The position of Kevass was part of the legacy of the long Turkish domination of the Levant, dating from the time when it was the custom for all VIPs to be accompanied and preceded by a member of their household, part steward, part bodyguard. Ambassadors had clearly qualified for this jealously guarded distinction; the Embassy Archives record a splendid early eighteenth-century wrangle between the Ambassador in Damascus and a Consul in Beirut, disputing the latter's right to the dignity. The British had continued the custom to the present day, long after all other Embassies had dropped it, partly because they could not bring themselves to get rid of Costi. Comparatively young though he was, he represented a direct link with the great days of the British presence in Lebanon, the 'Spears Mission' of World War II. It had been General Spears himself, according to Costi, who had engaged him, a young boy probably misrepresenting his age, as a messenger. Thereafter, he had graduated up the hierarchy of locally engaged staff to his present, uniquely privileged but still not very high-ranking position. He was well known in Beirut and in his smart uniform with campaign medal-ribbons (his entitlement to which was never the subject of close investigation – he ought to have earned them, we felt) and his gold buttons and badge came to symbolise the British Embassy at least as effectively as many of the civilian-clad Ambassadors he served. Indeed, when I went to call on the Prime Minister or Foreign Secretary Costi would brush aside the functionaries in the outer offices, knock loudly on the door and, flinging it open, would proclaim firmly, 'Safir Burrittania'; whereupon the great man would rise from his desk and say, in Arabic, something like 'Why, Costi, how nice to see you!' Then, and only then, would he give me, who had been hovering in the door, a more formal but always friendly greeting in French or English.

Costi was a devout Greek-Orthodox Christian and would cross himself at the slightest hint of bad news or difficulty, often muttering an Islamic proverb at the same time. He was, as most Arabs, highly emotional and had difficulty in not embracing me when we met on board the aircraft, as indeed he was to do publicly, and with copious weeping, when the time came later for him at last to leave the Embassy. His knowledge of the seamier side of Beirut life was encyclopaedic. I was the recipient of many of his confidences as he accompanied me on my morning constitutional along the sea front. We would invariably discuss personalities, Costi's opinion being summed up in the simple phrase, 'He very good man, Sir', or more often, 'He terrible bad man, Sir, Oh yes, Excellency'.

The formalities at the airport were over while I was still enjoying them, always the sign of a well-managed affair, and we were soon on our way, Daimler-encased and flag flying, to the Residence. The evening air was full of golden dust, and even the squalor of the Palestinian camps which we passed was muted in the soft flickering lights by which they lived after dark; only daylight would reveal the stark horror of their reality. As we drew up at the gates, a fresh wave of nostalgia struck me; the sight of the large, palatial building all lit up, the smell of the cypresses in the garden and of the damp earth after its evening watering; Wadieh, the butler, waiting smiling by the door; all these brought back comforting memories and cushioned me against the real, present world which I had inherited and which I knew would be far less comfortable than those past days of which the assault on my senses was reminding me.

Wadieh had served the Embassy almost as long as Costi; together with George, the Chauffeur (an Armenian, now retired), this powerful triumvirate represented nearly 100 years' service to the British Crown. They were all highly professional in their way, disliking change although the essence of their jobs was the need to accommodate themselves to a new Ambassador every few years. They were respected by the rest of the Embassy staff, who treated them warily and thought carefully before they interfered with their routine. They regarded the Ambassador, his wife and his family, as their personal collective responsibility, and enjoyed spoiling us. Wadieh and his family lived in a small cottage in the Residence grounds; his patient, almost saint-like character, was to prove one of the principal supports for our work in both good and bad times. When the moment came for us to leave, Babs was so overcome by emotion that she could not find words to tell him how much we owed him. He is still there, loyal and patient, having survived conditions far worse than the most pessimistic forecasts would allow.

We met like old friends. I brought him greetings from several of my predecessors. He led us across the cool, pillared hall, up the staircase to the *piano nobile* and into our own, private quarters. The house, although not very old, was built in the traditional Turkish pattern, a strong Venetian influence showing in its large rooms, high ceilings with everywhere a sense of light and quiet coolness. There was a good deal of handsome stone, still the most prevalent building material in Lebanon at both ends of the economic scale; there were marble pillars upstairs as well as in the hall, which one of Babs' predecessors had desecrated by covering with scarlet and gold Christmas wrapping paper. We could entertain twenty-four to a sit-down meal; three hundred or more for a reception if the downstairs was used as well. The spare rooms and guest sitting rooms were on the ground floor; we had our own three-room suite on the first floor, apart from the principal, formal rooms; here Babs could make the nest so essential to our well-being. There was a Bechstein grand piano, alleged by the Property Services Agency (which by now had taken over responsibility for Embassies abroad, in my view greatly to the detriment of the Service) to be unplayable, and only rescued from the scrap heap by my frantic appeal to leave it until I got there. Of course, it was perfectly playable; I took it to pieces myself (doubtless offending some rule or other) and cleaned it; after an excellent Lebanese tuner had been engaged, it was judged fit for John Ogden to give a recital on one evening when disturbances in the city had prevented the use of the University auditorium.

The garden was beautiful, with splendid luxuriant trees including a huge cypress of unknown but considerable age. Gardening could not be said to have been one of our favourite hobbies, even when we lived in Sussex and had land and ideal conditions of our own. Babs had a certain touch with roses which, it must be said, practically grew themselves on our light, downland soil. I was notorious in the neighbourhood for possessing black thumbs; anything I touched seemed to shrivel and die – useful for weeds but fatal for a herbaceous border. I could cut grass, however, so our Sussex garden had consisted of wide, gently undulated lawns and large weedless beds inhabited exclusively by roses. The garden at Beirut, like that at Kinshasa, was of a richness and a sophistication far beyond our experience or capabilities. Not so our predecessors, nor for that matter our successors, Peter and Felicity Wakefield, who devoted many hours during the worst of the appalling conditions which they endured with such bravery, to beautifying the garden with a true British combination of phlegm and fertiliser which the Lebanese will always remember as epitomising the British character at its best. One former Ambassador had prudently persuaded the Ministry of Works (the old, civilised department which used to look after us before the advent of the dreaded, and dreadful PSA) to buy a small plot of adjacent land when it became vacant, thus enlarging the garden and providing some mock ruins where bits of the original wall had been left standing. We used the garden frequently for entertaining, and were able comfortably to accommodate the six hundred guests who attended the annual Queen's Birthday Party.

I had not realised until I arrived as Head of Mission just how grand a personage the British Ambassador in Beirut was. The heir to General Spears, and many other distinguished predecessors, the representative of a Power which, together with the French, had championed Lebanese independence and done a great deal in the past to protect it, he was invested by the Lebanese with an aura of influence and power far beyond that which a more realistic assessment would have revealed him as possessing. And as if reflecting this attitude and responding to its romantic exaggeration, the trappings of the post and the way of life expected of its occupant had retained many elements of a more spacious past. I was soon, and often, to experience a sense of time having stood still in Beirut, an atmosphere distinctly *fin-de-siècle* which gave to the conduct of business and pleasure alike an Edwardian plushness, and which inflated the importance of the post in many eyes, my own included if I was not constantly on guard against such *folies de grandeur*. Certainly my daily life was ordered and stately, and my every need catered for. Costi accompanied me everywhere, ready always with explanations, cash – (like Royalty, I hardly ever carried any money, being afforded unlimited credit on sight) – an umbrella when it rained, and those words of encouragement which Arabs rightly believe to be a part of the civilised life. I had seen this happening before when staying with Moore Crosthwaite and had noted the stir created wherever he went. He was an indefatigable seeker after beauty and would comb Beirut antique shops in search of objects with which to supplement the meagre official furnishings of the Residence. The wily and obsequious owners of these emporia would always somehow know in advance of his visit, standing on the doorstep to welcome him with clasped hands, hoping (always in vain) to slip some fake past his discerning eye, and casting their faces extravagantly up to heaven as they swore that, *'Pour vous, Monseiur L'Ambassadeur, je ferais un prix derisoir'*.

There was a large and efficient staff to back me up; and countless people in official circles and in the no less influential private life of the capital seemed anxious to meet Ambassadors and to boast that they had done so. The social life of Beirut was fiercely competitive; it was also politically important, for one really did meet the Prime Minister frequently at receptions at which the Beirut hostesses struggled to out-glitter each other; and one was able to take him aside and to have the kind of conversation so often recorded in fiction but less frequently in history – mutual and provocative speculation, probes, hints, and calculated indiscretions. Other ministers, too, would drift in and out during an evening reminiscent, I suppose, of Londonderry House or Cliveden. The French Ambassador was equally intrigued by this aspect of Beirut life. Michel Fontaine was the only French diplomat in my career with whom I was able to develop a relationship which transcended the bounds of professional co-operation. We shared a respect and liking for each other's countries and an understanding of their policies which minimised the friction often so unhappy a feature of Anglo-French relations, especially where, as in Beirut, the French regard themselves as having proprietory rights. We worked intimately together with the well-being of Lebanon, of which we were both fond, as much in mind as the interests of our own countries; and where these conflicted, we did our best to soften the blows to Lebanese pride and morale which inevitably followed. We amused ourselves by pretending (perhaps not without some substance of truth) that the Lebanese hostesses worked on a kind of points system in their endless competition for social pre-eminence, gaining special points for securing the presence of one of the more important Ambassadors, say the French, British or American, and a jackpot bonus if they got all three on the same night. Certainly, they went to unusual lengths to catch us for a party, telephoning months ahead to ask for a free evening in the Ambassador's diary, a request that even the combined ingenuity and outspokenness of my Private Secretary found difficult to refuse.

My first months in Beirut were in the sharpest contrast to those frustrating beginnings in Kinshasa. To the regulated, disciplined European mind, the Lebanese were unpredictable; but whereas with Africans this meant delay and muddle, in Beirut it usually meant unnatural speed. They darted from one project to another with that nervous energy which is the hall-mark of all Mediterranean peoples; that this was, in practice, little more effective than the sleepier ways of Africa did not matter all that much – it looked better, and in the Arab world looks and words often count for as much, or more, than deeds. At any rate, it seemed that the Lebanese were flatteringly anxious for me to start work. I was received by the Prime Minister (who was also acting as Foreign Minister at the time) the very morning after my arrival, before I had had a chance to visit my own Chancery. Saeb Salaam was one of the small, senior group of Lebanese politicians who had divided the principal offices of state between them virtually since Independence. Being a Sunni Moslem, he was doomed always to be Prime Minister or nothing, that post being reserved for the Sunnis under a kind of gentleman's agreement known as the National Pact, which regulated Lebanese political life and kept the balance between the many Christian and Moslem sects. The others also had their ear-marked posts, and thus the whole Cabinet, and indeed Parliament itself, supposedly reflected the various religious elements of the population in proportion to their supposed numbers.

Instant history is the bane of the twentieth century. I have no desire to be wise after the awful events which have engulfed the Lebanon since we left in 1975. I can only record, as honestly as I can, what I saw and thought while we were there in the early seventies. The reader must judge to what extent I foresaw, or was able to foresee, the greatness of the tragedy which lay ahead.

Lebanon's traditional role in the history of the Near East had been principally as a sanctuary for persecuted minorities from the surrounding hinterland, her mountains providing a virtually impenetrable refuge for sects such as the Maronite Christians, who fled from the intolerance of Orthodox Islam, and who were to make up the patchwork population of the future state. Hence religious tolerance was, on the surface, something to which all Lebanese adhered, and which was enshrined in their constitutional structure. Half humorous references were made to the United Kingdom's need for Lebanese technical assistance in solving the problem of Northern Ireland. Alas, time was soon to prove how fragile was the vessel which contained these aspirations, and how tragically ill-fitted a model for the settlement of confessional conflict the Lebanese experiment was to prove.

But even in 1971, the distribution of power was not as fair as it seemed, since the Maronite Christians, who had long since ceased to be in the majority, still held at least two of the plums; the Presidency, modelled on the French system and hence very powerful; and the Commander in Chief of the army. Moreover, the resulting precarious balance was arrived at by a process of wheeling and dealing so Levantine in its sinuousness, and an electoral system so baffling in its complexity, that even the Lebanese were never prepared to commit themselves to any coherent explanation. To add to the whiff of fantasy from which Lebanese politics were never wholly free, no census had been held in the country since 1932, thus making the relative strengths of the various religious sects upon which the National Pact had originally been based purely theoretical and almost certainly wrong. With typical realism there existed a tacit, mutual agreement that everyone would risk losing something and no-one stood to gain by the new truth which would be revealed by an appeal to the demographic oracle; better to switch off sight, sound and critical faculty in an attempt to pretend that the political scene was as unchanging as the coastline which Alexander the Great and Richard Coeur de Lion had known.

Sitting opposite Saeb Salaam at nine o'clock on that October morning, I was only dimly aware of these paradoxes. His charm and air of confidence were reassuring; moreover, his uncanny resemblance to one of my favourite uncles gave, on my side at least, an impetus to our relationship from which it never looked back. He remained from that day a firm friend and we understood each other in those ways which can transform the drab arena of political relationships into a colourful, exciting stage. It was at this first meeting, also, that I experienced the technique at which he was a master – by no means the only one in the Arab world, but probably without a peer – which can best be described as loving blackmail; an emotional appeal to the past by which the British have repeatedly been tempted, sometimes successfully, to say the words and sometimes even to promise the actions, so dear to Arab hearts. I drove away from this breathlessly early engagement confident that I had made a friend, and hopeful that I had not encouraged any romantic ideas of my future role.

During the years since my last visit, the cosy, rather ramshackle

Chancery building in the old part of the town had been discarded in favour of a new, and more compact building designed to accommodate all departments of the Embassy under one roof, except the British Council which, in keeping with its obsessive concern for its political virginity, was housed separately and pretended that it had no connection with the Embassy apart from duty-free diplomatic liquor and other perks. The formidable new building was supposed to combine security with efficiency, but succeeded only by sacrificing beauty to both. Costi provided a running commentary on our route to and from the Ministry, couched in terms which politely acknowledged my previous visits – 'You remember, Excellency?' – while making me feel like a tourist, especially when we passed the old Chancery which, I noted, had become a conglomeration of cheap souvenir shops with one of Beirut's sleazier nightclubs in the basement. The ghost of General Spears (which at that time had not been separated from his body) haunted the place, as indeed it did the Residence, ignoring disdainfully the nightclub jiving which, no doubt, he would have thought typical of the political manoeuvrings in the state which he had helped to create.

My arrival at the Embassy verged on the ceremonial. Jock Given, the Counsellor, was on the steps to greet me; the other Embassy Kevasses, who acted as guards, guides and general Godfathers to the crowds who frequented the premises seeking visas, trade, favours, bribes and deals of all kinds, were lined up to salute the new Excellency, as they must have done many times before. I was whisked up to my modest but comfortable private office (with its own loo, always a reliable status symbol and, in this case, one up on Kinshasa which boasted no such luxury) and thus into a realm of which I was outwardly the sovereign, but which in reality was ruled over by my private Secretary, Miss Shirley Mordin (now MBE). Miss Mordin was one of the phenomena which made Beirut different. A gifted linguist – her French was hardly less fluent than her German; and her Russian only a bit rusty – she was also a trained singer with a slender but true and sweet soprano voice and a musician's sense of tempo and phrase. She sang Lieder delightfully, and although I am not a good enough pianist to have done her justice as an accompanist – she gave a recital once a year with her own, equally gifted partner at the piano which had become a fixture of the Beirut season long before my arrival – we were able to make satisfactory music together. I persuaded her to exploit her talent for popular music of the thirties (Noel Coward and such-like) with which I was more at home on the keyboard than with Brahms or the grander Schubert. This was an unexpected bonus on top of her efficiency and encyclopaedic knowledge of the Beirut scene.

Perfectionists, like saints, are sometimes difficult to live with. Shirley was no saint; she and I had our ups and downs; the Ambassador's PA, like *éminences grises* throughout the world, was in a powerful and central position, and Shirley's not infrequent inability to accept the imperfections of her colleagues did not always make for Schubertian harmony in the office. But her loyalty to me was fierce and absolute, and she contributed a major part of the success of our installation and subsequent mission for which Babs and I shall always be grateful.

We took the same pains as in Kinshasa to get to know our staff – nearly 100 UK-based, if the Regional organisations were included. We invited them all to a party in the Residence garden the night after our arrival. My speech on this occasion was, I believe, an improvement on that first, toe-curling effort in Africa, although I retained the family theme, telling them that Babs felt as if she had suddenly acquired a large number of children and grandchildren without having undergone the customary processes of fecundation and parturition. This made her blush but they laughed, thank goodness, and we were off to a good start. Then, meticulously organised by Shirley, I settled down to the laborious business of calls and counter-calls, my own presentation of credentials having taken place with almost indecent haste after my arrival.

At first I scoffed at those who warned that it would be six months before I completed this task, thinking that my experience of the hit-or-miss Kinshasa version of this time-honoured procedure was definitive. But they were right; we were well into 1972 before the circuit could be said to have been completed. There were over eighty Ambassadors, many of the smaller powers stationing representatives in Beirut who were additionally accredited to other countries in the area; there were Archbishops (including a Maronite Cardinal), Beatitudes, Monsignori, Coptic monks and Armenian Archimandrites; there were Sunni and Shia Moslem Imams, and the leader of the mysterious Druze, traditionally very pro-British; there were Cabinet Ministers and the leaders of the innumerable political parties, by no means always the same people; there was the large British Community with its school and the Hospital for Nervous Diseases of which I was ex-officio President; and there were the outlying parts of my 'empire', notably the Middle East Centre for Arabic Studies (MECAS), long established in the village of Shemlan in the mountains above Beirut and held in suspicious awe by most of the Arabs who were convinced that its primary task was to train members of the British Intelligence Services for their subsequent sinister role in the Middle East. This cherished belief – as an Egyptian friend once said to me, Arabs are capable of believing things which they know to be untrue – gave rise to some prime examples of the art of rumour-mongering. One venerable villager was overheard making the assertion that, 'Of course, it's a spy school. And what's more, they teach them to shoot there; up on the roof there's a hut and you can see them going in there in the afternoons, carrying their guns, and you can hear them firing in there – pfut, pfut, pfut – like that!' He was actually referring to the squash court wherein the swotting and sweating students took what little exercise their intensive schedule could afford.

Shirley treated the organisation of this mammoth merry-go-round as if she were planning an Everest expedition or an Atlantic crossing, with charts and time-tables. She would not allow me to do more than two calls in the morning, except in unusual circumstances – ('Well, he only speaks Kurdish and has a hopeless interpreter, so you can't stay long there . . .') – and I had to fit in the daily business of the Embassy, not to speak of the frequent crises in the region, political and military, which usually meant that I had to see the Prime Minister or Foreign Minister, and often the President himself, who complained if I did not go to see him sufficiently often. Thus, in those first months, I shuttled daily across Beirut, guided by the omni-present Costi, who would leap from the car before it had actually stopped and terrorise the junior member of the staff of whatever Embassy I was calling upon, whom custom dictated should be on the pavement waiting to greet me and escort me to his Ambassador.

There followed about half an hour's conversation in a variety of languages, sometimes through an interpreter if no common tongue of sufficient mutual fluency could be discovered; the talks being washed down by innumerable cups of very thick, very sweet Turkish coffee, an obligatory ritual impossible to avoid whatever the condition of one's stomach or liver, both of which began to show alarming signs of deterioration as the great diplomatic bandwagon began to roll. When, after about a month or so, the calls began to be repaid, as custom demanded, I was forced to reduce to half-speed; at one time it looked as if, like the Forth Bridge, I should never be finished. But mercifully the turnover in Beirut was slower than in Africa, due to the combination of its importance and desirability, so that I *did* eventually catch up and became the called-upon rather than the caller.

Superimposed on this excessively mobile life was a special task which had been laid upon me before I left London. My predecessor's illness had forced him to adopt what is called in contemporary jargon a low profile, an expression which, however military its derivation – tanks hull-down on the horizon – for me conjures up an unmistakably Bertie Wooster-like image of beetle-browed foreheads and receding chins. The Lebanese had noted this absence of traditional British hospitality and, with their Byzantine ingenuity, had deduced that it must be a deliberate attempt to deceive them into thinking that Britain was in decline. What mattered perhaps more was that morale in the Embassy had fallen like a barometer before a hurricane. The British may not have that overwhelming urge to win, so characteristic of their transatlantic cousins; but like most people, they would rather be winners than losers and enjoy the appearance of success, despite the fact that no nation is so skilled at the celebration of failure. But it is not easy to carry this off with conviction when awkward facts, such as falling productivity, rising unemployment, balance of payments deficits, strikes and other symptoms of economic and political sickness, have to be explained. I believe that these are just the periods when, far from visible retrenchment, Britain's representatives abroad should be encouraged to put heart and stuffing into their friends by adopting a business-as-more-than-usual attitude, especially in their lifestyle. At any rate, I was gratified to find that the Office shared my view in this particular situation. 'Things need livening up,' I was told. 'The Embassy needs putting on the map again; you know, push the boat out, old boy, all that sort of thing – you and Babs are so damned good at that kind of carry-on.' Detecting the overtones of flattery, a sure sign of a defensive attitude on the part of Personnel Department, I asked whether I would be given any extra allowances to help launch us on this spectacular but obviously desirable social career.(I knew that the post had just been inspected and was afraid that the Ambassador's allowances – or the *Frais*, as it is still called, no doubt to make the usually abysmally inadequate figures appear better by talking about them in French – had been set to reflect the low level of activity forced on my predecessor.) My not unreasonable request brought forth a good deal of shifting in the chair, mumble, mumble, lookings out of the window, hummings and errings, and traditionally meaningless phrases such as, 'Of course, we'll look very carefully at any proposal you care to make . . .' But, in short, no more money.

It was not long before we found ourselves beginning, *faut-de-mieux*, to fulfil this aspect of our task. Every hostess, it seemed, wanted to add the scalp of the new British Ambassador to her collection; we were pursued, in some cases persecuted, by the Beirut ladies for lunch, drinks or dinner. Three social engagements in one evening was not uncommon, with often a lunch as well. The scale of these entertainments was breath-taking; dinners of fifty with clothes and jewels that looked like advertisements in *Vogue* or *Paris Match* (no doubt in some cases fulfilling the same function); and mountains of delicious, expensive food, far too much for the blasé crowd which clustered round the groaning buffet tables. The food, like the guests, was provided as much to be seen as to be eaten; and if East and West were never to meet under any other circumstances, they certainly did on Beirut's dinner tables, spiced Arabic dishes side by side with smoked salmon from Scotland and Caviar from the Black Sea; and all washed down with French wines imported at great expense since the local Lebanese wines, which we found delicious, were considered unworthy of Ambassadorial entertainment. Although usually invited for half past eight, we were lucky if we actually sat down before half past ten. We soon got to know the right hour to arrive so as to avoid too long a period of pre-prandial drinking. There was a hectic, unrelaxed quality about many of these parties, as if the hostesses were driven by some uncontrollable impulse not only to compete but to go for the record. Perhaps, too, they were in a hurry, sensing the storm gathering outside their gilded world. They were greatly egged on by the profusion of newspapers and glossy magazines published in Beirut which appeared to thrive on social news and gossip with extensive pictorial coverage and treated each party as if it were the Duchess of Richmond's Ball, omitting to point out, of course, that Waterloo could be expected to follow. . . .

That a battle of some kind was indeed coming seemed plain enough to me, although what kind it would be and whether the Lebanese would win, indeed what would constitute victory, was not clear. I doubt whether many realised the size of the storm into which this glittering, frivolous and some ways corrupt throng was so gaily sailing. It worried me a good deal, despite our own natural gregariousness and our enjoyment of such a high-quality social life. But the contrast between the rich life, which all this reflected, and the poverty which was always near the surface was deeply disturbing, particularly as very few of the rich made any effort to conceal their wealth; moreover, there were seeds of political poison in the all-too-obvious fact that many of the rich were Christians and nearly all the poor were Moslems. We felt uncomfortable at the amount of attention paid to us; descriptions of Babs' clothes and jewellery (more remarkable for originality than cost if the truth were known); where we had been, what we had done and said, received a degree of public attention which delighted the Embassy Information Department, who behaved as if they were paid by the column-inch, but which worried me. In those first months we became the fashion. But gradually we managed, without undue offence, to trim down this indiscriminate activity to dimensions which could be better justified and yet make the most of the undoubted political advantages of the social whirl. The Press, too, began to get tired of us and we became mercifully no longer news. The fact that it was all so enjoyable and that many of the people involved were so charming and civilised made the problem all the more acute. Diplomacy being essentially the art of reciprocity, we were led inexorably to entertain generously in our turn. We decided to make one big splash by having an after-dinner reception and dance just before Christmas, a festival kept in Beirut by Christian and Moslem alike. It was a huge success, attended by *le Tout Beirut*, as the newspapers reported, with carol-singing by candle-light. According to custom, we were deluged with flowers before and after; huge plants and enormous bouquets of gladioli as big as trees, and roses like grains of pink sand on some exotic beach. They were so profuse that they lined the path from the gate to the front door and on up the stairs inside the house.

Generosity is one of the Arabs' most endearing qualities; they will not only part with hard cash to buy expensive presents on the most trivial occasion, but will readily give a prized personal possession to a friend on the sole grounds that it has been admired. It is a society that would have perfectly understood the late Queen Mary. During my first weeks I had been foolish enough to admire a man's tie, probably because I could think of no other conversational gambit. To my intense embarrassment, I found it on my desk the next morning, with a charming and flattering note; and when, as if unwilling to learn, I repeated the mistake, the tie's owner whipped it off there and then, having made sure, I suspect, that a photographer was within range, and would not be satisfied until I had substituted it for the one I was wearing. The flash-bulb was so built-in a feature of Beirut society that I soon ceased to protest, or even to notice, drawing the line only when a guest at one of our smaller dinner parties arrived with her own photographer in tow; she found it quite baffling that we did not want her presence in our house recorded for posterity.

Many hours have been spent by aspiring and ultimately perspiring, Second Secretaries on tennis court, golf course, or at the chess board or bridge table, making up a fourth or a pair and working just that little bit harder to ensure that, even if H.E. did not win (as most undoubtedly preferred to do), he did not lose by any but the slenderest and most respectable of margins. 'A good game, thank you, Simpkins; would you care for a cup of tea before going back to the office?' There were also more unusual occupations. 'I wonder if you would mind feeding the tortoises, my dear fellow, before we draft that telegram . . .' Gladwyn Jebb, my first Ambassador, invented a form of croquet with rules so complex that only his intellectual equals could be expected to compete. The late Sir Paul Mason, another of my mentors and my boss in The Hague, used to alternate between long spells of silent rowing on the calm Dutch waterways and playing Mozart violin sonatas with Baroness van Tuyll, a very grand lady of the Dutch aristocracy who fulfilled a post at Court bearing the title 'La Grande Maîtresse'. The entries in the Ambassador's diary marking this rendezvous, which took place regularly each Thursday afternoon, at first confused me by their apparent explicitness until I discovered their true and charming significance. Others spent their time collecting French watercolours, translating late Latin verse, or preparing to write their memoirs. The nature of the profession imposes certain restrictions on the pursuit of leisure for which, in most posts, there is little time or energy to spare; nearly all social occasions were too much like work to be relaxing.

As a matter of fact, he who is bored at a diplomatic dinner has only himself to blame. I have spent many happy hours trying to figure out what it was that made my neighbour at lunch or dinner – a worthy Scandinavian wife, perhaps, or a deadly female diplomat – so excruciatingly dull. There is plenty of amusement to be had for those who know what to look for. Some years before, in Cairo, I had suffered from a mild stomach complaint which required me to take two small white pills immediately before eating. These I carried around in an elegant, late Georgian snuff-box which Babs had cleverly identified and bought as being just the thing. At a rather grand dinner party of the kind still possible and permissible in the middle years of Nasser's Egypt, I whipped out my little box and took my two pills as soon as we had sat down. I then turned to my neighbour as custom demanded. She was an extremely handsome Coptic lady of the kind liable to drive strong, silent white men into the Foreign Legion. I was just recovering from the long, sultry look which she gave me when she spoke in a voice which in every way matched her appearance.

'What were those pills you just took?' she asked.

'Oh,' I said, casually, as if used to such discussions with complete strangers. 'They're just something I have to take from time to time.' She appeared to consider this carefully, and then asked, 'Are they aphrodisiacs?' My answer will have to be paid for in the next world, but I hope the reader will agree that in this one there could be no other.

'Yes,' I replied, looking deep into her smouldering eyes, 'as a matter of fact, they are.' This did not seem to surprise her, but she paused thoughtfully again before saying, 'May I try one?'

'You mean now?'

'Why not?' With a solemnity which I felt the occasion demanded, I counted out a couple of pills and pushed them over to her.

'They're not very strong,' I said, apologetically, 'I daresay you ought to take two; I always do.'

She acknowledged this advice by a silent bow of her head and took the pills in a reverent kind of way, washing them down with little sips of white wine. It was difficult to know what to say next. I turned to my other neighbour and awaited developments. There was none. The Coptic lady exhibited no sign that anything unusual had taken place between us, although I did detect an occasional look of quiet anticipation cross her features, like the shadow of a cloud on a sunlit field. In reality, of course, her bile was being thinned (for that, so my doctor had told me, was the effect of the pills), but I doubt if she was aware of it. I have often wondered what she expected would happen; a sudden surge of passion? a declaration of lust? an invitation for later, nocturnal games? an attempt, even, at surreptitious gratification between the fish and the meat? I never discovered. Perhaps she blamed the British for yet another broken promise.

When we first arrived in Beirut, I began to ride horses again, the Congo not having been very suitable riding country. But this was soon denied me on security grounds; I was considered too vulnerable on horse-back, although this was always put so as not to appear to reflect on my horsemanship which, I must say, after a year and a half of hard riding almost daily in the desert outside Cairo was not too bad. A certain amount of swimming was possible, and I could sometimes manage a walk into the mountains, although my policemen hated this, being, like their colleagues the world over, allergic to footwork. But the marvellous air and spectacular scenery helped to put into perspective the sophisticated urban life which I was compelled to lead. Our dog, a golden Labrador appropriately named Lady Hester Stanhope, never refused exercise; fortunately, our garden was big enough to give her a good run, and there were glorious days when she could romp on the beach. I never took her to the office; like all Labradors she was a dreadful flirt and could be relied upon to disrupt all human activity with her demands for attention.

Bridge was a definite danger; we had played a good deal in Kinshasa, but mainly with close friends –Mohammad Kamel, the Egyptian Ambassador and his wife Rashika (he was later to become Sadat's Foreign Minister for a brief period); and with our Indian colleague Surrendra Alirajpur, who invented the delightful expressions *chota-slam* and *burra-slam*. Beirut, however, was in a different class; high-powered bridge was played for high stakes, enamelled ladies rattling the cards for hours on end in smoke-filled rooms deeply shuttered against the sunlight. This was not Babs' style at all, nor did I relish its male equivalent; so we concealed our bridge-playing, such as it was, from all but a few intimates.

Babs, in fact, went one better and enrolled in the American University under the distinguished Professor of History, Zein Zein. Although this provided her with a perfect alibi with which to escape the bridge table, it was in reality to fulfil her long held ambition to follow the example of her mother and grandmother both of whom had re-entered the academic world comparatively late in life. Her classes were rewarding and regular except when her professor telephoned to say that the situation at and near the University was unsafe and that she should not risk coming that day.

Travel could, in some circumstances, be classed as recreation. Not in the Lebanon itself, of course; everywhere I went I was on duty, which meant being on show. There was no corner of that little land that I did not come to know intimately; beautiful and ancient, the names of its ruined, majestic cities read like pages from the Bible; Tyre and Sidon; Baalbec and Biblos. Thither I would take my visitors to see the mysterious stone and marble foundations of the ancient world, lying gaunt and silent in the hot sun. Babs and I would visit schools, hospitals, provincial officials, bishops and imams; attend local festivals, eating and drinking on the mountain sides while the stars shone over a warm, dark sea. It was all very romantic, marred only by the ever-present reminders of twentieth-century strife – an Israeli fighter plane high in the sky, distant gun-fire, and rumours of unrest.

My most exciting official journey was a trip along the entire length of the southern frontier with Israel. The Lebanese Government asked me to do this so that I could see for myself the damage caused by Israeli raids across the border and, in one or two cases, the presence of Israeli military outposts on Lebanese soil. I was driven in a civilian car with a couple of Lebanese Colonels in plain clothes. Neither I nor the Lebanese wished to advertise my presence and we had to be careful to confine pauses for observation through field-glasses to known Lebanese military establishments or UN observation posts. It was an eerie experience. For some miles the road runs parallel to an Israeli road only metres away; at some points the frontier itself was a wire fence dividing a two-lane highway (rather better surfaced, I noticed, on the other side). At one moment we passed an Israeli armoured car so close that I could have talked to its crew without raising my voice. Israeli soldiers were quite often to be seen. A story is told of a Lebanese military guide who stopped close to one of these frontier guards and began to point out landmarks on the Israeli side to his VIP visitor; whereupon the Israeli soldier standing nearby on his side of the boundary corrected him at one point, saying, no, the Kibbutz is further to the left. However resolute my professional neutrality, it was difficult not to think of Israel as 'enemy territory' and to experience that thrill of watching an unknown, hostile and forbidden land through my glasses, wondering at the lives that were being led there, alien perhaps but not as alien or as hostile as my guides tried to make out, and human enough when it came to the shared experiences of birth, love, sorrow and death.

Travel outside the Lebanon was surprisingly easy, given the state of unrest usually to be found in the area. We visited Cairo twice, renewing old friendships and revisiting the scenes of our past. On one trip we took the boat trip from Luxor to Aswan, surely one of the most beautiful and peaceful of holidays. The limpid river slides silently beneath us, its banks dotted with villages which any Pharaoh would have recognised, the great temples waiting for us to violate their secret beauties. Jordan was a treasure-house easily accessible, but the West Bank and Jerusalem itself, which we had known in earlier years, were now denied to us. I do not believe the Lebanese would have been upset if I had visited Israel, but it would have been too tempting an incident for trouble-makers and the Lebanese, as usual, would have been compelled to react to prove their Arab solidarity, whatever they might privately have thought. The risks were thus too great; but we visited the rest of Jordan two or three times, basking in the hot January sun at Aqaba, getting up at five o'clock in the morning to see the rose-red sun greet another day in Petra's long history as we plodded through the Suq on our sad little donkeys; wandering through the sweet-smelling ruins of Jerash as the spring winds ruffled the wild flowers where Hadrian once walked.

Syria, although our closest neighbour, was both the most difficult and, for me, the most rewarding to visit. Damascus itself presented no difficulty once we had re-established relations with the Syrians. One of the most consistent errors in British Middle Eastern policy has been a stubborn refusal to admit the importance of Syria in the affairs of the region. For centuries geography alone has ensured that whoever controlled Damascus must be reckoned with as a central factor in the area's political and military development. The creation of Israel with its fragile, artificial borders (none more so than the Golan Heights) only enhances this importance.

When I arrived in Beirut, there was no British representation in Damascus; our Embassy was responsible for reporting whatever we could learn at second hand of Syrian affairs and policies. For some time the Syrians had been dropping hints that they would welcome a resumption of diplomatic relations with Britain providing, of course, that this could be achieved without their losing face after the precipitous and unnecessary rupture in 1967. It seemed to me to be greatly in our interests to make friends in Damascus and to be as well placed there as possible before the next storm, already on the horizon, broke. The Foreign Office were markedly reluctant to take any initiative, arguing that public opinion in the UK would not take kindly to the spectacle of a British Government courting a supposedly left-wing, none-too-respectful, Arab regime. I thought this bosh, and said so. In the end agreement was reluctantly and painfully reached; David Roberts, an able Arabist and former member of my Department in the FO, arrived as British Ambassador in Damascus the day before the war of Ramadan broke out.

The Syrians received him well and since they were now at war, allowed him to operate without having presented his credentials which, understandably, they were too preoccupied to receive. But he had no communications, so we organised a daily run to the frontier where we collected his telegrams and classified bag material and despatched them from Beirut. I went up on two occasions to meet him and we paced the dirty strip of road on the Lebanese side of the Frontier post, between the parked and broken-down lorries while we discussed the war, whose noise came up quite clearly from the guns on the Golan Heights, twenty miles to the south.

After the war the rest of Syria north of Damascus became free, thus opening up the magical desert with Palmyra at its heart and Aleppo, with its labyrinthine Souks and its hinterland of Christian cities long since abandoned to the Asian winds. We took the chance of a week's trip beginning with a visit to the Krak des Chevaliers during a dramatic thunderstorm which created a Tennysonian setting for that most perfect of Crusader ruins. Then after a night in the cold splendour of Palmyra, reached through the purple and gold carpet of wild flowers which the desert wears in spring-time, we arrived at Aleppo and stayed at the famous Baron's Hotel, as solidly English as Cheltenham and, during the cold April nights, about as draughty. From this base we explored the northern part of Syria, marvelling at the great ruined city of Resafe, its curious crystalline stone glinting behind the huge, Byzantine walls at last crumbling before the final enemy; and stood by the pillar of St Simeon (surely the most eccentric of saints), now reduced to a stump by the faithful chippings of centuries of pilgrims and enshrined in the golden stone of its ruined basilica. I was not, however, left undisturbed during this idyll so far from the polished life of Beirut. The plain-clothes detective who had come with us spotted a well known (to him) Palestine guerrilla having his breakfast two tables away from me, and I was hustled away to my room until the coast was clear. Later in the week the BBC, a world life-line for all those unfortunate enough to have to take account of the news, reported student riots in Beirut, and after a miraculously clear and rapid phone call I decided to return ahead of time, not wishing to be absent or, still worse, unable to get back if real trouble was brewing.

Nevertheless, Beirut provided me with one major consolation – music; and, more important, music to be made as well as heard. A number of professional musicians lived and worked there. The music department of the American University was excellent. There were several good pianists, including a Lebanese concert professional, Henri Ghoraieb who became a close friend; a number of good concerts by visiting artists; an amateur choir and orchestra which gave respectable performances of the easier Handel and the flashier Offenbach, with the usual programme of Christmas carols; and, of course, Shirley on the doorstep. I was not shy in letting it be known that I was musical and quite soon the Residence became a meeting place for musicians. We made music together and listened politely to each other; I found great joy in playing four hands with the other pianists, most of whom, like Henri, were much better than me; as in tennis, your game improves when you play with the pro. It must have occurred to me that music-making with the British Ambassador conferred a certain cachet which was anything but musical; but whenever it did, I dismissed the thought, determined to enjoy to the full the sense of musicianship with which my friends surrounded me, and let my critical faculties take care of themselves. So these enjoyable *folies de grandeur* persisted and indeed were intensified by the discovery, promoted discreetly by Babs perhaps, that I had written two carols for unaccompanied voices years ago in Paris, coupled with a request that the Beirut amateur choir should include them in their Christmas concert. This was pernicious enough, but what finally undermined my attempts at self-realism was an invitation to conduct them in person. We rehearsed a small group of the best voices in the choir and, naturally, this item was widely advertised and written up in the Press; the audience was swelled by many who sensed a social rather than a musical occasion. I turned a resolutely deaf ear to those small voices who whispered that H.E.'s name on the programme was worth more than his notes on the score. Although consumed by pre-concert nerves I thoroughly enjoyed the experience and the thunderous applause which followed.

Emboldened by this event I wrote a couple of works for chorus and orchestra which were given in following years and which, if truth be told, were too ambitious for performers and composer alike. I also wrote some instrumental and chamber music suitable, as I thought, to be performed by my friends who loyally and patiently blew and scraped their way through it. The atmosphere was a little like that at the court of a minor German State in the eighteenth century although quite lacking the purity and discipline of that demanding epoch.

But it would be fair to say that there was an element of Doctor Johnson's dog about the whole affair; musical composition is not a prerequisite for entry into the Diplomatic Service. As soon as I had settled in London after my retirement I enrolled in the Composition class at Morley College. The class was taken by Hugh Wood, himself a distinguished composer of modern music which I admire but do not always like, and a good teacher.

He did not need to spell out how juvenile and immature was my work when subjected to the standards which he applied. Music is an exact science and a demanding mistress. My first few periods with the class soon showed me how much I had to learn and, more painful, confirmed my secret belief that my apparent successes in Beirut had owed little to my music. Nevertheless, the experience was painful, and one for which my sheltered, privileged life as a diplomat had done nothing to prepare me. Indeed, it had only increased the force with which I hit the ground after a delicious glide beneath the Ambassadorial parachute. But such experiences in the end only serve to emphasise the salutary lesson which all but a handful of mandarins have to learn, namely that the vapour-trail of glory which follows them into retirement is unlikely to last much longer than that of a jet fighter on a windy day.

A little musical talent is a dangerous thing. I am not normally envious, but I envy the professional. I enjoy watching professionals at work, gaining pleasure from the absolute certainty of technique and judgement which they appear to command. But whether through laziness, lack of will or of confidence, I have never been able to tear up the surface with the ruthlessness of the professional and to sink myself in the lonely task of dedication. Certainly music had never compelled me to make the kind of sacrifices for which my experiences at Morley College only served to underline the need. For those, the vast majority, who are not blessed with genius or an overwhelming compulsion to devote their lives to a single cause, profession or creative activity, it is hard to decide whether to try to be very good at one thing or fairly good at a number. Without a conscious decision I seem to have ended up in the latter category and hence, perhaps by accident, to have achieved a degree of professionalism in the one career which requires its Jacks to be expert in, if not masters of, all trades relevant to its demands. Although I left Lebanon still, in some senses, a learner, the last two explosive years forced me to draw on all my experience and found me ready for a final test by the most exacting of professional standards. Beirut has never been a place for amateurs.

CHAPTER TEN

In childhood all gardens flowered in the perpetual sunlight of constant early summer, except for short periods of deep clean white snow at Christmas. There was magic behind every shop window, the long shadows of summer evenings standing still so that bed-time was forever suspended; or the secure glowing nursery fire making safe the mysterious winter afternoon outside with its glowering grey sky. Aunts behaved with uncharacteristically affectionate warmth; parents never scolded and commanded an inexhaustible supply of gifts and treats; fairyland was a short walk to the end of the road where the real open countryside still dozed in the gentle haze. Perhaps our time in Beirut is still too recent to have been overlaid by such a comforting patina; at any rate, my memories are not exclusively rose-tinted, although there is a sufficient afterglow to make me believe that I enjoyed pleasures and privileges of a kind unique in my own life and not given to many late-twentieth century Englishmen. Certainly I have never before or since detected in myself a sense of importance, perhaps also of power, although any serious student of politics will know that the two are not synonymous. A nice distinction of this kind was made recently by an American journalist – a White House correspondent – who had suggested in some television programme that a British Ambassador in Washington now no longer wielded the kind of influence enjoyed by his predecessors. 'But surely', said another member of the discussion panel, 'the British Ambassador can see the Secretary of State whenever he wishes, and doesn't have much difficulty in reaching the President?'

'That's not influence,' rasped the correspondent, glaring balefully at the camera, 'that's access.'

It was palpably intoxicating to enter a room and to sense that slight turbulence of the air and hesitation in the rhythm of talk which marks the sudden presence of a well-known figure; to have one's opinion sought and listened to respectfully; to see the Foreign Minister break off a conversation with some lesser figure because he needs to talk to you; to catch that look of genuine interest in the eyes of a beautiful woman which denotes the advantage that can be an Ambassador's for the asking. All this was the essence of the novelette, frothy, saccharine, undemanding and, to be honest, not a little addictive. But in the case of Beirut a piquant flavour was added by the knowledge, tentative at first but growing in certainty as we plunged deeper into the complexities of Beirut life and politics, that this was the end of an epoch and that we were playing a part which might in the end turn out to be not merely prominent, as it was already and likely to remain, but important.

With hindsight I see that in those first months I could have discerned the seeds of the disasters which were to overwhelm that poor defenceless country in 1975; seeds wrapped in tinsel, hidden from all but the most perceptive while the silk dresses rustled in the perfumed air. At the beginning of 1972 security in Beirut gradually began to show signs of cracking. There were student demonstrations and rioting, internecine quarrels between factions on the fringe of Lebanese politics, an odd shooting here and there; nothing significant but enough to put one on one's guard in a city where the sight of large Palestinian refugee camps was unavoidable – near-autonomous areas in which Lebanese law could not be enforced and whose misery and squalor bred the viruses which were to attack, perhaps fatally, the whole Lebanese state.

In face of this slight but unmistakable deterioration we reluctantly came to the conclusion that I must be given more efficient protection than had been considered necessary in the past. I talked the problem over with the Lebanese Prime Minister and appropriate authorities; they were sensible and unemotional, recognising that the responsibility for my safety, according to international law and practice, rested with them. They assigned two armed police officers as a permanent escort, the Embassy supplying transport for them by agreement since this, in fact, gave us greater control over the operation. From then on until we left in 1975, I was never free of these friendly but determined policemen. They followed me to and from the office and every outside meeting; to the beach, to the mountains, to every party and only let me go when I was safely locked up for the night in the Residence. They took their instructions literally and maintained radio communication with their Headquarters. As part of these precautions, my daily routine was constantly varied. I left and returned to the Residence by a different route and at a different time each day; and whereas when I first arrived I found that my days' engagements were typed out by Shirley to read rather like the Court Circular, and distributed in advance on a broad basis to the Embassy staff, now not even Costi or my Chauffeur knew my movements ahead of time. It made life very difficult for everyone. Costi, in particular, began by deeply resenting the police and the general upheaval in what had become a hallowed routine; but when once convinced that the threat was sufficient to justify these innovations, he became very security-minded himself and, indeed, demanded to be armed, like the police, with an automatic weapon. When this was refused – I was firmly against the arming of any Embassy personnel and, unlike some of my foreign colleagues, never carried a gun myself – I noticed one day a swelling under the sleeve of his coat which he reluctantly and shamefacedly revealed as an ugly-looking, weighted stick with which he intended, if called upon, to defend his Safir. The private lives of the Lebanese policemen were, of course, completely wrecked, but neither would take even a day's leave for fear that they might be replaced; they liked the job, it seemed, in spite of the long and uncertain hours, and did not wish to forego the exciting lack of routine, free meals all over the place, even an occasional visit to the cinema at Her Majesty's expense.

For Babs and me it was a constriction which we felt increasingly as time went on. It removed all spontaneity from our lives, for there could be no sudden dashes to the beach, no slipping off *à deux* to a cosy little bistro; all had to be planned to make sure that the escort was there and that those responsible in the Embassy knew exactly where I was at any time; and since, like the Embassy drivers, the police could not be on duty permanently for twenty-four hours a day (although there were occasions in real crises when they achieved very nearly that), we were sometimes prisoners inside our own house. Babs used to joke about this, saying that she felt secure in leaving me alone in Beirut since my chances of straying from the path of strict matrimonial fidelity must be virtually nil with all that surveillance – a build-in private eye for wayward husbands. But like most jokes which attempt to hide an unpleasant truth, it grew quickly threadbare. Moreover, I felt uncomfortable with my diplomatic col-leagues, very few of whom took such elaborate precautions; it was only after attempts had been made on one or two of them that the security practices of other embassies began to fall in line with our own. The risk of extremist Palestinian or other Arab groups attempting murder or kidnapping was, by this time, considered high; but the British Ambassador had also the Irish to contend with. I occasionally received phone calls, usually anonymous, but purporting to come from the IRA, threatening my life or my family. It was tempting, and even soothing, to think of these as hoaxes, which no doubt most of them were. But the first rule in security is to take everything seriously, and so all such calls were reported to the Lebanese and analysed by them and by us, in so far as any analysis was possible.

One day I received a letter in the open post. The envelope was in

189

obviously feminine handwriting and postmarked Dublin. Not having had at that, or at any other time, a girlfriend in that city, I was sufficiently suspicious not to tear it open, but picked it up gingerly and felt, through the envelope, the tell-tale metal flanges which we had been taught were evidence of a possible letter bomb. I was cross rather than frightened. Officials came and took it away, with suitable precautions, for scientific examination. I spent a reflective morning wondering whether someone really had tried to blow me up. Later in the day I was handed, with some embarrassment, the contents of the envelope – a thick wad of advertising material, all stapled together, promoting the Irish sweepstake. As far as I was concerned, the promotion cannot be said to have been a commercial success, for I did not feel like buying any tickets. It was only later in the evening that the full implications of this little object lesson were borne in on me; it was disturbing to think how plausible were our fears, how easily it might have been the real thing. I felt a little wobbly at the knees, and persuaded myself that I needed an extra drink. Although the Lebanese failed to publicise this particular episode, they did release to the Press details of one or two other threats against me, usually with implied congratulations to the Lebanese Security authorities for having, once again, prevented my assassination. I found this disturbing and embarrassing. Those who pose as heroes, even if against their will, end up looking slightly ridiculous if nothing happens. I dreaded the reaction at home; genuine concern by my family and friends, perhaps, but a knowing look on the faces of my colleagues in the Service, some of whom would not believe my innocence and others who would know that much greater risks were to be encountered at other posts, perhaps their own. This unwelcome publicity also led to Lebanese attempts to exploit it; they were always quick to sum up a situation of potential advantage to themselves and seldom inhibited from trying to cash in on it. One prominent Parliamentarian telephoned me immediately after seeing a Press report of an incident, and in the same unpunctuated, breathless sentence said how glad he was that my life had been saved and asked if I could give his cousin a job.

The Foreign Office Security Department were kept fully informed of these plans and also of the parallel tightening up which we instituted in the Embassy itself; more restricted and controlled access, even to the public parts of the building such as the Visa Office and the Commercial Department; stricter rules about the escorting of visitors to other parts and so on. But I was still not entirely satisfied and asked for an expert from London to come out and advise us. He was a quiet shy man who gently but firmly analysed our system like a family doctor, and pronounced us in good health; his principal additional recommendation was for me to be provided with a specal bullet-proof car with what he called anti-abduction devices. It arrived a few months later, looking outwardly the same as my original Daimler, but containing a number of James Bond-like gadgets – sirens, flashing lights, immobilising switches and so forth, which I occasionally set off by mistake but which would certainly have been effective in a crisis. The weight of all this gadgetry, plus the allegedly bullet-proof glass and sides (again, mercifully, never put to the test) sometimes proved a little too much for the engine. Although perfectly all right on the flat, it tended to overheat when going up hills. As Beirut is built on a series of small mountains, and most roads in and out of the city climb precipitously, there were times when H.E. had to complete a journey in the escort car (which, incidentally, always carried a spare flag for such emergencies) or, most humiliating of all, accept a lift from a colleague whose car, Citroën, Mercedes or Honda, did not break down at the sight of a sand dune.

All this was oppressive but we tried not to let it become obsessive. Security was made for Man, I kept telling myself, not the other way round. Desperate men who regard their own lives as expendable in a given cause and who perhaps seek martyrdom or for whom it is sought by others, cannot ultimately be prevented from violence unless their target remains permanently invisible and immobile. This is clearly unacceptable; life and work must go on, whatever the threat; all that can be done is to reduce the risk as far as possible and then accept whatever remains as part of life's hazards. It was only when some incident elsewhere – a kidnapping or assassination – reminded me of my own vulnerability that I worried about the problem as I moved around Beirut and the countryside with my armed escort and Costi grimly in the front of the James Bond Daimler, wondering what would happen if I did not get to my destination. Otherwise, it all too soon seemed to be the natural order of things. When I was next in London and found myself able to hop on to a Number 11 bus like any other passer-by, I understood what was meant by the precious reality of freedom.

As the incidence of violence, and especially kidnapping, increased and hence, I suppose, the threat if only marginal to me personally, my own reactions in the event of my being a victim began to weigh on my mind. The behaviour of that other senior British diplomat, Sir Geoffrey Jackson, during and after his ghastly experience, had been a model of courage and faith which I knew I could never equal. As Ambassador to Uruguay Sir Geoffrey was kidnapped in 1971 and held hostage for eight months. But I held fast to the principle that terrorists must never be given in to, least of all by governments; and I tried to reconcile this moral and theoretical stand, this strength of the spirit with my own weakness of the flesh. I seriously considered sending, and in fact had tried to draft, a letter to the Head of the

Diplomatic Service making it clear that I would not wish any kind of deal made on my behalf with any terrorists and that, in the event of my being nabbed, the letter could be published if the Government's hand would thereby be strengthened. But I discarded the idea as being too dramatic and hence embarrassing; moreover, I found the letter itself extraordinarily difficult to draft without giving the appearance of attaching undue importance to my own survival and of questioning, in advance, a decision which would almost certainly be taken in the way suggested without my prompting and irrespective of my views.

In the dead of night, when I was able to do my thinking in those hard-pressed times, I recognised that my motives were not as altruistic or noble as I would have had the public believe; the temptation to strike attitudes is infectious for those in the public eye. Fortunately I was never put to that particular test.

I suppose it was inevitable that I and my colleagues should be preoccupied with the risks of my own position. The Head of Mission had invariably been the target in previous incidents, whether successful or otherwise; it seemed logical that the major, perhaps the only, threat would be against him – more junior officers were considered less valuable as hostages in proportion to their rank and presumed inside knowledge; women, in the Arab world at any rate, were regarded as improper subjects for negotiation. It came as something of a surprise, therefore, when the one incident of this kind with which I had to deal involved a junior member of my staff. As it turned out, the drama which unfolded was the result of an accident rather than a premeditated attempt.

Shortly before the outbreak of a Lebanese Civil War in 1973, a young junior officer arrived at the Embassy on temporary attachment. During one weekend when there was a lull in the fighting, Henry took it into his head to carry out a 'personal recce', as he afterwards described it, and simply disappeared from sight. He set out on a Saturday afternoon; his absence was not noticed that evening, but it should have been on the Sunday. Somehow it was not. He was a bachelor, living alone, with no family to get agitated at his non-appearance. By Monday morning it was clear that he was missing, and I had to report this dismal fact to London by Emergency Telegram. According to the drill laid down in the case of a suspected kidnapping of a diplomat, alarm bells went off all over Whitehall. The regulations specify an impressive list of Ministers and others who must be immediately informed on receipt of a telegram of the kind I was so unhappily forced to send – the Prime Minister, the Secretary of State for Foreign Affairs, the Chiefs of Staff, and several others. Quite a performance, it might be said, and one calculated to bring one's Embassy into the Whitehall limelight in a manner not every Ambassador would wish.

The solution to this crisis was, in the event, swift and merciful. We received enough information to make us pretty certain that Henry was being held prisoner in the main Palestinian camp of Sabra, not half a mile from the Embassy. It is at moments like this that the long cultivation of a relationship of friendship and mutual trust pays a priceless dividend. Abou Hammad, the Foreign Minister, and his enchanting wife, had become just such friends. He was a lawyer by profession, and about as non-political as anyone in Lebanese politics could be. Although his spiritual home was Paris, he had developed a respect and liking for the British and an understanding of our policies which owed a certain amount to our friendship. He even set himself to learn English, which I encouraged by relating and explaining where necessary a number of slightly risqué stories which he greatly enjoyed. If anyone could help in this situation, it was he. I eventually tracked him down in a Cabinet meeting, out of which he came at my urgent request to speak to me on the telephone – a very personal favour not likely to be accorded to many of my colleagues and unthinkable, for example, in London. I told him, very guardedly, what had happened and of our suspicions. 'I understand,' he said crisply. 'An officer will be with you within half an hour.' And hung up. The officer duly arrived, a senior Colonel in the Lebanese Military Intelligence, who was rapidly briefed and departed leaving behind him a faint aroma of hope and Gauloises. By seven o'clock that evening, Henry was handed back to us under an elaborate procedure worked out between the Lebanese Army and the Palestinians. He was shaken but unharmed. His de-briefing revealed that during the commendably courageous but politically ill-advised 'recce', which he carried out in his rather too conspicuous white sports car, he had taken a wrong turning and driven slap into the middle of the Sabra camp. The Palestinians were, understandably, at first baffled and then suspicious. They popped him into a basement cell where he stayed locked up, except for periods of interrogation, until the Lebanese managed to secure his release.

Palestinian suspicions, which require very little stimulus to be brought to fever pitch in their love-hate relationship with the British, were confirmed when they discovered that the boot of Henry's car contained some old American Army maps of Syria and that he possessed a diary in which were noted – (to aid his memory, but who would believe that?) – certain key events, viz: 'Israeli raid'. All these facts spelt the letters SPY to the Palestinians as clearly as if they had been in neon lights on the Embassy roof. Fortunately, the episode was over before the Press got wind of it. But the repercussions on the Embassy were considerable. We judged it unsafe for Henry to remain in Beirut longer than absolutely necessary. Indeed, we did not allow him to return to his own house; he stayed a couple of nights with us at the Residence and then was shipped home, much complaining, under cover of an invented suspected illness which could not be completely diagnosed or cured in Beirut. This was bad luck on Henry but, I am sure, the right decision. One could hardly blame the Palestinians for being suspicious in the light of the circumstantial evidence which his sudden appearance in their midst revealed. They must have released him only with great reluctance, no doubt as part of some complicated deal with the Lebanese in which he figured only as a convenient bargaining counter. We could not be sure that they would not try to confirm their suspicions by attempting to recapture him; adequate protection would have been virtually impossible. So off he went, having redeemed his initial mistake, by a commendably stiff-upper-lip performance during his short captivity. He told me that he had made up his mind that he might be in for a long stretch and had organised himself to count the hours and days, and to get as much exercise as his cell would allow. Moreover, he must have been very resolute during his interrogations, sticking as far as possible to the principle, no doubt culled from World War II fiction, that you give your name, rank and number and nothing else. The Palestinians treated him well; no threat, or use of force; no psychological pressure. But it must have been uncomfortable to say the least. We were lucky to have got away with it so lightly – lucky to have stumbled upon the clue that helped us to find Henry and lucky in Henry himself, whose qualities proved exactly right for the difficult role he was so unexpectedly called upon to play.

The demands of security filled a considerable proportion of the days and nights; they made me anxious and fretful from time to time, but they also caused the adrenalin stimulated by risk and action to flow. If there was danger, it remained at the back of my mind where the daily, sometimes hourly, need for practical decisions conveniently pushed it. A more constant and more threatening cloud was the prospect of war; a shadow which could not be dispelled by action, since I was essentially a neutral spectator, unable to affect the issues except by the remote, roundabout effect, if any, of such comment or advice that I might give to London. The great, historic conflict between Jew and Arab, which was never for long quiescent, dominated all men's minds by its unanswered, perhaps unanswerable, questions and by the ever-present menace of the bullet and the bomb.

The 1973 War of Ramadan was therefore not altogether a surprise when it came. We were in London when we heard on the BBC news that hostilities had broken out. It was the day before we were due to return to Beirut. I immediately rang up the Foreign Office and got through to James Craig, the Head of the Near East Department. He confirmed the news, but was unable to give me many more details, particularly about Beirut, from which there had so far been very little information.

'Too bad you can't get back,' he said gloomily. 'You'd better pop in tomorrow and we can have a chat.'

'Is the airport closed?' I asked innocently.

'Well, I assume so,' said James; 'All the others are.' I was not so sure. The Lebanese, despite their outward air of frivolity, are courageous and resourceful people; they would go far to avoid being sucked into the war and hence would carry 'Business as Usual' to its utmost limit.

'I'll ring you later,' I told James.

He was far too busy to prolong our conversation. Early the following morning, after a hurried pack up, we took a taxi to Heathrow, cancelling the official car which was due to collect us later. We had been booked on the Lebanese line, Middle East Airlines. I usually alternated my journeys between this excellent company and British Airways in an attempt to balance diplomacy with patriotism. I had a feeling that this time they would do their utmost to keep flying, and so it turned out. On arrival at Heathrow we were greeted by a totally unflustered airline manager. Yes, indeed, there was space on the flight, which would take off on time. No, no trouble at Beirut airport. How nice to have your Excellencies on board – may I offer you a glass of champagne? Trying not to feel or sound smug, I rang up James again.

'Hallo,' I said cheerfully, 'I'm at Heathrow.'

'Really,' said James. 'Whatever for?'

'Well, MEA say Beirut airport is open and the flight is leaving on time.' James sounded a little put out that the Lebanese, as so often, had failed to conform to the situation as seen by HMG.

'All right,' he said, rather doubtfully. 'I suppose you know what you're doing.'

'Well, I'm not staying here if I can help it,' I said ungraciously. Ever since first hearing the news I had been haunted by the fear of getting stuck in London. It was not a question of courage; there was nothing much to be courageous about. It was rather that Nanny hates to be away in a crisis, even if it's only the Baby next door having measles.

'Bye Bye,' I said to James. 'I'll send you the usual telegram when I get there,' and hung up before he had time to argue.

We had a perfect flight and landed without incident, to be met by Costi in what seemed completely normal conditions. Beirut was quiet and indeed remained so throughout the short war. The Lebanese had no desire to join the fighting and were, in fact, anxious that their territory should not become part of the battlefield. The Palestinians were also quiescent, confining their activities to hit and run raids over the border in the south, which attracted the inevitable Israeli aerial response unopposed, so far as we could tell, by the Lebanese Air Force. The Israelis bombed the oil refinery at Sidon but did not interfere with the much larger installation at Tripoli in the north. This surprised us since the Lebanese allowed Syrian petrol tankers to cross the border, refill at the refinery and drive straight back to the battle-front – a gesture of solidarity requiring courage and strong nerves, since it so obviously invited Israeli reprisals. Relations between the Lebanese Government and the Iraq Petroleum Company, which owned and operated not only the Tripoli refinery but the pipe-line of which it was the terminal, had not been good for some years and were to worsen during my time to the point of nationalisation of the installations by the Lebanese, following similar action by Iraq and Syria. Each side, with some justification, blamed the other; I spent many hours with the President and Prime Minister trying to promote a settlement which was still not in sight when I left in 1975. During the war, however, I was at least able to point out to the Lebanese the advantages of having an international flag flying over the refinery. I doubt whether this had, in fact, deterred the Israelis, but the Lebanese were not slow to get the point and to give me one of their ironic, but appreciative, smiles in response. They played their hand with their customary skill, judging to a nicety exactly how far they could go in giving aid to their Arab neighbours to prove their solidarity, without incurring too great a risk of being sucked into the fighting and becoming themselves a theatre of war. It was not the first, nor the last time that I was to admire the subtlety of these beleaguered people, who had so much to lose and so little to gain from the great conflict on their doorstep; and who maintained their precarious but beautiful sanctuary with their *savoir-faire* and impeccable manners unimpaired.

Indeed, it might have remained that way, had it not been for the Palestinian presence, that crucial factor which had dominated Lebanese politics since 1970 and which would eventually lead to the most severe upheaval the country had ever known. This problem overshadowed my life also. Not only was it responsible for the restricted, security-dominated existence which I was condemned to lead, but it complicated my political work and my position with the Lebanese, let alone with the Palestinians themselves. It is not surprising that any British Government, let alone a Labour one as was then in power, should wish to keep the Palestinians at arm's length; and in particular, to have no dealings with the Palestinian

Liberation Organisation, the quasi-governmental instrument chosen by the Palestinians themselves, with Yasser Arafat at its head, but regarded by a large part of the world, with ample justification, as a terrorist organisation. In 1972 the PLO had established an office in London, and the Government had survived the predictable force eight gale that blew up immediately in Parliament and the Press. It was quite wrongly supposed that this meant 'recognition', whereas in fact it was merely a sign that the Government had given up the difficult business of pretending that the PLO did not really exist, and had concluded that it was on balance better to have some contact with them, however indirect. In any case, the Government took the view that it had no power to prevent it. It made the task of trying to explain Palestinian actions and motives to London considerably easier. The situation was also helped by the appointment of the late Said Hammami as PLO representative in London. He was a man of great charm, intelligence and ability. He used to come to see me privately in Beirut whenever he was there; together we would compare notes about our respective problems over monumental whiskies. He was murdered in London in 1974, a tragic end for one who had worked hard for peace – his kind of peace, admittedly, but one with which we would not necessarily have found it impossible to live.

These meetings, innocent though they were, gave rise to concern in the Foreign Office. Contact of any kind with the PLO was bad news and if one or other of the correspondents in Beirut had decided to make a story out of my meetings with Said, which must have been known about, I would have been ordered off the field. Of course, it was not entirely possible to avoid circumstances in which I might meet Arafat. He circulated fairly freely in Beirut, except in times of tension, and was usually to be seen at, for example, the Soviet Embassy at their larger parties to which I, and all the diplomatic corps, were invited. So seriously did I take my irritating instructions that I would go to considerable lengths to avoid him, fearing that one of the ubiquitous photographers would snap us together – I could hardly have turned my back on him if brought face to face – and sell the result to a British newspaper, which might have been glad to run a speculative story on a dull day. So I dodged behind the potted palms and stayed only as long as bare decency required. I was convinced, however, that contact was useful and should be maintained.

The PLO naturally shared my view; we received from time to time indirect messages from Arafat, sometimes through Said, to the effect that he would like to talk to a representative of the British Government, and could that not be me, as we both lived in Beirut? The Lebanese were keen on this as well, perhaps in the forlorn hope that we might act as honest brokers. I discussed the question privately with the Foreign Minister, who undertook to get me to a rendezvous with Arafat and back again without anyone knowing. I argued the case with London. Why not, I said, take a risk? Of course, Arafat was no innocent where terrorism was concerned and was easily painted in the most lurid colours. But he was not unique; remember Kenyatta? – the Stern gang? Besides, Arafat, for better or worse, represented the moderate element in the tangled Palestinian undergrowth. That might not be saying much, but he was the best Palestinian we had, so to speak. Surely it was in our interests to strengthen his hand against the extremists; contact with us could only help him do this. I added that I, personally, had great sympathy with the plight of these tragic people and, moreover, believed that real peace could never come to the Middle East without a solution to their problem.

All this was of no avail when set against the strength of feeling at home and the political risks involved. I even went so far as to suggest that I could make contact with Arafat without being instructed to do so; if news of the meeting subsequently leaked, Ministers could publicly disown me, saying that I had acted on my own authority and against the tenor of my instructions. Not surprisingly, this offer was turned down; the news would certainly have leaked – the Palestinians would have seen to that – and the manoeuvre would have been revealed in all its transparency. But to propose it seemed to be the only way left of demonstrating my concern.

My indignation can, therefore, be imagined when the French coolly pre-empted us by doing precisely what I had been advocating, and at a much higher level than the modest plan I had suggested. Monsieur Sauvagnargues, the French Foreign Minister, arrived in Beirut and held a highly publicised 'secret' meeting with Arafat at the French Ambassador's Residence. Everything was carried out with the utmost skill and propriety. The French Ambassador had not been present, to emphasize the unofficial nature of the meeting. Sauvagnargues met the EEC countries' Ambassadors immediately afterwards and briefed them fully. He had conceded nothing; he had left Arafat in no doubt that the West's commitment to Israel's survival was permanent and unshakeable, and that terrorism could not be condoned. But within these limits, he had been sympathetic to Palestinian aspirations without, however, any commitment for specific action to advance them. The effect was, of course, to give Arafat's prestige and morale a considerable boost, besides earning the French some very useful marks with the rest of the Arabs. The Israelis reacted predictably, sending fighters to produce sonic booms over the French Embassy while the meeting was in progress and mounting a shrill, spluttering propaganda barrage. The French remarked drily that the

Israelis need not have expended so much effort in proving their ability to over-fly Beirut, a fact well known to all. Later that evening, before a dinner in his honour, Sauvagnargues took me aside and asked what I thought of his meeting with Arafat.

'If you are asking me officially, Monsieur le Ministre,' I replied, 'I shall have to ask for instructions; but if you are asking me personally, I will say that I can see nothing but good from it.'

However much the Palestinians were courted by outside powers and however great the patience displayed by the Lebanese in the face of the considerable problems which their presence posed, it was clearly only a matter of time before the resulting tensions became unbearable. The Palestinian refugee camps had always maintained a degree of autonomy in the conduct of their own affairs; but as they became more crowded and the clandestine flow of arms from a variety of sources accelerated, they acquired strength and independence to the point where the Lebanese authorities could no longer exercise any control within their confines. They had become sovereign enclaves, inaccessible to Lebanese law and its enforcement agencies. Such a situation was clearly intolerable.

In early May 1973 something happened to ignite these powder barrels. The exact nature of the incident was never clear; Lebanese–Palestinian relations were by then so bad that a *casus belli* could have been produced by either side almost hourly. Nor do we know whether the Lebanese were prepared for a battle; whether they manufactured a situation to suit their own timing, or simply reacted to a developing situation. The fact remained that fighting broke out with the sudden violence of a Mediterranean storm which can blow up in minutes out of a clear sky. The early morning had promised only some grumbling tension of the kind so familiar that few any longer took much notice. By eleven o'clock a full scale battle was raging across the scruffy sand dunes and ramshackle shanty towns which lay between the city and the airport. We set up an emergency operations room in the Embassy and put in hand the various military-like steps required in such circumstances – assessment of the seriousness and likely duration of the fighting, and of the threat to the Embassy; securing our communications and transport, so that we would not be immobilised; maintaining contact with the British community and deciding what protective measures for them should, or could, be taken; reporting to London and to neighbouring posts. By mid-day it was clear that the fighting was serious, involving heavy weapons on both sides and drawing in more and more Lebanese troops; it seemed set for a drawn-out battle which might last for days.

What gave us most concern was the grim fact that the British school, situated on the road to the airport, lay in the middle of the battlefield. Since there had been no reason earlier to treat the day as anything but normal, some one hundred and fifty children had arrived as usual and were now huddled in the basement, while mortar and machine-gun fire was exchanged over their heads. Fortunately, there was one telephone line still open, although its use entailed a dangerous dash across the school's open courtyard. The school buses had left and were safely in an unaffected part of the town; there was food for a mid-day meal. I spoke to the headmistress, a brave and resourceful woman who sounded as if this sort of thing was part of the school curriculum. We decided that we could not risk evacuating the children; they would have to stay where they were and we would review the situation later in the day.

The fighting, which showed no signs of letting up, was curiously localised – in other parts of the city, life went on as usual and people wandered in and out of the Embassy expecting to be given visas, information and other comforts. We were flooded by calls from the community, mostly from school parents, some of whom were angry and frightened, and tended to blame me for the plight of their offspring. Several fathers announced their intention of going to fetch their children, pooh-poohing as alarmist and defeatist our strong advice not to try this. It took a near tragedy to lend sufficient authority to what we told them; one young father was seriously wounded and his car wrecked in an attempt to reach the beleaguered school.

By five o'clock there was still no sign of a lull, although the Lebanese Sureté told us privately that they were trying to get talks going with the Palestinians. It would be dark in an hour or so. Clearly a decision had to be made soon; whether to leave the children over-night at the school, where there were now no provisions, no bedding and no light; or to send in the buses in a risky attempt to bring them out before it was dark and then, if successful, face the additional problem of dispersal to their homes through the dark and dangerous curfew. As we stood around in the operations room, now littered with empty tea-cups and full ashtrays, listening to the distant crackle and crump of the battle, it was equally clear whose decision that had to be. The little group fell silent as they looked at me, unwilling to volunteer advice, thankful no doubt that the responsibility was not theirs, and yet anxious for me to make the right choice. I am not very good at incisive, instant action, but this was a time when to dither would have been fatal.

Inwardly calling upon the Christian and Moslem deities as well as, for insurance purposes, a few pagan Gods and Goddesses no longer represented in the Lebanese Constitution, but very much alive in the country, I plumped for what I believed to be the lesser of the two evils – to leave the children where they were and hope that, somehow, sometime the following day we would be able to bring them out. I was fortified in this decision by having been able, earlier in the day, to talk by telephone to the Lebanese General in charge of the battle, being put through, much to my surprise, direct to his Command HQ in response to a casual enquiry as to his whereabouts. He told me that he could not guarantee the safety of the children if they were moved from the school that night, and was clearly unhappy about any such attempts being made.

This decision brought a number of secondary problems in its wake; some parents were furious and asked what authority I had for taking it. A good question, to which the only answer was that someone had to decide; so I replied, 'Only common sense and the Queen's Commission, in that order.' More important, we had somehow to find enough food, blankets and candles and get them to the school. There were enough candles for at least one night between the Embassy itself and the Residence, where our scale of entertaining dictated a certain reserve quantity; we were able to buy bread and some rather evil-looking tins of jam. Blankets were the real problem; finally the Lebanese Red Cross, a marvellous organisation run by dedicated women and supported by many of our friends, came to the rescue. From them we were able to collect a sufficient number to provide a little over one between two children. Next question, how to get them to the school? I successfully made another call to my friend the General, who did not seem at all put out at having to pause in his battle to talk to the British Ambassador. He had been my guest for dinner not long before; we liked one another and, unlike some other nations, the Lebanese do not discard their impeccable manners in a crisis. When I asked if he could provide an escort for these supplies, he said that he could but strongly advised against doing so.

'Send in one of your own vehicles,' he told me, 'with an Arabic-speaking escort, preferably locals.' As I thanked him and rang off, the solution came to me in a flash. I need hardly say that Costi had been hanging about all day, fetching cups of tea, listening to the radio and wearing a martyred expression designed to indicate frustration at his enforced inaction. I realised that his moment had come, for if anyone could manoeuvre our pitiful, but vital supply column through the lines to its scholastic destination, it was Costi. I called him over and explained the situation. His eyes gleamed, and drawing himself up almost to attention, said, 'They are there already, Excellency.' I half expected a salute, but the impression was more that of a Levantine Captain Oates about to sacrifice himself for the

British Raj. Whatever part he was privately playing, Costi was soon off with an Embassy lorry packed with our hard-won supplies.

We sat biting our nails, unable now to communicate with the school, the telephone line having been finally knocked out. In a little over half an hour he was back again and telling me nonchalantly, 'No trouble at all, Excellency, no problem. Everyone happy at school.' This time there was a distinct whiff of Walter Mitty as he took himself off into the night, his duty done, his shoulders squarer and his stance more upright for having played the kind of role he relished, and played it well. I learned afterwards that his journey had, indeed, been relatively trouble-free. The truck had been fired on once, at which Costi had let fly such a stream of invective – Arabic is particularly rich in this vocabulary – that all contestants and their weapons were stunned into a respectful silence.

I went home dead tired after nearly fourteen hours continuous strain. Babs had been immured for most of the day since the Residence was nearer to the battle and she reluctantly agreed that it was not safe to wander about. I left everything ready for an early start, with a first check call at five o'clock – before dawn – and went to bed, too tired and too worried to sleep. Arab cities have a way of becoming unnaturally quiet when there is trouble, the advent of which used to be, and in some cases still is, heralded by Greek shopkeepers putting up their shutters. They always knew what was afoot before anyone except the trouble-makers themselves; it was a signal for those who could to get out fast. That night Beirut was no exception. I lay listening while periods of silence, so deep that a whisper in the next street echoed round the stone corners, were shattered by the savage, maniacal chatter of machine-guns and the disgruntled cough of a mortar. I thought about the children, imagining each distant crash as a direct hit, and lay there a prey to the indecision which, fortunately, I had resisted earlier in the day. Had I done the right thing? Would we be able to get them out and if not, what could we do? Those imaginary headlines in the popular Press formed and reformed against my tired eyelids, my hot pillow beat against my head, the world was against me, I should be disgraced, retired prematurely . . . suddenly the telephone rang. It was just after five o'clock. The duty officer had been in touch with the Lebanese. The buses were standing by. If we could get the children out by six o'clock, it would probably be all right; did I agree? 'Yes,' I replied, almost shouting with relief. Without bothering to shave I threw on some clothes, mobilised Afif and the police, and drove down to the Embassy still uncertain that some last minute hitch might not have wrecked this, perhaps the last, chance. I was greeted by a heart-warming sight. A group of Embassy wives had already turned up and were setting up an impromptu canteen; parents were gathering to collect their loved ones; there was an atmosphere of relief, of celebration, an early morning gala almost. Soon the first busload of excited children arrived, to be greeted with cheers and the sovereign British remedy for all ills – steaming mugs of hot sweet tea. The other buses followed and I was surprised to see the rear of this convoy brought up by a Palestinian truck with a machine gun mounted on the roof; they gave us a cheerful wave and then roared off to continue the battle. I found myself answering a number of questions from the Press, some of them for once quite flattering.

But the real heroine was, of course, Miss Hammond, the headmistress, who appeared totally unruffled, every hair in place as if she had just walked out of Harrods' fitting room. The children, needless to say, had had the time of their lives and seemed genuinely sorry that they could not continue their exciting, candle-lit basement existence with school magically transformed into real-life adventure. Indeed, there were a few tears when they were reclaimed by thankful parents. I shed no tears when reclaimed by a thankful Babs who, against all the rules, had come down after me with one of the wives. I went back to breakfast, shave, and to face that day, and the ten remaining before a cease-fire was eventually arranged.

The ebb and flow of battle was never very far from the Residence, the crump of high explosive often rattling our windows and sending up columns of smoke only a block or two away. But apart from the restrictions on our movements, and the inevitable strain of such circumstances, our lives were not all that abnormal – indeed the forced inaction was first boring, then irritating. The Lebanese finally ended the hostilities by putting in the Air Force to bomb the camps, a step which they had obviously been loath to take recognising, perhaps, that the emotive image of air action against primitive or lightly armed foes can inflict propaganda damage on its user out of all proportion to the military advantage which it may bring. In this case it proved to be the point at which the Palestinians, bitter but exhausted, turned aside and negotiated a settlement in which, as it happened, they did not have to give much away. The political and spiritual damage was deep and lasting; hatchets were not so much buried as put on the shelf and kept oiled for future use. There was no-one who doubted that they would be needed again. From then on it became increasingly clear that the precarious political and religious balance of Lebanese society on which they rightly prided themselves had been finally destroyed. Christian and Moslem would be set against each other in defence of what each thought right for their country, a bloody and tragic conflict in which, for the first time, not even the Jew, as the common enemy, was able to unite them in drawing back together from the brink.

In our last months we watched sadly, silently and helplessly while scars as old as time were re-opened and the blood began to flow. Our Lebanese friends all seemed to be in the grip of some hypnotic dance which whirled them and all they loved ever closer to the precipice. An ominous hush descended on the city as people waited for what they knew was coming and felt powerless to prevent. Our social life remained busy; the generosity of the Lebanese and our diplomatic colleagues in giving farewell parties for us seemed to exceed what custom and protocol required. These functions took on an added dimension both for us, who were saying goodbye to a country and people we had come to love, and for our hosts and their guests who appeared to gain comfort from this huddling together before the storm. Often, however, there were not enough to make a huddle, some incident in the city having temporarily closed roads or otherwise made moving about inadvisable.

The Indian Ambassador had arranged a farewell lunch for us about a week before we were due to leave. I had been looking foward to this occasion; he had a wide circle of interesting and influential friends, some of whom were not normally seen at social gatherings. That morning, however, produced more than the average crop of explosions; as we drove down to the office the police were chattering away on their radio and I could see a black and grey column of smoke rising slowly over an area close to where my Indian colleague lived. When I got to the office I telephoned him to ask how things were in his neighbourhood – in those days embassies spent a good deal of time sending to know for whom the bell was tolling – and said that I assumed his lunch would be cancelled.

'Not at all, my dear friend,' he said. 'We are perfectly all right. I am looking forward to seeing you both.' Clearly the honour of Britain and the Commonwealth demanded a supreme effort. Much against the wishes and advice of the experts, Babs and I set forth, having obtained a not too unpromising forecast from the police and an extra escort car. We flew the flag, still respected as the symbol of a Power as friendly as could be reasonably expected, one at least which had managed to avoid direct involvement and whose reputation still counted for at least as much as its actual policies. As we drove across the city, now become suddenly silent and empty, I reflected that perhaps we had added a little to the comparative respect which the British seemed to be able to command, that perhaps not all my colleagues would have had so smooth a ride, being waved through the innumerable road-blocks erected by the various factions with a minimum of delay, and sometimes even a friendly wave.

I was very glad we had made the effort. Much to my Indian colleague's embarrassment most of his guests failed to turn up; in fact out of some

204

thirty invited, only two besides ourselves had braved it – the Soviet Ambassador and his wife! This was an added bonus; opportunities to talk to my Russian colleague in so relaxed, informal an atmosphere were very rare indeed. Mr Soldatov had only recently arrived in Beirut, his posting setting off waves of speculation through the Western Foreign Ministries. He was a very high-powered official, having served as Ambassador in London for six years, followed by four in Havana. Neither post was exactly a sinecure; and although Beirut had its own importance, it was not usually considered a rung on the professional ladder above, or even parallel to, London or (from the Soviet point of view, no doubt) Havana. What was he doing in Beirut, we asked ourselves. He was a highly skilled diplomat of frightening charm and plausibility. Unlike his predecessor, a very dull Russian Moslem who spoke no languages and never moved without at least one interpreter by his side, Mr Soldatov spoke English fluently and paid his first call on me unaccompanied. He was wearing a distinctly middle class pair of grey flannel trousers and a well-cut tweed jacket. He sat cross-legged in my office, as if we were old colleagues in the same service ('How's Gladwyn these days?'). One would almost have thought that we had been to the same school.

We had an amicable, if rather noisy lunch, the conversation general and relaxed, the periodic explosions seeming to recede as the meal, with its generous alcoholic content, progressed. Mr Soldatov was at his most charming, creating an impression of complete and disarming frankness, without giving away anything of importance. I cannot say that I detected anything behind his bland, practised smile. It was a polished performance. This slightly bizarre encounter (the last time I was to see him) added an extra spice to the excellent curry which our Indian hosts served for their gallant but forlorn lunch party.

During our last few days in Beirut we became numb with fatigue, with sorrow at leaving our friends, and particularly Wadieh, in such circumstances, and with the effort not to let our true feelings show. For, added to the steadily worsening situation in Lebanon, and the growing certainty that it was about to plunge into a conflict which would change it beyond all recognition, perhaps for ever, there was the knowledge that for us, too, this was the end of one kind of life; we had reached the frontier of that land which, for so long, we had tried to pretend did not really exist – the land of the pensioner, the has-been, the departed glory, the recollected crisis and the imagined triumph. We put the thought of this away in our luggage so that we could get it out and face it properly at sea when the hectic present had slipped over the horizon to become the past.

The last bag before we left brought a letter from London saying that my name was to be submitted to the Queen for a KCMG, and asking if I would accept the honour if it was awarded. I was very touched and moved by this, especially since it would afford recognition also to Babs giving her, rightly, an equal share in the symbol of a successful career in which she had played so vital, irreplaceable a part. We did not pretend to each other that we were not proud and pleased. It was all, of course, to remain a deadly secret until publication of the Birthday Honours in June; only Shirley, who had to type my reply, was in the know. That reply was not easy to draft, I found, without sounding too anxious, too complacent or too pompous; it is not something one does every day; there were no precedents to guide me, and no-one I could consult. The same bag also brought the gratifying news that Shirley would receive a well-deserved MBE in the same list, and that the few other honours which I had recommended as my last fling, so to speak, rather like an out-going Prime Minister's dissolution Honours, would be agreed.

Even now I find it painful to write about our last day; if I did so, I could not guarantee the accuracy of any description, so blurred are the memories of the last hours and moments, of the farewells, the promises to return and of continued friendship – a striking contrast to the clarity of my arrival, of which I can remember, even now, every detail down to what tie I was wearing. Somehow we found ourselves being driven to the docks, walking up the gang-plank, to be welcomed by the Captain of the Italian ship which was to take us to Venice, and being embraced by a host of colleagues and friends who had braved the crumbling stability of the city to bid us farewell. The Italian sailors excitedly shepherded everyone ashore; the gangway swung up; the gap of oily water slowly widened; three mournful hoots sounded our departure; we slipped silently into the warm night, a little group on the quayside waving until the last shed blotted them out. I turned to Babs as the engines began to throb. 'Well, that's it,' I said ruefully. She hid her emotion behind her habitual briskness.

'I've got to get us unpacked before dinner,' she said. A new life was waiting; whatever our feelings about the future, it was now too late to look back.

CHAPTER ELEVEN

As our comfortable Italian ship ploughed across the Aegean Sea, all but scraped her sides going through the Corinth Canal, and steamed up the Adriatic towards Venice, the numbness caused by the strain of those last, sad weeks gradually wore off and we began to contemplate the future. The problem was not so much to shed the past – that would have been impossible even if desirable; and we had no wish to forget much, if any, of our experience – but to place it in perspective. Generations of diplomats returning to London, on retirement or a home posting, have summed up the process as going 'from mink to sink'. It was the psychological as well as the material adjustment implied in this apt phrase with which we had to come to grips. We had chosen to come back by sea to Venice and thence by car to London, all in easy stages, giving ourselves time to begin making these adjustments as well as providing the first real carefree relaxation we had enjoyed for years. Even so I was not allowed to shed my Ambassadorial role with the ease that I had alternately hoped for and feared. The Captain and crew of the ship treated us with an elaborate and courteous formality, referring in every other sentence to Their Excellencies, thus alerting the other passengers to our invisible but special status. Those who knew about sea-faring might have guessed what was afoot for, in a touching gesture, he insisted on flying the Red Ensign from the masthead in my honour throughout the voyage.

In many other countries Ambassadors retain the rank for life, enjoying a good deal of its glamour and even a few of its privileges. Foreigners often find it incomprehensible that the British should discard their senior diplomats at the early age of sixty, sometimes with nothing more to show for a long career of service than a few mysterious letters after their name and a greatly reduced standard of living. They are also baffled by the evident suspicion which has inhibited successive British Governments, alone among civilised nations, from providing their representatives with Diplomatic Passports. None of this worried Babs and me unduly; indeed we were, I believe, genuinely anxious to become private citizens again, to do what we wanted and say what we thought without that political calculation which had become almost second nature to us. Our last few posts had not been without their drawbacks, particularly, of course, Beirut where the heavy hand of security had become increasingly hard on us. Nevertheless, we both recognised that if asked to continue we would have done so. There is a remark attributed to Lloyd George which underlines the addictive property of power and deflates those who try to persuade themselves of their own altruism. Towards the end of World War II he is said to have asked Harold Laski what Churchill intended to do in the future, once victory had been won.

'I don't know,' said Laski. 'He talks of retiring.'

'Ah,' said Lloyd George, 'so did I – and Margaret was very keen that I should. But, you know, when you stand on the balcony of Buckingham Palace between the King and the Queen and there are a million people down there in the Mall cheering, you tend to say to yourself, for their sakes, I must go on.'

No cheering crowds, however, awaited our return. We had barely time to identify the problems ahead, let alone solve them, before we were sailing into Venice on a bright May morning, the magical white and gold city winking at us as if to say, 'The world is not as real as you feared; stay with me and put off the day of reckoning'. We stayed for eight days, cosseted and protected by our beloved cousin, Anna-Maria Cicogna, whose hospitable house has meant so much over the years, and who represents for us that precious European civilisation whose standards we had tried, in our modest way, to maintain and preserve against the ugly, destructive forces of the late twentieth century. We left her to drive slowly north, our eyes becoming gradually accustomed to the soft light and dappled skies of France and rekindling some of our happier memories of that limpid land. We avoided Paris and drove on to Calais, catching an afternoon boat to Dover.

The Channel crossing was calm, cold and grey. All the way over, indeed all through France, the Glory had been oozing quietly away from us like juice from an over-ripe peach. As the ferry nosed into the jetty and the car engines started up, I realised that my first big test was about to begin; the Customs! Of all the minor perks available to an Ambassador, that of VIP travel is one of the most desirable, certainly the most missed. Now, after some years of travel as an ordinary, often packaged, citizen, of long stationary queues in hot airports, of lost luggage, of hostile officialdom, of inexplicable delays and cancellations, of the loneliness of foreign ports and airports, it seems almost impossible that once upon a time we were met by a car at the gangway, whisked off to a private, air-conditioned waiting room, our passports stamped and our luggage waved through, unseen by us in our VIP cocoon, led out to a waiting limousine and bidden goodbye by officials who actually seemed to care what happened to us.

We drove off the boat and were immediately diverted by a uniformed official into a bay like a railway siding. Our car was still wearing its Lebanese plates and had already been the object of puzzled and suspicious glances all through France. The Arabic numerals stood out boldly, and although the wonderworking but by now devalued CD letters were visible, they were not prominent; the car's special status in Beirut had been determined by the shape and colour of the licence-plate, a fact not likely to be known to the French or British police. I sat rather nervously behind the wheel waiting to be told what to do. The hostility which officers of HM Customs and Excise display towards homeward-bound members of the Diplomatic Service is legendary and deeply-rooted – almost a matter of genes, you might say, like cat and dog. Somehow these normally polite, hardworking men become transformed into pitiless inquisitors at the sight of a British diplomat, their minds perhaps overheated by the picture of the sybaritic life which these pampered beings are supposed to lead; no stone, certainly no suitcase, is left unturned to prove the point that whatever a diplomat's privileges abroad, they vanish like the Emperor's clothes on entering British territorial waters. In the past, a retiring Ambassador was allowed to bring in, free of duty, what was usually termed his 'cellar' – a limited quantity of drink, usually sufficient to keep him going during the painful months of adjustment to ordinary retail prices. But even this last modest privilege had now been withdrawn; the Exchequer cannot have stood to lose or gain much either way, but it was clearly a victory for the Customs who dislike all exceptions on principle.

Fortunately I was not without experience of this particular battlefield and so was tensed for a difficult passage as a Customs Officer walked, with lazy purposefulness, towards the car. Long before he reached us, he spotted the Lebanese plates.

'Arabs this time, Bert,' he said laconically over his shoulder, and sticking his head into the car window, said loudly and slowly, 'Do you speak English?'

It had been a long day's drive and was now about five o'clock on a May evening; I did not trust myself to reply and so merely handed him our British Passports.

'Oh,' he said, clearly baffled; and then, 'Ah!' as he riffled through the pages and came across the tell-tale entry describing my profession. 'Home on leave, then?' he said hopefully, with visions, I suppose, of costly exotic gifts hidden away beneath the undies.

'No,' I said, hoping my voice was quiet and even, 'we're home for good. Retiring,' I added, in a tone meant to sound helpful.

'I see, Sir,' said the Customs Officer, making the mode of address sound vaguely threatening, as policemen do when they stop you for speeding. 'Would you mind stepping out of the car, please?'

It was thus that I set foot on my native soil as a permanent resident of the country which I had represented abroad for so many years. The moment of truth had arrived; the final note of the glorious trumpet had shivered away in the evening air. It would be tempting to invest the journey to London with some symbolic meaning, to invent metaphors for a transition from one life to another; but the truth is that, tired as we were from the long day, we felt much the same, apart from the effort of driving on the left once more, as we had done since we left Venice. It was now dusk; a pale sun had made a brief appearance before sinking into the weald; there was a sweet smell of early summer, the first mowings, the harvest to come; it was all painfully English. We did not say much to each other, being perhaps a little afraid of releasing emotions that, like the future, would be better faced after a night's sleep.

★ ★ ★

INDEX